London's Monuments

by Andrew Kershman

London's Monuments
Written by Andrew Kershman
Photography by Andrew Kershman & Susi Koch
Edited by David Gluck
Fact checking by Tony Whyte
Design by Susi Koch & Lesley Gilmour
Maps by Lesley Gilmour
Cover Design by The Partners

First published 2007 by Metro Publications Ltd.

Published in 2013 by Metro Publications Ltd,
PO Box 6336, London, N1 6PY

Metro® is a registered trade mark of Associated Newspapers Limited. The METRO mark is under licence from Associated Newspapers Limited.

Printed and bound in India
© Metro Publications Ltd 2013

British Library Cataloguing in Publication Data.
A catalogue record for this book is available from the British Library.

ISBN 978-1-902910-43-7

In Memory of Meinrad A. Koch
(1930-2006)

Acknowledgements

This book has involved the help of a great many people, most especially my colleagues, Susi and Lesley, at Metro who have worked hard to make this book as good as it can be. Thanks also go to my editor, David Gluck who went to such lengths to ensure my writing was fit for publication. Tony Whyte has been a learned, enthusiastic and painstaking fact checker, drawing my attention to numerous mistakes and misunderstandings and placing these pages on a much sounder footing. Tim Mackintosh-Smith deserves my thanks for providing an accurate translation at a moment's notice, and my friend Brynmor Lloyd-Evans was kind enough to read through my book and offer advice and most importantly encouragement.

I have required permission to gain access to both Westminster Abbey, St Paul's Cathedral and the Guildhall and the press officers at these institutions have been very helpful. Likewise the press office at the Bank of England was kind enough to provide me with information and photographs of their monument of William III which I would not have been able to find elsewhere. Other institutions which merit thanks include the Corporation of London, Tower Hamlets Council, the National Archive at Kew and the London Metropolitan Archives.

Contents

"Monuments are for the living, not the dead"
Frank Wedekind

Dante Gabriel Rossetti, see p.317

Introduction

This book has taken over two years to research and write and has cost the author a considerable amount of blood, sweat and tears. The blood was shed after falling on wet paving while walking around the monument to the Duke of Bedford in Russell Square. Perspiration should not be elaborated on too much, but I have walked many miles to find a monument in Hyde Park that, despite assurances, has never existed, and put as much effort into tracing the statue of Pocahontas in Red Lion Square which has since disappeared into a private collection. There have been a few tears, but these have largely been shed over the lives of those immortalised on London's streets, whether the tragic betrayal of General Sikorski and the Polish people or the generosity of Quintin Hogg, who disregarded his father's wealth to dedicate his life to teaching street children.

The people commemorated in London are not all worthy of our admiration or our tears. George IV has one of the most prominent monuments in Trafalgar Square and yet history has judged him to be a profligate and foolish monarch. He squandered the money raised for a monument to his daughter, Princess Charlotte, but expended considerable time and money on his own memorial. Likewise, standing on a 123ft column is George IV's brother, the Duke of York, whose monument is as prominent as were his debts and the scandal which surrounded his corrupt sale of army commissions to pacify his creditors. The tablet to W.T. Stead on the Embankment makes him sound like a great and principled journalist, but in reality he was the first tabloid hack who led a campaign to send General Gordon to Khartoum which resulted in the soldier's death and the fall of Gladstone's government. Stead later spent time in prison for perjury having fabricated a salacious story about the white slave trade.

One man's hero is often another man's villain and there are quite a few people commemorated in the capital that are figures of controversy. Lord Palmerston was the Victorian prime minister who led the country into a disastrous war in the Crimea and suffered several sex scandals and yet, through skill and charm, kept his job. It is also worth remembering that when Nelson Mandela's monument was first erected by the soon-to-be-abolished Greater London Council, the Conservative government of Margaret Thatcher still regarded the man as a terrorist. The monuments of London demonstrate that Britain has a culture that manages to swallow controversy and argument with barely a murmur of indigestion. Oliver Cromwell has a place, as does the king he dethroned and executed. James II is not forgotten but nor are the treacherous son-in-law and daughter who took his throne, and the arch enemies William Pitt and Charles Fox are also commemorated – although kept at a distance.

The idle and the feckless, the corrupt and the incompetent, all manner of persons can find themselves immortalised on the streets of London through luck or privilege, but there are many who have gained their place by virtue of their genius and achievements. Many of the great names from the arts and sciences feature, including Shakespeare and Dickens, Virginia Woolf and Oscar Wilde, Sir Henry Irving and Charlie Chaplin, Isaac Newton and Isambard Kingdom Brunel, Reynolds and Hogarth. Explorers are also well represented with great names like Captain James Cook, Scott and Shackleton all receiving their due. Giants of British industry and commerce, such as Julius Reuter and George Peabody, are also recognised – despite many being migrants from other shores.

In the course of my travels I have often been struck by the invisibility of many of London's monuments. One parks police-woman assured me that the monument of Dr Jenner was not on her patch and yet within five minutes I was standing by the seated figure of the great man. Likewise, the café staff close to the monument to Brunel on the Embankment did not know of its existence. I do not think this ignorance is an indication of indifference for I was often asked questions by curious passers-by as I took photographs of a monument. I hope this new edition of my book stimulates further interest by animating these lifeless effigies and bringing their fascinating and surprising stories to life.

TRAFALGAR
SQUARE

King Charles I, see p.19

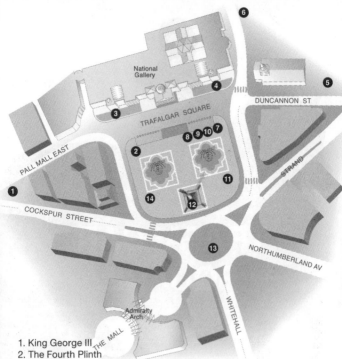

1. King George III
2. The Fourth Plinth
3. King James II
4. George Washington
5. Oscar Wilde
6. Edith Cavell
7. King George IV
8. Admiral Viscount Cunningham
9. John Rushworth, Earl Jellicoe
10. Admiral Earl David Beatty
11. Sir Henry Havelock, Major General
12. Horatio Nelson, 1st Viscount Nelson
13. King Charles I
14. General Sir Charles Napier

4

Trafalgar Square

The area occupied by Trafalgar Square was cleared of its old stable buildings in 1830 by John Nash (see p.259), but it was not until 1840 that the paved public square we recognise today was created by Sir Charles Barry. A year later the square was named after Nelson's great naval victory and in 1843 the great man was placed upon his vast 170ft column from where he has continued to look down upon the city. Trafalgar Square has for centuries been considered the capital's centre and all measurements of distance from London are taken from Charles I's monument on the south side. Since its creation Trafalgar Square has been a place of political protest and national celebration from the Chartist protests of the 1840s, to the VE Day celebrations of May 1945 to the more recent anti-war marches of 2003.

Over the years Nelson has been joined in the square by the great naval and military men of later generations. Sir Henry Havelock and Sir Charles Napier defended the interests of Britain's 19th century empire and stand either side of Nelson. Behind the fountains are busts of admirals Beatty and Jellicoe from the First World War and the great Admiral Cunningham from the Second World War. A less worthy occupant of the square is the vain and profligate George IV, whose large equestrian monument was placed here as a temporary measure but has remained to this day. The former mayor of London, Ken Livingstone, has suggested that Napier and Havelock should be replaced by statues 'ordinary Londoners would know'. The use of the empty fourth plinth for the display of public art since 1999 has been part this democratisation which has been continued by his successor. Just outside the National Gallery stand the figures of James II and George Washington with monuments to George III, Charles I, Oscar Wilde and Edith Cavell within easy walking distance.

1. King George III (1738-1820)

Junction of Cockspur Street and Pall Mall East, SW1
Sculptor Matthew Cotes Wyatt, Bronze, 1836

This equestrian statue commemorates Britain's longest serving king, his 59-year reign straddling the latter half of the 16th century and the first two decades of the 17th. Though the third of our Hanoverian monarchs, this George was the first to call himself an Englishman, his predecessors all having been very much German in character and loyalties. His reign, during a time of factional politics, endured considerable difficulties, not least those engendered by colonial unrest in America. George disliked the nature of British politics and was often in conflict with unstable Whig governments as he tried to assert the crown's authority. He is widely thought to have mismanaged Britain's American colonies and precipitated their loss, though much blame also lies with his politicians.

Catastrophic though losing the American War of Independence in 1783 was to Britain's esteem and influence, the latter part of George's reign proved more stable and less fraught with difficulties as stronger and more effective governments were formed. Pitt the Younger's administration, in particular, helped lessen the crown's responsibilities. The French Revolution boosted the constitutional role of the British monarchy by contrasting it to the disorder and tyrannous terror that reigned over the channel. But the King's worsening mental health – now recognised as the symptoms of porphyria – also helped evolve a constitutional monarchy and inadvertently increased the popularity of the crown.

If he was not the dominant political figure he aspired to be, George III was at least that rare being, a popular king. Lampooned as 'Farmer George' in the popular press for his preference for the simple country life, this only heightened public affection for him. His last years were spent in the virtual seclusion of mental illness and in 1811 the Regency Act gave royal responsibility to the Prince Regent who, as George IV, did so much to undermine the respectability of the British monarchy (see p.13).

2. The Fourth Plinth

Trafalgar Square, SW1
Current sculpture: Hahn/Cock
Sculptor Katharina Fritsch, Fibreglass, July 2013

The fourth plinth of Trafalgar Square remained largely empty for 160 years. This state of affairs changed in 1999 when the plinth was used to display three successive artworks. The experiment's success led to the establishment of the Fourth Plinth Commission and on the 15th September 2005 Marc Quinn's spectacular statue of the disabled and heavily pregnant artist, Alison Lapper, became the first of many artworks to occupy the site. Since that time the occupancy of the fourth plinth has changed every 18 months with memorable occupants including Yinka Shonibare's 'Ship in Bottle' and Antony Gormley's fleeting use of the plinth for living statues in 2009. The monument in situ at the time of writing is the ninth to occupy the site and depicts a cobalt blue Cockerell by the German artist Katharina Fritsch.

For the latest news about the fourth plinth see
www.london.gov.uk/fourthplinth.

3. James II (1633-1701)
Trafalgar Square, SW1
Sculptor Grinling Gibbons, Bronze, 1686

This is a companion piece to the monument of Charles II which stands in the Royal Hospital, Chelsea (see p.315) and was commissioned by the same man, Tobias Rustate to depict both monarchs in Roman costume. James II was the second son of Charles I but the failure of his brother to provide an heir, combined with James's Catholic faith triggered the Exclusion Crisis, a campaign to prevent him being crowned. James won the day and became king on the death of his brother in 1685. James's religious zeal and wilful nature soon turned many against him as he attempted to abolish anti-Catholic laws and place Catholics in prominent positions.

The birth of a son in June 1688 increased the prospect of a Catholic dynasty and proved the trigger for James's overthrow by his son-in-law William of Orange and his daughter Mary. James avoided the initial battle and fled in December 1688 to Ireland, where he had more support. His reforms were popular among the majority Catholic population, but even here his forces were crushed and he was forced into exile. He spent the last few years of his life in France in a state of religious mania, praying constantly and seeing his downfall as a punishment from God for his many affairs. The overthrow of James II has been termed the Glorious Revolution and this monument has, not surprisingly, been treated with a similar lack of respect, having been moved many times since it was first placed in St James's Park. James now enjoys a position of some prominence outside the National Gallery, looking towards his father on the other side of Trafalgar Square.

4. George Washington (1732-1799)

Trafalgar Square, SW1
Sculptor Jean Antoine Houdon, Bronze, 1785

The marble original of this statue stands in Richmond, Virginia. This bronze copy was a gift from the Commonwealth of Virginia in 1921, to commemorate the first President of the United States. George Washington was born in 1732 into a planter's family and received the education of an 18th century Virginia gentleman. He trained as a surveyor before taking command of the Virginia militia and fighting on the side of the British during the French and Indian War. From 1759 to the outbreak of the American Revolution in 1775, Washington managed his lands and served in the Virginia House of Burgesses.

Washington was not initially in favour of independence but the bad administration of the British and the writings of Thomas Paine helped to persuade him. From May 1775 Washington fought for six gruelling years against the well-trained British troops with his own poorly equipped militia forces. Finally, in 1781 – with the aid of French allies – the Continental Army forced the surrender of Cornwallis at Yorktown. Washington could easily have assumed power at the head of his army, but instead retired from the military and set about establishing a constitution enshrining the rights of the citizen and placing limits upon government. It was as a civilian that Washington was elected America's first president in 1789. He served two terms of office but retired in 1797 and died only two years later from a throat infection.

5. Oscar Wilde (1854-1900)
Adelaide Street, SW1
Sculptor Maggi Hambling, Bronze, 1998

Oscar Wilde, among the best playwrights, essayists and short story writers of his generation, was also a noted wit and public figure whose ascent was as rapid as was his downfall. Wilde was part of a talented Dublin family, his father was a surgeon and his mother a writer. A brilliant scholar he first studied classics at Trinity College, Dublin before winning a scholarship to Magdalen College, Oxford, where he joined the aesthetic and decadent movements espousing the importance of art and pleasure in life. He left Oxford in 1878 with a double first in classics, a sharpened wit and the manners of a dandy, soon coming to the public's attention as a spokesman for the Aesthetic movement by giving lectures both in England and the United States. He was engaged to Florence Balcombe, a noted Irish beauty but she broke off the engagement to marry the writer Bram Stoker. Wilde was already aware of his homosexuality when he married Constance Lloyd in 1884, and had two children with her but also led a second life as a promiscuous gay man.

While leading this complicated private life Wilde began to achieve success and recognition as a writer. His book of fairy tales (1888) was well received and his only novel, *The Picture of Dorian Gray* (1891) was an instant success. It was Wilde's comic plays that were to prove his greatest triumph with *Lady Windermere's Fan* (1892), *A Woman of No Importance* (1893) and *The Importance of Being Earnest* (1895) establishing his reputation and fortune.

At the height of his success Wilde became embroiled in a scandal that was to destroy his reputation and his life. He had begun a passionate affair with Lord Alfred Douglas which brought him into conflict with Douglas's father, the Marquess of Queensbury, who confronted Wilde in several ugly public scenes. Wilde was disastrously persuaded to take legal action against Queensbury which failed and encouraged counter prosecutions leading to his imprisonment for acts of 'gross indecency'. The scandal and two years incarceration, combined with the death of his wife in 1898, were to take a terrible toll on Wilde. He died in poverty and isolation in Paris in November 1900, his reputation and stature only fully recognised once homosexuality was decriminalised in the 1960s. Wilde's own words are inscribed on this contemporary monument, 'We are all in the gutter, but some of us are looking at the stars.'

6. Edith Cavell (1865-1915)
St Martin's Place, WC2
Sculptor George Frampton, Marble, 1920

The execution by German firing squad of the English Red Cross nurse Edith Cavell, for spying, quickly became a *cause célèbre* in 1915. The propaganda posters depicting her death, together with that of her Belgian accomplice, Phillipe Baucq, with the exhortation 'remember the murder of Edith Cavell', did much to stir up anti-German feeling in Britain. The notoriety of her martyrdom belied a life of hard work and dedication to the care of others which began as the daughter of a Norfolk rector. Her aptitude for languages gained her a position as a governess in Belgium but she returned to England to nurse her dying father and afterwards took up nursing as a profession.

After completing her training, Edith worked on the Continent, becoming the first matron of the Berkendael Medical Institute in Brussels. During the First World War Cavell worked in occupied Belgium for the Red Cross, treating soldiers from both sides. It was here that she became involved in the smuggling of wounded Allied troops to neutral Netherlands from where they could return home. After the plot was discovered Edith admitted her role in the escape of over 200 troops and was executed despite a campaign for mercy. Edith Cavell's last written testament contained the words 'patriotism is not enough, I must have no hatred or bitterness towards anyone'. These words are inscribed on this vast monument that was erected in 1920, just one year after her body was returned for burial in the grounds of Norwich Cathedral.

7. George IV (1762-1830)
Trafalgar Square, SW1
Sculptor Sir Francis Legatt Chantrey, Bronze, 1843

This massive equestrian statue was commissioned by George IV in 1829 and was intended for the top of Marble Arch – then located in front of the newly built Buckingham Palace. The king died in 1830 before the statue was completed and it was placed in Trafalgar Square as a temporary measure, one which has now become very much permanent.

The future George IV had the misfortune of having to wait until the age of 58 before becoming monarch, and in many years of inactivity failed to acquire any of the skills of statecraft but instead accumulated vast debts, a taste for opium and alcohol and a reputation for scandal. George was a dashing and fashionable young man, but by the time of his coronation in 1821 he was forced to wear elaborate corsets to hide his enormous girth. He resorted to similar measures for this statue which represents him in Roman dress and on horseback even though he was by then too large to ride. Although George IV was extravagant when it came to immortalising himself, he spent the funds allocated for a memorial to his daughter and heir, Princess Charlotte, when she died in childbirth in 1817. There were insufficient funds to pay Sir Francis Legatt Chantrey for this statue and it was left to his estate to pursue payment from the state after his death. When the King died in June 1830 national apathy was summed up by the comment in The Times 'There never was an individual less regretted by his fellow-creatures than this deceased king. What eye has wept for him?'

8. Admiral Viscount Cunningham (1883-1963)
Trafalgar Square, SW1
Sculptor Franta Belsky, Bronze, 1967
Andrew B. Cunningham was known, unsurprisingly, as 'ABC' in
the navy. His distinguished naval career led to his becoming
Commander-in-Chief of the Mediterranean Fleet in 1939. His
seamanship and Nelsonian instinct to attack the enemy at every
opportunity were to have considerable success against the Italian
fleet. In March 1941 at the Battle of Cape Matapan his fleet sank
three heavy cruisers without any British casualties. However,
during the evacuation of Crete in the spring of 1941, his fleet
suffered heavy casualties, but succeeded in evacuating over two
thirds of the Allied Troops. Cunningham directed the invasion
of North Africa from mid-1942 and having gained control of the
Mediterranean in October 1943 became First Sea Lord and was
present at the Yalta and Potsdam conferences. He retired from the
navy in 1946.

9. John Rushworth, Earl Jellicoe (1859-1935)
Trafalgar Square, SW1
Sculptor William Macmillan, Bronze, 1948
The son of a merchant seaman, Jellicoe joined the Royal Navy in
1872 and was appointed to the Admiralty in 1888. He was shot
during the relief of Peking in 1900 – the bullet remaining in his lung
for the rest of his life. Jellicoe was promoted to Commander-in-
Chief of the Grand Fleet on the eve of the First World War and was
involved in the Battle of Jutland in 1916 for which he received some
criticism, including from Winston Churchill, which contributed to
his replacement by David Beatty as Commander-in-Chief. Jellicoe
was by this stage exhausted and was sacked by Lloyd George who
successfully introduced the convoy system against Jellicoe's advice.
He retired in 1917 and was raised to the peerage the following year.
Jellicoe became Governor-General of New Zealand between 1920-
24 and was made an Earl in 1925.

CUNNINGHAM
1883-1963

JELLICOE
1859-1935

BEATTY
1871-1936

10. Admiral Earl David Beatty (1871-1936)
Trafalgar Square, SW1
Sculptor Sir Charles Wheeler, Bronze, 1948

This monument elegantly captures the handsome features of David Beatty who became the youngest British admiral since Nelson. Beatty came to the Admiralty's attention when forced to take command of HMS Alexandra during Kitchener's invasion of Sudan in the late 1890s. At his time he became friends with Winston Churchill, a friendship that was to help him in later life. Beatty was promoted to Commander in 1898 and was wounded in 1900 during the Boxer Rebellion, as was his contemporary Jellicoe.

Beatty was a glamorous and charismatic figure who married an American heiress in 1901 and so became financially independent of the navy and a member of high society. In 1910 he was promoted to Rear-Admiral but fell out with the Admiralty and was only found a post when Churchill became First Lord of the Admiralty.

During the First World War Beatty had a number of successes commanding the Battle Cruiser Squadron. After Jutland Beatty replaced Jellicoe as Commander-in-Chief and issued new instructions allowing more initiative to be used in battle. His finest hour came when he accepted the surrender of the High Seas Fleet on 21 November 1918. Beatty become Admiral of the Fleet in 1919 and spent the interwar years arguing for greater expenditure on the navy. He died in 1936 and is buried close to Nelson in St Paul's.

11. Sir Henry Havelock, Major General (1795-1857)

Trafalgar Square, SW1
Sculptor William Behnes
Bronze, 1861

Sir Henry Havelock joined the army in 1815 and saw action in the Burma War (1824-26), the first Afghan War (1839) and the Sikh Wars (1843-49), eventually rising to the rank of General. His greatest military achievement was during the Indian Mutiny, when he fought a number of battles across India, recapturing Cawnpore from mutinous forces in July 1857 but was too late to prevent a massacre. Havelock fought on and gained public attention when he relieved Lucknow from siege in September 1857. Unfortunately, Havelock's forces were too small to liberate the city and a new siege began which only ended in November when further reinforcements arrived. Havelock died of dysentery within a few days of the relief of the city and so assured himself a place as one of Britain's military heroes, his death causing widespread public grief.

Havelock had become a committed evangelical Christian and his heroic exploits did much to gain acceptance of non-conformists within the British army. This monument was erected soon after his death and was the first to be based on a photograph. The legacy of Britain's empire is now a matter of political debate and Havelock has become another Victorian with huge sideburns whose exploits have largely been forgotten by the British public. In 2000 the then Mayor Ken Livingstone suggested that both Havelock and Napier be removed from Trafalgar Square and replaced with more recognisable figures. With the departure of Mr Livingstone, Henry Havelock's position on the square seems likely to continue.

12. Horatio Nelson, 1st Viscount Nelson (1758-1805)

Trafalgar Square, SW1
Sculptor E. H. Baily (Statue), W. Railton (Column),
E. Landseer (Lions), Bronze, 1843

The design and construction of Trafalgar Square was begun 25 years after the eponymous battle and the death of Britain's greatest naval hero, Lord Horatio Nelson. Sir Charles Barry designed the square 'fit for a hero', while the towering column and statue of Nelson are (like the Albert Memorial) the work of a great number of artists and cost the then remarkable sum of £50,000. The 17 foot statue of Nelson was erected upon the column in 1843, once the square was completed. The reliefs illustrating Nelson's life are made from captured French cannon from his four greatest victories (St Vincent, the Nile, Copenhagen and Trafalgar). Sir Edwin Landseer's four enormous lions were added in 1867 and are now rarely seen without a vast number of gleeful tourists sitting upon them posing for photos. Unlike Wellington, Nelson was a down-to-earth man who would probably have enjoyed the irony of French school children climbing upon this symbol of British maritime glory.

Horatio Nelson was a sickly and slender child. His mother died when he was only nine years old and in 1771 at the age of only 12, with the help of his seafaring uncle, he joined the navy. Nelson was not an obvious choice for a maritime hero. He stood only 5'4" and suffered from sea sickness throughout his life. Despite these disadvantages by the age of 20 Nelson had seen service in the West Indies, the Baltic and Canada and risen to the rank of captain. It was at this stage in his life, after several affairs, that he met and married a young widow by the name of Fanny Nisbet.

Britain entered the French Revolutionary Wars in 1793 and Nelson served in the Mediterranean helping to capture Corsica, losing an eye at Calvi and achieving his first great victory at the Battle of St Vincent. Within a year of losing his arm at the Battle of Santa Cruz de Tenerife (1797) Nelson captained H. M. S. Vanguard and destroyed the French fleet at the Battle of the Nile in 1798.

It was while in port at Naples after his victory that he met and fell in love with Emma, Lady Hamilton, embarking on a very public affair which effectively ended his marriage, though Lady Hamilton's marriage continued with the indulgence and understanding of her elderly husband. It was partly because of his personal life that Nelson was sent to the Baltic under Sir Hyde Parker. The Battle of Copenhagen was to prove one of Nelson's greatest victories when he ignored Parker's command to retreat and decisively defeated the Danish fleet. He was made a Viscount for this victory and soon after allowed to retire. His retirement lasted for a brief two years, spent in domestic harmony with the Hamiltons despite – or perhaps because of – fathering a child, Horatia, with Emma. All too soon he was back at sea on HMS Victory in the Mediterranean, a two-year stint with only one brief shore leave before his last famous Battle at Cape Trafalgar in 1805. Struck by a bullet on the first day of battle he died a few hours later to the grief of both navy and nation. While the Battle of the Nile was Nelson's most notable victory, effectively annihilating Napoleon's navy and with it his dreams of an empire to the east, it is Trafalgar that is forever associated with his name and which captured the popular imagination. Unless you're a pigeon, it is impossible to see any of the detail of his statue, being over 170 feet up, but there is a very fine bust in Queen's House at Greenwich (see p.338).

13. King Charles I (1600-1649)

Trafalgar Square, SW1
Sculptor Hubert le Sueur, Bronze, 1633

This equestrian statue of Charles I was originally commissioned by the High Treasurer Lord Weston just before the English Civil War. The defeat of the royal armies made the statue an embarrassment to the Commonwealth government and it was given to brazier John Rivett to be destroyed. Rivett buried it in his garden and sold trinkets claiming they were made from the same metal. After the restoration of the monarchy the statue came into the hands of Charles II who had it erected here in 1665. The location is particularly appropriate as Charles I looks down towards Parliament, the disagreements with which helped bring about the civil war. It is also the site where the last remaining signatories to the King's death warrant were executed after the monarchy's restoration, and within walking distance of the Banqueting Hall where the king was executed on the 30th January 1649. The Royal Stuart Society lays a wreath here each year on the anniversary of the king's death. It is thought that the pedestal is the work of Grinling Gibbons from a Wren design, but over the centuries much of the detail has been lost due to erosion. For more details about the Civil War and its aftermath see the statue of his nemesis Cromwell (page 74).

14. General Sir Charles Napier (1782-1853)

Trafalgar Square, SW1
Sculptor George Cannon Adams, Bronze, 1855

Born into an illustrious military family – his father was a colonel and his brother also a distinguished soldier – Charles Napier first saw action in the Irish rebellion in 1798. He went on to fight in the Danish campaign in 1807 and was a prominent figure in the famous retreat of Corunna of 1808. Despite being wounded several times Napier continued to play a leading role in the Napoleonic wars and was then put in charge of a regiment fighting against the United States forces between 1812-13. One of his greatest achievements was his governorship of Cephalonia from 1822-30. He became an eloquent advocate of Greek independence and a friend of Lord Byron (see p.275). Napier left Greece after a fierce quarrel with the high commissioner and spent time writing and bringing up his children after the death of his wife. He became commanding officer in the north of England during the height of the Chartist troubles and showed considerable restraint when preserving law and order.

Napier went to India in 1842 to command the region of Sind. He decided that the ruling emirs were the obstacle to effective British rule and adopted a brutal policy to defeat them. His actions in India were the most controversial aspect of his career and ran counter to the wise council of General Outram (see p.137). Napier left India in 1847 and received public acclaim for his military success. He is credited with anticipating the uprising in India in 1857, but died in Portsmouth before his warning came true.

LEICESTER SQUARE & PICCADILLY

Eros 7th Earl of Shaftesbury, p.31

Leicester Square & Piccadilly

Leicester Square was laid out in the 1670s as a fashionable residential area and in the 17th and 18th centuries it was the home to several aristocratic families as well as famous artists and scientists. Hogarth and later Reynolds both lived in the square, Reynolds' house serving as a meeting place for notable characters such as Burke, Goldsmith and Johnson. In 1748 Burchard's statue of George I was bought by the wealthy residents of the square as a monument to George II and erected where Shakespeare's statue stands today.

During the 19th century Leicester Square was abandoned by its wealthy residents and became a place of entertainment with grand hotels, Turkish baths and theatres. The imposing equestrian figure at the square's centre fell to ruin along with the square itself, and after the tatty statue was painted to look like a cow by a prankster the monument was removed and destroyed. The square was rescued by the flamboyant MP and businessman Albert Grant who bought the land in 1874 and commissioned James Knowles to design the gardens complete with all the statues found here today with the exception of Chaplin's, which was added in 1981.

The square is now largely known for film premieres and as one of London's most central meeting places. It has again been redeveloped in recent years and, with the exception of Shakespeare, all the monuments have changed their location with most now clustered within the ticket office on the south side.

Included in this chapter are five monuments which are a few minutes walk from the square but still worth visiting. Among these is the famous Eros statue, which is in fact dedicated to the great Victorian philanthropist, the 7th Earl of Shaftesbury. This chapter concludes with a monument to this country's first great leader of fashion – George 'Beau' Brummell.

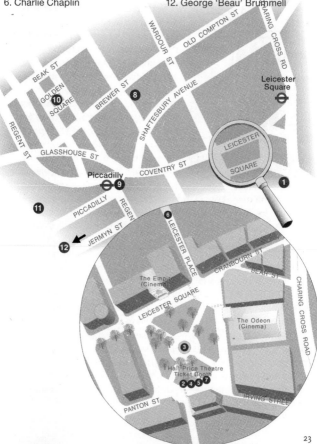

1. Sir Henry Irving
2. Sir Isaac Newton
3. William Shakespeare
4. John Hunter
5. William Hogarth
6. Charlie Chaplin
7. Sir Joshua Reynolds
8. Earl of Derby
9. Eros – 7th Earl of Shaftesbury
10. King George II
11. Sir Joshua Reynolds (RA)
12. George 'Beau' Brummell

1. Sir Henry Irving (1838-1905)

Charing Cross Road, WC2
Sculptor Thomas Brock, Bronze, 1910

Henry Irving was born John Brodribb in Somerset to a Methodist mother who disapproved of the theatre. Despite his upbringing he became the most successful actor of his generation and the first to receive a knighthood. As a young man he attempted to follow his mother's advice and took up a career as a clerk, but the lure of the stage proved too strong and in 1856 he first stepped on stage under the name of Henry Irving. For the next ten years Irving played over 600 parts in provincial stock companies and gradually acquired the mannerisms, timing and presence that were to make him famous. In 1866 he moved to London, but it was not until 1871 that he finally gained public recognition as the lead in *The Bells* at the Lyceum Theatre. For the next 30 years Irving was to dominate the English stage as actor-manager of the Lyceum, playing all the great Shakespearian roles – most notably his 200 performances of Hamlet in 1874 – usually accompanied by his leading lady Ellen Terry. In the last 20 years of his career Irving toured North America eight times to great public acclaim and as a manager introduced the convention of lowering the curtain to denote a scene change and pioneered gas lighting in the theatre. Irving's acting was equally innovative with his emphasis on realism rather than showmanship, but his choice of material was conservative, ignoring the contemporary works of Wilde, Ibsen and Shaw. Irving died not long after leaving the stage in October 1905 during his farewell tour. He is buried in Westminster Abbey.

2. Sir Isaac Newton (1643-1727)

Leicester Square, WC2
Sculptor William Calder Marshall, Stone, 1874

This small bust of Isaac Newton commemorates probably the greatest scientist and mathematician this country has produced. The bright lights of Leicester Square make it hard to imagine that Newton kept an observatory near this site.

Newton's early life showed little sign of his genius and it was only his failure to manage his country estate that persuaded his mother to send him to Cambridge. It was in 1666 when Cambridge shut its doors during the plague that Newton returned to his country estate and began his ground-breaking work on calculus and later, optics, mechanics and celestial dynamics. Within three years he was made Lucasian Professor and came to the attention of the Royal Society through his invention of the refracting telescope. The publication of *Mathematical Principles of Natural Philosophy* in 1687 unified his ideas of gravity and motion and were to remain unchallenged until Einstein's *Theory of Relativity* over two centuries later.

In 1787 Newton abandoned his studies and moved to London to become Master of the Mint and president of the Royal Society. He spent the next 40 years defending his achievements against his critics and amassing a considerable fortune. There was a darker side to the character of Newton – he suffered from severe bouts of depression, mental breakdown and many bitter disputes with his rivals. After his death in 1727, Newton's assistant, Whiston, wrote that 'Newton was of the most fearful, cautious and suspicious temper that I ever knew'.

3. William Shakespeare (1564-1616)
Leicester Square, WC2
Sculptor Giovanni Fontana, Marble, 1874

William Shakespeare left a huge body of plays and sonnets to posterity and yet very little is known of the man and there remains considerable controversy about his identity, sexuality and the authorship of some of his plays. Even the famous Chandos Portrait in the National Portrait Gallery is of dubious authenticity. It is certain that William Shakespeare was born and brought-up in Stratford-upon-Avon, Warwickshire, that his family were prosperous gentry and that he did not go to university. His marriage to Anne Hathaway in 1582 is recorded, as are the births of his children, but little else is known of his personal life. His professional life is better documented and it is certain that he came to London during the 1580s to become an actor and playwright and that he was a leading figure in a theatrical company known as The Lord Chamberlain's Men, which later, under the patronage of James I, became The King's Men. English theatre underwent a revolution during this time as the traditional academic and morality plays were replaced with a form of secular theatre that could be both entertaining and profound. Shakespeare was in the vanguard of this revolution and by the age of 30 had become a great success as a playwright, actor, theatre-owner and manager. His reputation in life has been far exceeded by his pre-eminence in the centuries that followed his death in 1616. It is perhaps fitting that a man who could write so profoundly of the human condition should have become such an enigma. This monument is a copy of an original by Scheemakers which stands in Westminster Abbey (see p.80).

4. John Hunter (1728-1793)

Leicester Square, WC2
Sculptor Thomas Woolner, Stone, 1874

John Hunter was one of the founding fathers of modern surgery whose skill with a knife was matched by a rigorous scientific approach to the study of nature. Hunter's Scottish childhood in East Kilbride showed little promise and he left school at the age of 13 to spend his time exploring the countryside and studying wildlife. His life changed when he came down to London to join his brother William who was a successful anatomist. The young John soon showed his promise as a medical student and he quickly rose to became Master of Anatomy at Surgeons Hall in 1753, at the age of only 25. Due to poor health Hunter joined the surgical staff of the army in 1760. He served in France and Portugal during the Seven Years War and managed to make significant advancements in the treatment of gun-shot wounds during this period. On his return from war he set up his own anatomy school in London in 1764 and started a private surgical practice; three years later he was elected to the Royal Society. In 1783 Hunter moved to a house on Leicester Square where he was able to arrange his vast collection of anatomical preparations of over 500 species of plants and animals. It is this collection that formed the basis of the Hunterian Museum after his death in 1793. John Hunter made advancements in the study of teeth, inflammation, venereal disease and the digestive system. He was known to be an irascible man, but with a good nature, who would frequently offer his services to the poor free of charge and who cared little for money and status.

5. William Hogarth (1697-1764)
Leicester Square, WC2
Sculptor Joseph Durham, Stone, 1875

Born in Smithfield in 1697 in the reign of William III (see p.102), after whom he was named. His father was an unsuccessful businessman who, after the failure of a coffee shop, was sent to debtors' prison in 1707. Young William began his career as an engraver, under the instruction of Sir James Thornhill, whose daughter he later married. By his early 20s Hogarth was a portrait painter and engraver and started to produce the political satires that were to bring him fame and fortune. Hogarth was living in a time of unparalleled corruption as Whig politicians enriched themselves through political intrigue. Hogarth's satire of prime minister Robert Walpole – *The Punishments of Lemuel Gulliver* – was an instant success in 1726 and he followed it with *The Harlot's Progress* (1732) and *The Rake's Progress* (1733-35). Hogarth was to be instrumental in the passing of the Engravers' Copyright Act to prevent the widespread illegal sale of his work and with his new-found wealth established a school for young artists. He made a fortune painting conventional portraits of the aristocracy, but it is the works of satire such as *Gin Lane* (1751), *The Election* (1754) and *The Times* (1762) that have brought him lasting fame. The later work is an anti-war satire that is still relevant today. William Hogarth died in October 1764 having lived for some time in the square in which his statue now stands. The National Gallery and Sir John Soane's Museum both have fine examples of his work. A further monument to Hogarth and his dog, Trump, was unveiled in Chiswick in 2001.

6. Charlie Chaplin (1889-1977)
Leicester Place, WC2
Sculptor John Doubleday, Bronze, 1981

Charlie Chaplin was born to theatrical parents, he made his entrance in 1889 in Walworth, London and appeared in music hall as a child. His family life was unstable and they were forced into the workhouse when their father abandoned them. Chaplin was always a natural comic and as a teenager found acting work which eventually took him to America. It was while touring the States in 1913 that Chaplin was spotted by the movie producer Mack Sennett and began his career in comic silent movies. Chaplin was intelligent and ambitious and within a year he had begun writing and directing his own films – slowing the pace and developing characters. During this period he made *The Tramp* (1915), *Easy Street* (1917) and *A Dog's Life* (1918) and became the first movie star to sign a million-dollar contract in 1918. Chaplin's success was only matched by his ambition and within a year he had established a film studio with other film stars of the day – United Artists. Directing and producing his own films, Chaplin was one of the few actors to make a successful transition to talking pictures. Despite having very little formal education he formed friendships with some of the leading intellectuals of his day including H. G. Wells, Harold Laski and Albert Einstein. Chaplin was a socialist with strong sympathies for Soviet Russia and made some of the most overtly political films of the period – *Modern Times* (1936) and the *Great Dictator* (1938). During the war he devoted his energies to Soviet war relief and the campaign for the opening of a second front in Europe. With the rise of anti-communism and the start of the Cold War, Chaplin fell under suspicion by J. Edgar

Hoover's FBI and in 1952 Chaplin's right to enter the United States was revoked and he became an exile in Europe. He made several films in Europe – none of which were distributed in the US – and was only allowed back into the country in 1972 to receive an award. Chaplin died in Switzerland on Christmas Day 1977 having become one of the most successful and controversial figures of the 20th century. This monument has avoided any political controversy, representing Chaplin in his early days as a loveable tramp with the inscription 'The comic genius who gave pleasure to so many'.

7. Sir Joshua Reynolds (1723-1792)
Leicester Square, WC2
Sculptor Henry Weekes
Stone, 1874
Joshua Reynolds lived at 47 Leicester Square which is now demolished. For more details about the life of Reynolds refer to his statue at the Royal Academy on p.33.

8. Edward Stanley Earl of Derby (1799-1868)
Great Windmill St, W1D
Stone, 1877
Earl Derby was a generous benefactor of St Peter's Church and they built this school in his honour in 1877. Soho Parish Primary School now occupies the site. See p.67 for more details about the Earl of Derby.

9. Eros 7th Earl of Shaftesbury (1801-1885)

Piccadilly Circus, W1

Sculptor Alfred Gilbert, Aluminium (fountain), 1893

Few people who sit at the foot of Eros in Piccadilly realise that this London landmark was erected in memory of the 7th Earl of Shaftesbury – one of the great Victorian reformers. Anthony Ashley Cooper was an aristocrat, educated at Harrow and Oxford and destined to inherit his father's title. Despite his privileged background, Ashley spent most of his adult life fighting for the rights of the poor and downtrodden, inspired by his Christian Evangelical faith. Lord Ashley entered parliament in 1826 having assumed the seat through his family's control of the rotten borough of Woodstock. The young MP did not seek power but reform and was soon involved in a committee concerned with the treatment of lunatics. This achieved little in terms of legislation at the time, but Ashley kept a keen interest in the subject and was later involved in the passing of the Lunatic Act of 1845 which helped improve the treatment of the mentally ill. Lord Ashley joined the movement to limit child labour in factories and although his bill was rejected the government passed the limited Factory Act in 1833. He continued to press for further reforms to improve the conditions of working-class children and in 1840 helped establish the Employment Commission to investigate such issues. Ashley was instrumental in some of the key reforms of the day including the Coal Mines Act (1842), the Ten Hours Act (1847) and the Lodging House Act (1851) which attempted to improve the living conditions of the working poor. He became 7th Earl of Shaftesbury in 1851, but continued his reforming work in the House of Lords and as chairman of the

Ragged Schools Union which established elementary schooling for the poor. During the Crimean War (see p.100) Lord Shaftesbury was able to give considerable assistance to his friend and ally Florence Nightingale (see p.99) and so improve the treatment of soldiers wounded in the conflict. Shaftesbury's evangelical zeal was popular with those who benefited from his efforts and he played a key role in calming the mood of revolt on the streets of London in 1848 – when revolutions were widespread on the Continent – through his work with the City Mission. The Earl was a popular figure in public life and his 80th birthday was celebrated in grand style at the Guildhall. This famous monument depicts a Christian angel of charity upon a fountain which states the virtues and efforts of the Earl of Shaftesbury. The Christian nature of the monument and the man it commemorates have been forgotten by most people and it is now commonly known as Eros.

10. George II (1683-1760)
Golden Square, W1
Sculptor John Van Nost,
Portland stone, 1753

The origins of this monument are not certain but it is believed to have come from the Duke of Chandos's country estate and to have been purchased by an anonymous bidder at auction there in 1848 and presented to the public. The statue has been in residence in this fine square since it was built in 1753 and is briefly mentioned by Dickens in *Nicholas Nickleby*. For a biography of George II see the review of his monument in Greenwich (see p.330).

11. Sir Joshua Reynolds (1723-1792)
The Royal Academy, Burlington House, W1
Sculptor Alfred Drury, Bronze, 1931

Joshua Reynolds was a schoolmaster's son from Devon who rose to become the outstanding portrait artist of the 18th century. In 1740 he was apprenticed to Thomas Hudson, with whom he studied for two years before embarking on his own career. Reynolds continued to develop his own style, greatly influenced by his travels in Italy between 1749 and 1752, where he was inspired by the works of Roman antiquity and the artists of the Venetian renaissance. Reynolds returned to England determined to establish the 'Grand Style' of Continental painters on home soil and set up house and studios in London's fashionable Leicester Square. He was an instant success, painting portraits of the country's leading aristocratic families – even being commissioned to paint several allegorical works for Catherine the Great of Russia. Despite having lost his hearing while in Rome, Reynolds had a considerable talent for friendship and was close to many of the leading figures of his day including Dr Johnson, Oliver Goldsmith and Edmund Burke. Reynolds founded the Royal Academy with Gainsborough in 1768 and in the same year was knighted by George III. He was a man of considerable intellect and gave a series of 16 discourses on the classical ideal which are still referred to today. Reynolds's health was beginning to fail by the 1780s but his studio, with its team of apprentice artists, continued to be remarkably productive – exhibiting 244 paintings at the Academy until 1790. Reynolds died in February 1792 and was buried with great pomp in St Paul's Cathedral.

12. George 'Beau' Brummell (1778-1840)
Jermyn Street, SW1
Sculptor Irena Sediecka, Brass, 2002

George 'Beau' Brummell was without doubt the most fashionable man in England and at the very heart of a particular change in culture and fashion associated with the Prince Regent and known as Dandyism. After Eton and Oxford, Beau joined the Regent's own regiment, the Tenth Royal Hussars in June 1794, and having captivated the prince was soon promoted to captain.

Brummell resigned his commission in 1798 and for the next 15 years became the epicentre for the Regency set. He spent five hours every day washing, shaving and preparing his wardrobe, the afternoon shopping and the evening attending the most fashionable parties and gentleman's clubs. The high necktie and the introduction of the long trouser were all fashion innovations attributed to Brummell and assiduously followed by the future George IV, who would often visit his mentor to observe his bathing and clothing preparations.

Brummell's downfall was as sudden and calamitous as his rise had been glittering. He fell from favour with the new Prince Regent in 1813 and without Royal patronage creditors soon began to chase him. Brummell managed to survive on his wits, but in 1816 was forced to flee to France to avoid his creditors. White's betting book still has 'not paid, 20th January 1816' against his name. The man who resigned his commission to avoid living in unfashionable Manchester was forced to live out his days in Calais and Caen, spending time in a debtors prison and eventually dying in an asylum from syphilis in 1840. Brummell has remained a figure of beauty and elegance and this monument captures him in his fashionable prime.

WHITEHALL

THE WOMEN OF WORLD WAR II

Women of World War II, p.45

Whitehall

Whitehall has been the administrative centre of British government since before the eponymous Palace of Whitehall was destroyed by fire in 1698. Most of the grand buildings that line the wide thoroughfare of Whitehall and Parliament Street are Victorian and 20th-century creations, but Banqueting House is an original Inigo Jones building dating from 1622. Charles I was beheaded outside this building in 1649 and a small bust now commemorates this infamous regicide.

The unfortunate king is one of the few political figures to be commemorated in Whitehall along with the domineering full-length figure of the Liberal politician Spencer Compton Cavendish, which stands opposite the entrance to Horse Guards Avenue. The Department of Health is located in Whitehall but there are no monuments to famous nurses or doctors. HM Treasury also has fine offices here, but there are no influential economists immortalised in the area.

It is the Ministry of Defence which seems to exert a dominant influence over the choice of monuments that surround its modern concrete offices complete with wired fences, security cameras and armed guards. In this area can be found no less than five field marshals, three commander-in-chiefs of the British army, one admiral, five war or army memorials as well as a vast monument to the military adventurer and capitalist Robert Clive, who with guile, cunning and brutality founded British rule in India. Those who agree with the late foreign secretary Robin Cook's argument that British government is dominated by the interests of the military, would find their opinion reinforced by a walk around Whitehall. The small bust of perhaps this country's greatest novelist, Charles Dickens, on the second floor of a public house on Parliament Street, does little to weaken the strength of such an argument.

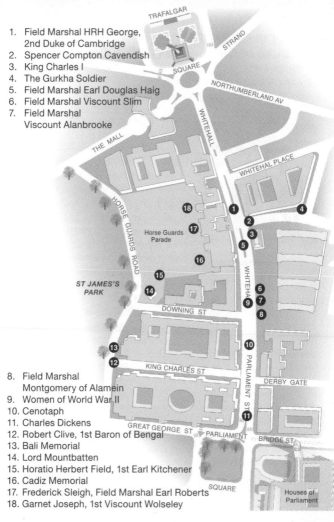

1. Field Marshal HRH George,
   2nd Duke of Cambridge
2. Spencer Compton Cavendish
3. King Charles I
4. The Gurkha Soldier
5. Field Marshal Earl Douglas Haig
6. Field Marshal Viscount Slim
7. Field Marshal
   Viscount Alanbrooke

8. Field Marshal
   Montgomery of Alamein
9. Women of World War II
10. Cenotaph
11. Charles Dickens
12. Robert Clive, 1st Baron of Bengal
13. Bali Memorial
14. Lord Mountbatten
15. Horatio Herbert Field, 1st Earl Kitchener
16. Cadiz Memorial
17. Frederick Sleigh, Field Marshal Earl Roberts
18. Garnet Joseph, 1st Viscount Wolseley

1. Field Marshal HRH George, 2nd Duke of Cambridge (1819-1904)

Whitehall, SW1
Sculptor Adrian Jones, Bronze, 1907

The Duke of Cambridge was Queen Victoria's cousin and a career soldier who saw action in the Crimea (see p.100). In 1856 the Duke was promoted to Commander-in-Chief of the British Army and spent the next 39 years preventing any kind of military reform. Under his command the army stagnated while continental rivals made major advances. The Duke also promoted officers on the basis of their class rather than merit and so filled the higher ranks of the army with men of little talent. He once said 'There is a time for everything, and the time for change is when you can no longer help it.'

The victory of Prussia in the Franco-Prussian War (1870-71) demonstrated the need for reform and Gladstone's government passed the War Office Act (1881) which attempted to remove powers from the Commander-in-Chief and pass them to the Secretary of State. This reform was resisted by the Duke and the senior officers that owed their positions to him. It was only after a royal commission ,led by the 8th Duke of Devonshire (see opposite), published a critical report in 1890, that reforms were finally made. It took a further five years before the Duke of Cambridge was finally forced to resign. The only imagination or divergence from precedent the Duke demonstrated was his marriage to actress Sarah Louisa Fairbrother (in contravention of the 1772 Royal Marriages Act). It is a surprise to anyone with knowledge of the Duke's career that a grand monument should stand in his honour.

2. Spencer Compton Cavendish, 8th Duke of Devonshire (1833-1908)

Horseguards Avenue, Whitehall, SW1
Sculptor H. Hampton, Bronze, 1910

Cavendish served in several of William Gladstone's reforming administrations. As Secretary of State for War (1882-1885) he was widely criticised for his policy in Sudan which led to General Gordon's death in Khartoum (see p.140). In 1886 Cavendish broke with Gladstone over Irish Home Rule and ended his career as a minister within Lord Salisbury's Conservative government. Cavendish is now relegated to the margins of British history but was one of the most important parliamentary figures of his day.

3. King Charles I (1600-1649)

Banqueting House, SW1
Sculptor Unknown, Lead, around 1800, placed here 1950

This small lead bust of Charles I stands just above the entrance to Banqueting House. A plaque below the bust explains that it is situated close to the spot where the King was executed on 30th January 1649. On each anniversary a service of dedication and wreath-laying is carried out here. A much larger equestrian statue stands at the top of Whitehall (see p.19).

39

4. The Gurkha Soldier

Horse Guards Avenue, SW1
Sculptor Philip Jackson, after work in India by Richard Goulden
circa 1924), Bronze, 1997

The Gurkha regiments have their origin in Britain's colonisation of India under the auspices of the East India Company. To the north of the British-controlled regions of India was the northern city-state of Gurkha in a region that was later to become Nepal. Disputes arose between the Nepalese and British which eventually led to war in 1814. The Gurkha army managed to hold the British at bay for two years and a peace treaty was signed in 1816. The British were so impressed with the ability of these hardy mountain men that provision was made for the Gurkha soldiers to volunteer for service in the East India Company's army. It is from this 19th-century treaty that the regiments of the Gurkha Brigade were formed which have served in the British army to the present day. The Gurkhas played a major role in the Second World War in Burma (see Viscount Slim page 42) and the 4th battalion of the 10th Gurkha Rifles formed the core of the Chindits (see p.145). This bronze statue of a Gurkha Soldier commemorates the bravery and skill of the Gurkha regiments. The plaques below the statue detail Gurkha regiments and campaigns and outline their service during the First and Second World Wars. A simple plate at the front of the monument reads 'Bravest of the brave'.

5. Field Marshal Earl Douglas Haig (1861-1928)

Whitehall, SW1
Sculptor Alfred Hardiman
Bronze, 1937

As a young officer, Haig fought in the Sudan, the Boer War and held administrative posts in India. He joined the War Office in 1906 and was responsible for establishing the British Expeditionary Force. The high point of his career came as Commander-in-Chief of British Armies in France between 1915-18. It was in this post that Haig expressed his strategy for fighting the war as 'Kill more Germans'. This blunt and unthinking approach to warfare was to lead to the terrible casualties of the Somme and Passchendaele between 1916-17 in which hundreds of thousands of British and French soldiers were sacrificed for the gain of very little territory. Haig planned his strategy in the comfort of his staff offices and knew nothing of the conditions under which his soldiers were fighting. Despite these failures and the opposition of Lloyd George, Haig remained in his post and had greater success towards the end of the war once the Americans had joined the conflict. After the Allied victory there was little mood for recrimination and Haig was made an Earl and given a tax free sum of £100,000. This statue won the Royal Society of British Sculptors award in 1939, despite Haig's horse being in a posture for urination.

6. Field Marshal Viscount Slim (1891-1970)

Raleigh Green, Whitehall, SW1

Sculptor Ivor Roberts-Jones, Bronze, 1990

William Slim led the 14th Army in Burma from 1943-45 – one of the most important and least recognised fields of battle of the Second World War. As a young soldier he had fought in Gallipoli and Iraq during the First World War. In the early years of the Second World War he was to command British forces in Sudan, Iran and Iraq, but it was in the jungle conditions of Burma that Slim was to prove his qualities as a military leader. In 1942 he took charge of British and Indian troops as they were driven back by the Japanese over 1000 miles to the borders of India. Slim and his troops held their position and when reinforcements arrived fought the Japanese back to Mandalay and Rangoon between 1943-45. The conditions of the Burma campaign were the toughest faced by British troops but the 14th Army and the Indians that fought along side them have never been given the credit they deserve. Earl Mountbatten was probably right when he described Slim as 'the finest general World War II produced'. After the war Slim served as chief of the Imperial General Staff from 1948 to 1952 and was made Field Marshal in 1953. He served as governor-general of Australia from 1953 to 1960 and was created a viscount in 1959.

7. Field Marshal Viscount Alanbrooke (1883-1963)
Raleigh Green, Whitehall, SW1
Sculptor Ivor Roberts-Jones, Bronze, 1993

Alan Brooke had a distinguished military career which included active service in Ireland, India and on the Western Front during the First World War. At the start of World War II Brooke was head of Southern Command and went to France as a member of the British Expeditionary Force. In June 1940 he played a leading role in the evacuation of British troops at Dunkirk. Brooke was a forceful character and had several disagreements with Churchill before he was surprisingly appointed, by the Prime Minister, Chairman of the Chiefs of Staff in December 1941. Brooke continued in the role until the end of the war, acting as a vital brake upon the wilder plans of Churchill. He was promoted to Field Marshal in January 1944 and finally received both the GCB and GCVO in 1953.

8. Field Marshal Viscount Montgomery of Alamein (1887-1976)

Raleigh Green, Whitehall, SW1
Sculptor Oscar Nemon, Bronze, 1980

Bernard Law Montgomery was known as 'Monty' to his troops and the British public. As a young soldier he served in India and was seriously injured in the First World War. He became the most famous soldier in the British army during the Second World War when as commander of the British Eighth Army he defeated Rommel's Afrika Korps at El Alamein (Egypt) in October-November 1942. Winston Churchill said of the victory 'Before Alamein we never had a victory, after Alamein we never had a defeat', although this probably had more to do with the US joining the war than the victory in North Africa.

Montgomery went on to command British forces in Sicily, France, the Netherlands and Germany between 1943-45. The last few years of war saw him in conflict with the Americans as he sought a more prominent role in the invasion of Europe. His plan to concentrate on the North was not universally supported by Allied Command and failed in its main objective of taking Arnhem. Despite this failure and his increased marginalisation within Allied Command, Montgomery was made Field Marshal in 1944 and Viscount in 1946.

This statue was unveiled by the Queen Mother in 1980, just four years after his death, and shows him sporting his famous beret. Montgomery's reputation has been tarnished in recent years with the publication of previously secret papers from 1947-1948 which show him to be against African independence and in favour of a 'racist master plan' for postwar Africa.

9. The Women of World War II

Parliament Street, SW1
Sculptor John W. Mills, Bronze, 2005

When the war started in 1939 men left their work to enlist in the forces and this created a vast labour shortage which women helped to fill. The Women's Land Army (WLA) recruited women to work on the land and provided much needed food during Germany's U-Boat blockade. Women also worked in Britain's factories to provide the munitions and armaments needed to wage war. When times are hard Britain reaches for the kettle and many women too old to work on the land or in factories joined the Women's Voluntary Service (WVS) to provide tea and refreshments to firemen and those sheltering from German bombing. Women also served in the various non-combat roles within the military, with a select few joining the Special Operations Executive, working as spies behind enemy lines (see pages 158 and 246). By the end of the war in May 1945 there were 460,000 women serving in the military and 6.5 million in civilian work. Many women were forced back to the kitchen when the men returned from the war, but progress had been made towards greater equality and a recognition of the skills and abilities of women. This large bronze memorial was unveiled by the Queen just over 60 years after the end of the Second World War and is a much-needed reminder of women's contribution to the Allied victory.

10. The Cenotaph
Parliament Street, SW1
Sculptor Sir Edward Lutyens, Portland Stone, 1919

The Cenotaph was initially built as a temporary structure for the Allied Victory Parade of 1919. The Cenotaph was the idea of Lloyd George who, impressed by French victory celebrations, commissioned Edward Lutyens to design a structure similar to that seen in Paris. The design was initially made in plaster but a permanent Portland Stone version was constructed in 1920. Since 1945 the Cenotaph has been the national monument for the fallen of both world wars.

11. Charles Dickens (1812-1870)
Red Lion (2nd Floor), Parliament Street, SW1
Sculptor Unknown, Terracotta, 1900

No writer of any period is so strongly associated with London as Charles Dickens – people even use the term 'Dickens' London' to refer to his fictional vision of the city. One of the great qualities of Dickens' work are his characters and the diversity of life he was able to convey. He was able to write about such a broad section of London's society because he had managed to escape an impoverished childhood in Camden Town to attain a position of wealth and fame. The Dickens family experienced great deprivation, after moving to London in 1822. At one point they were sent to debtor's prison, while Charles worked in a shoe blacking factory at the age of 12. They were eventually saved from penury by a small inheritance and Charles was able to receive a basic education which he completed at the age of 15 without distinction.

Dickens worked in a solicitor's office but soon decided that he wanted to be a writer, teaching himself shorthand and becoming a court and later parliamentary reporter. He had a good deal of success as a journalist and campaigned in his writing for parliamentary and social reform. It was at the age of 21 that He first came to the public's attention as a writer of fiction under the pen-name 'Boz'. The publication of The Pickwick Papers (1836-7) was the first work of fiction in his own name and marked the start of the most productive period in his life which saw the publication of Oliver Twist (1837), Nicholas Nickleby (1838-39), The Old Curiosity Shop (1840-1), Barnaby Rudge (1841), Martin Chuzzlewit (1843-4) and A Christmas Carol (1843). Dickens was a famous figure in his own lifetime partly because all his works were published in popular periodicals rather than in book form. Each installment of his stories was eagerly anticipated by the increasingly literate public. The serialisation of The Old Curiosity Shop engrossed the public in the fate of Little Nell and the country went into mourning when the tale of her death was published. Never has an author cast such a spell over his readership.

Dickens enjoyed the public's attention and embarked on readings of his works to packed theatres both in Britain and also during tours of America in 1842 and later in 1867-8. He was thought by many to be the greatest actor of his generation, but such talent and energy took its toll on his health. Like his contemporary, Isambard Kingdom Brunel (see p.119), Dickens worked himself to a state of exhaustion and died prematurely at the age of 58. There are several small memorials to Dickens, but it is a shame that there is not a major statue in the city with which he is most associated.

12. Robert Clive, 1st Baron Clive (1725-1774)
King Charles St (on the steps at the St James's Park end), SW1
Sculptor John Tweed, Bronze, 1912

In the latter part of the 18th century Britain lost its American colonies while gaining dominance over the vast domain of India. One of the key reasons for Britain's success in India was the role played by Robert Clive. Through military conquest and political intrigue Clive rapidly brought India under the control of Britain's East India Company. The bronze reliefs on the plinth of this monument illustrate the beginning and end of this process; the siege of Arcot (1751) and Clive receiving the grant of Bengal, Behar and Orissa at Allahabad (1765).

Clive went to India as a young man after a difficult childhood in which he exhibited a troubled and sometimes violent nature which led to his expulsion from Charterhouse School. When he first arrived in India at the age of 18 in 1743 he was employed as an administrator, but the capture of Madras (now Chennai) by the French forced him to flee the city and later enlist in the East India Company army. Clive came to national prominence in 1751 when he occupied the city of Arcot and held it under siege against a much larger French and Indian army. This was to be the beginning of a long series of campaigns which first secured southern India and later established the supremacy of the East India Company in the north with the defeat of Siraj-ud-daulah, the Nawab of Bengal, at the Battle of Plassey in June 1757. The aspirant to the Nawab's throne, Mir Jafar, was induced to throw in his lot with Clive and the war was won in a matter of hours, illustrating Clive's skill as a politician as well as a soldier. The Treaty of Paris in 1763 confirmed the gains Clive had made and recognised the British rule of Muhammad Ali in the north.

Clive returned from India for the final time in 1767, but a life of extravagant expenditure (he made and lost more than one fortune), battling in harsh conditions and years of opium addiction had taken their toll on his mental and physical health. An unsuccessful attempt was made to impeach him for financial wrong-doing which was enough to drive him into a depression, to which he was always prone, and in November 1774 he killed himself. It is the manner of his death that perhaps explains the passage of nearly a century and a half before this monument was erected in his honour.

13. Bali Memorial
Horse Guards Road, SW1
Sculptor Gerry Breeze and Martin Cook, Marble, 2006

This memorial was unveiled by Prince Charles on the fourth anniversary of the Bali terrorist bombing which it commemorates. The attack was carried out by an Indonesian Islamist group with links to Al-Qaida on the holiday resort of Kuta on 12th October 2002. The ensuing carnage claimed the lives of 202 innocent people, making the Bali attack the most deadly Al-Qaida related terrorist incident since the attack on the World Trade Centre on September 11th 2001. The monument consists of a 5ft-high marble globe to symbolise the international nature of the atrocity and has 202 doves carved upon it to represent each victim. On a curved wall behind the globe are inscribed the names of all those who died – 28 of whom were British.

14. Louis Mountbatten, 1st Earl Mountbatten of Burma (1900-1979)

Foreign Office Green, Horse Guards Parade, SW1
Sculptor Franta Belsky, Bronze, 1983

Louis Mountbatten, who was the grandson of Queen Victoria, spent the interwar years as a naval captain and glamorous socialite, marrying the heiress Edwina Ashley and forming a close friendship with Edward, Prince of Wales. He played a major role in the Second World War firstly as Chief of Combined Operations (1941-3) and later as Supreme Allied Commander in South East Asia (1943-6). Mountbatten was a popular leader but his only major military initiative was the disastrous Dieppe Raid of August 1942. While in South East Asia he was constrained in his actions by more experienced American planning staff.

After the war Mountbatten's socialist sympathies won him favour in Attlee's Labour government and he was appointed the last Viceroy of India in 1947. He was a significant figure in the events leading to India's independence and the formation of Pakistan but has been criticised for his handling of the situation which contributed to the bloodshed. Despite such criticism, Mountbatten was made an Earl in 1947 and later became the First Sea Lord in 1955. His marriage to Edwina was troubled, suffering infidelities on both sides – most famously her affair with Nehru (see p.163). In 1960 Edwina died and Mountbatten spent his latter years as a mentor to the young Prince Charles and fending off newspaper stories regarding his personal life. He was assassinated by an IRA bomb while holidaying at his summer home in Ireland in August 1979. This monument stands behind the Foreign Office and shows Mountbatten in naval uniform.

15. Horatio Herbert Field, 1st Earl Kitchener (1850-1916)

Horse Guards Parade, SW1
Sculptor John Tweed, Bronze, 1926

Kitchener joined the Royal Engineers in 1871 and served in Palestine (1874-78) and Cyprus (1878-82). The young Kitchener came to the nation's attention through the successful campaign in Sudan (1883-85) and after his victory at Omdurman he was knighted. During the Boer War (1899-1902) Kitchener was chief of Staff to Earl Roberts (see p.53) and developed the strategy of burning Boer farms and placing civilians in concentration camps. The policy was effective but criticised for its brutality by politicians such as Lloyd George.

Kitchener was made Minister for War at the start of the First World War. His face was used on the famous 'Your Country Needs You' recruiting poster which helped to enlist three million young men to the army. Many of these recruits were killed during the Somme and Dardanelles Campaigns, partly because of the leadership of Earl Haig (see p.41) and partly because of the old-fashioned views of Kitchener who supplied unsuitable munitions and refused to use tanks. Following these disasters and the further catastrophe of Gallipoli (1916) Kitchener offered to resign, but was kept on by Prime Minister Asquith. Later that year he was killed when HMS Hampshire struck a German mine. Sir Arthur Conan Doyle was probably right when he wrote 'Kitchener grew very arrogant. He had flashes of genius but was usually stupid.'

16. Cadiz Memorial
Horse Guards Parade, SW1
Sculptor Not known, Cast-iron, 1816

The Cadiz Memorial consists of a French mortar mounted on a
cast-iron Chinese dragon. It was a gift of the Spanish government
to the Prince Regent in memory of the lifting of the siege of Cadiz
following the defeat of French forces near Salamanca in July 1812
by the Duke of Wellington's army. The battle was a decisive one in
the Peninsular War and helped establish Wellington's reputation as
a great battlefield strategist. Despite the serious intention behind
the memorial the general public and caricaturists were tired of war.
The memorial became satirically known as the 'Regent's Bomb'
and, given the Prince's many mistresses, cartoons made lewd
references to the size and angle of the cannon. One such satirical
drawing is entitled 'A representation of the Regent's tremendous
thing erected in the park'. For a more serious assessment of the
future George IV and the Duke of Wellington see pages 13 and 198.

17. Frederick Sleigh, Field Marshal Earl Roberts (1832-1914)

Horse Guards Parade, SW1
Sculptor Harry Bates, Bronze, 1923

Frederick Sleigh Roberts was born in India to a military family and joined the Bengal Artillery in 1851. He fought with distinction during the Indian Mutiny (1857-58) and was awarded the Victoria Cross. He came to the public's attention for the relief of Kandahar during the Second Afghan War (1878-80) and became a military hero in the same way that Sir Henry Havelock had been for the relief of Lucknow (see p.16). Roberts was rapidly promoted after the relief of Kandahar and became a Field Marshal in 1895. In 1899 the British army encountered set backs during the Boer War and Roberts was appointed to take charge. With the aid of Kitchener (see p.51), he set about reforming the army in South Africa and reversed the course of the war in Britain's favour. On his return to Britain in 1900, he became the last Commander-in-Chief of the British army but soon found himself in conflict with the government and resigned in 1904. He died of pneumonia in France in 1914 while visiting Indian troops fighting in the First World War. Roberts was such a popular soldier that he was one of only two non-royals in the 20th century whose body lay in state in Westminster Hall, the other being Winston Churchill. He is buried in St Paul's Cathedral.

18. Garnet Joseph, 1st Viscount Wolseley (1833-1913)

Horse Guards Parade, SW1

Sculptor Sir William Goscombe John, Bronze, 1920

Garnet Joseph Wolseley followed his father into the military at the age of 19, serving with distinction in the Second Burmese War (1852-53). Despite being injured in battle, he soon returned to service in the Crimea (1854-56), India (1857-58) and China (1860). It was in India that Wolseley made his name serving under Sir Colin Campbell (see p.96) in the relief of Lucknow and defending Alambagh under the command of General Outram (see p.137). In 1862 Wolseley spent some time as an observer during the American Civil War and served in Canada where he established Canadian sovereignty over the Northwest Terrritories. On his return home Wolseley received the Order of the Bath (CB), and began work in the War Office to institute the Cardwell scheme of reform against the wishes of the Duke of Cambridge (see p.38). Wolseley became the most prominent advocate for reform while also successfully commanding forces in Ashanti, South Africa and taking a seat on the Council of India in 1876. His most brilliant campaign was to defend the Suez Canal against a rebellion in 1882 for which he was promoted to the rank of General and awarded a peerage. It was Wolseley who attempted the rescue of General Gordon (see p.140) from Khartoum in 1885. He briefly became Commander-in-Chief in 1895, a position he held until 1901. By the time of his death, in 1913, Wolseley had established his reputation as the most capable soldier of his generation. He wrote numerous books on soldiering and history and was a close friend of the author Henry James.

PARLIAMENT
SQUARE

Sir Winston Churchill, p.72

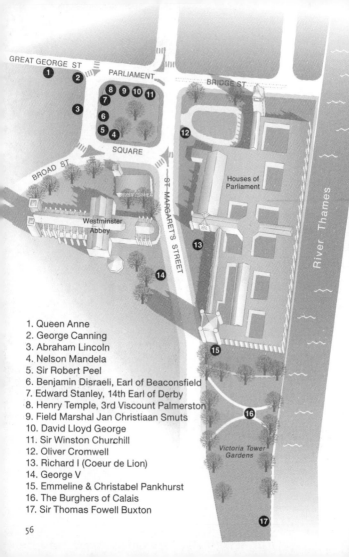

1. Queen Anne
2. George Canning
3. Abraham Lincoln
4. Nelson Mandela
5. Sir Robert Peel
6. Benjamin Disraeli, Earl of Beaconsfield
7. Edward Stanley, 14th Earl of Derby
8. Henry Temple, 3rd Viscount Palmerston
9. Field Marshal Jan Christiaan Smuts
10. David Lloyd George
11. Sir Winston Churchill
12. Oliver Cromwell
13. Richard I (Coeur de Lion)
14. George V
15. Emmeline & Christabel Pankhurst
16. The Burghers of Calais
17. Sir Thomas Fowell Buxton

Parliament Square SW1

This area of Whitehall is dominated by Sir Charles Barry's Palace of Westminster, built in 1858, and Parliament Square which was laid out ten years later to complement the neo-gothic edifice. Parliament was heavily bombed during the Second World War and the site was partially re-developed by George Grey Warnum in the late 1940s without changing its nature. The greatest intrusion upon the Victorian and Edwardian uniformity is Westminster Abbey which dates from medieval times (see p.80) and the post-modern structure of Portcullis House, completed in 2001. The area has been the focus of British parliamentary democracy for over 400 years and many leading British politicians and royalty are commemorated here as well as a few politicians from abroad – South Africans Jan Smuts and the more recent Nelson Mandela and president Abraham Lincoln.

It would be comforting to suppose that the characters commemorated in stone and bronze outside the Houses of Parliament were more dignified in their conduct than our political contemporaries, but history is never comforting and there are just as many tales of power, ambition and scandal among the statuary. Disraeli hated Robert Peel after being turned down for a cabinet place as a young man and exacted revenge by bringing down the Peel administration over the Repeal of the Corn Laws. The two now stand mute alongside each other on Parliament Square. A seated George Canning looks passively towards one of the great Victorian politicians, Lord Palmerston, who was his assistant and prodigy at the Foreign Office. Palmerston was an adventurist in his foreign policy, but a reactionary at home and always distrusted the democratic spirit of the United States. He was not a supporter of the Union during the American Civil War, much to the annoyance of Lincoln who sits alongside Canning looking towards Parliament. Oliver Cromwell stands apart from the fray behind concrete barriers within the grounds of a fortified parliament which he did much to establish after victory in this country's own 17th century Civil War.

The suffragette Emmeline Pankhurst is the only radical political figure to be found here and she is consigned to a corner of Victoria Embankment Gardens along with the much put upon Burghers of Calais.

Radicalism for a while thrived on Parliament Square in the living form of Brian Haw who began a lone vigil outside parliament in June 2001 in protest at the government's policy towards Iraq. His dogged presence led politicians to introduce many adhoc laws to try to remove him and the Serious Organised Crime and Police Act of 2005 was in part designed to make his protest illegal. Visitors should be aware that any form of unauthorized political protest in this area is now an offence. In the end Brian Haw was forced to abandon his protest because of ill health, he died from lung cancer in June 2011, ten years after his occupation of Parliament began.

His protest inspired many and was a thorn in the side of many politicians who would far rather 'move forward' from the war in Iraq and its consequences. The artist Mark Wallinger recreated Haw's many protest banners for an exhibition entitled 'State Britain' which won the Turner Prize in 2007.

In recent years Parliament Square has become a more hospitable, if sanitised, place. The road crossings – removed to discourage protest – have been reinstalled, and visitors can now wonder among the monuments, including recent arrivals such as Mandela and 'the Welsh wizard' Lloyd George.

1. Queen Anne (1665-1714)

Queen Anne's Gate, SW1

Sculptor unknown (perhaps Francis Bird), Stone, 1708

This monument commemorates the second daughter of James II, who reigned in ill health from 1702 till her early death. Queen Anne died without leaving an heir and so was the last Stewart, ushering in the reign of the Hanovarians. The unspoiled Georgia road which bares her name is worth a visit in its own right with many blue plaques commemorating famous politicians. For more details about Queen Anne see the review of her statue outside St Paul's Cathedral (p.218)

2. George Canning (1770-1827)

Parliament Square, SW1

Sculptor Richard Westmacott, Bronze (Erected in Palace Yard 1832, moved to present site in 1867)

George Canning's statue in Parliament Square shows him as a toga-clad Roman senator which is fitting as his eloquence and reason had earned him the title "The Cicero of the British Senate". He came from a modest Irish family, but the patronage of a wealthy uncle allowed him to acquire a gentleman's education and an introduction into the Whig party. Canning was soon to change allegiances due to his antipathy towards the French Revolution (which many Whigs supported) and his admiration for and friendship with Pitt the Younger. Under Pitt's war administration, Canning was an effective minister and in 1808 devised the seizure of the Danish fleet preventing it falling into the hands of Napoleon. It was at this time that Canning fell out with the aristocratic war minister, Castlereagh. The feud became so bitter that the two fought a duel in September 1809, in which Canning was injured. Both men were obliged to resign following the incident.

Canning held a few minor positions in government after his resignation, but only achieved a position of prominence after the suicide of Castlereagh in 1822. Canning took over the position of foreign secretary and adopted a more populist approach to Britain's foreign policy than any before him. He pursued a more liberal stance in response to the reactionary states of France, Austria and Russia who dominated Europe after 1815. He was unable to prevent the suppression of independence in Spain by the French, but used Britain's naval power to successfully promote independence for the Spanish colonies of South America and the liberation of Greece from Ottoman rule. Canning's populist style was much disliked by more reactionary Tories such as Wellington and Eldon, both of whom refused to serve in his brief administration which was formed after the death of Lord Liverpool in 1827. Canning was only to serve as prime minister for 100 days. He died in office from a lung infection brought on by a cold caught at the funeral of the Duke of York. He was a progressive foreign minister, but a conservative when it came to domestic policy, a style of politics that was to be adopted by his young pupil Palmerston. Disraeli was later to credit Canning with being one of the originators of progressive Conservatism. Canning's own account of his philosophy is worth quoting:

'I consider it to be the duty of a British statesman in internal as well as external affairs, to hold a middle course between extremes; avoiding alike extravagancies of despotism or the licentiousness of unbridled freedom'

3. Abraham Lincoln (1809-65)

Parliament Square, SW1
Sculptor Augustus Saint-Gaudens, Bronze, 1920

Abraham Lincoln was the 16th president of the United States and one of the most controversial. He was born in a log cabin to a humble second-generation frontiersmen family and as a youth worked as a farmhand. The young Abraham was an avid reader and would often get into trouble with his father for showing too much interest in learning. Lincoln struggled to make a living and did all kinds of jobs as he made his way in the world. In 1831, while a store clerk in New Salem, Illinois, Lincoln fought a famous wrestling match with Jack Armstrong, the leader of a rowdy gang of youths. Lincoln stood 6'4" tall and although slight of build was renowned for his physical strength. It is said that Lincoln had the better of the fight but the two protagonists shook hands and became life-long friends. Lincoln later successfully defended Armstrong's son against a murder charge and asked no fee for his work. Had Lincoln become president during less troubled times he may have achieved a great deal; however his presidency was to be overshadowed by the bloody civil war which was already imminent when Lincoln took office. When the southern confederates overran Fort Sumter in 1861, Lincoln had little choice but to raise an army to maintain the Union and so the Civil War began. After four long and bloody years of war the Confederate General, Robert E. Lee, surrendered on April 9, 1865. Two days later Lincoln gave a speech outside the White House which so infuriated a southern-sympathising actor by the name of John Wilkes Booth, that he determined to assassinate the president. On April 14th Booth shot Lincoln while he was attending the theatre. As Lincoln was set upon reconciliation and a just peace, this act did little to help Booth's cause.

There is a very fine bust of Lincoln at the Royal Exchange in the City (see p.200). This statue is a copy of the one that stands in Chicago. These statues and Britain's history as a pioneer in abolishing slavery lead most people to assume that Britain supported the Northern cause during the civil war. In fact the British political establishment was divided over the issue and prominent figures such as Gladstone, Palmerston and Russell were supporters of the South. After the Northern victory and Lincoln's assassination, fulsome speeches were made in praise of the fallen president in parliament and the establishment's southern sympathies quickly forgotten.

4. Nelson Mandela (1918-)

Parliament Square, SW1
Sculptor Ian Walters, Bronze, 2007

Categorised as a terrorist by Margaret Thatcher's government and imprisoned for nearly 30 years by South African Apartheid government, Nelson Mandela was released in 1990 and witnessed the unveiling of this monument in 2007. Mandela is depicted on a lower plinth than the other monuments on the square and is shown addressing a crowd in one of his famously colourful shirts. A large and more imposing bust of Mandela, also by Ian Walters, can be found on the South Bank (see page 150).

5. Sir Robert Peel (1788-1850)

Parliament Square, SW1
Sculptor Matthew Noble, Bronze, 1851

Born in Lancashire, the son of a wealthy cotton mill owner, Robert Peel was a man of considerable intellect and the most important figure in Parliament between 1820 and his death in 1850. His political importance is all the more remarkable for a man who was said by contemporaries to be rather cold and haughty in his manner, and to suffer bouts of mad temper which did not make him many friends in parliament.

Peel entered the Commons in April 1809. When Lord Liverpool became prime minister he took up the position of chief secretary for Ireland in which capacity he became renowned for his opposition to Catholic Emancipation. Peel nearly fought a duel with the Irish nationalist Daniel O'Connell in 1815. O'Connell had called him 'orange Peel' for his support of the Protestant cause. As with O'Connell's later attempted duel with Disraeli, the authorities intervened to prevent any blood shed.

Peel soon resigned his post in Ireland, exhausted by the constant travel involved. He was to return to ministerial office as home secretary for both Lord Liverpool and Wellington. It was as home secretary under Wellington that Peel performed one of his first major changes of mind. Having opposed Catholic Emancipation for many years, Peel was persuaded that change was necessary to avoid crisis and so in March 1829 he introduced the Emancipation Act. It was also at this time that Peel created the Metropolitan Police Force for which he is most famous. The term 'peelers' or 'bobbies' for police officers derives from Peel's name. As Tory leader through most of the 1830s, Peel also had to make an accommodation with the 1832 Parliamentary Reform Act which he had formerly opposed. It was Peel's attempt to accommodate such change which was to mark the beginning of the transformation of the Tory party into the modern-day Conservative party.

Peel was to head several Tory ministries, passing major reforms such as the introduction of income tax and several laws to lessen the problems in Ireland. In 1843 there was an attempt made on Peel's life by a mentally deranged Scottish woodsman named Daniel M'Naghten. Peel was unscathed, but his personal secretary was killed in the incident. The subsequent trial established the rules on insanity pleading in law that are still used to this day and bare the mad woodsman's name. Peel's final change of mind came when he repealed the Corn Laws in 1846, after years of opposition to the proposal. The Corn Laws kept corn prices high for farmers, but in so doing impoverished the weakest in society. The Tory party was split on the issue and the repeal brought an end to Peel's ministry and let the Whigs into power for many years. Peel remained active in politics after the end of his government. He fell from his horse on 28th June 1850 and died from his injuries several days later.

6. Benjamin Disraeli
Earl of Beaconsfield (1804-1881)

Parliament Square, SW1
Sculptor Mario Raggi, Bronze, 1883

Benjamin Disraeli was probably the most interesting and certainly the most exotic politician of his day. He was a dandy, a wit and a successful novelist whose character can be contrasted with the rather worthy seriousness of his contemporary, Gladstone. Disraeli was also the first and last Prime Minister of Jewish decent, although he was christened after his father converted to Christianity.

As a young man Disraeli travelled through Europe, had several affairs, contracted venereal disease and began his career as a novelist and politician. Before entering parliament he became embroiled in a long-running dispute with the Irish nationalist Daniel O'Connell. The two were to have fought a duel in 1835, but the police intervened to prevent it.

After several attempts he was finally elected as a Tory MP for Maidstone in 1837. When the party won the 1841 general election, Disraeli presented himself to prime minister Robert Peel as a suitable candidate for ministerial office. Peel did not share Disraeli's high opinion of his talents and declined the offer. Disraeli took his revenge by becoming a leading figure of the 'Young England' group who criticized the government from the back benches. It was during this period that Disraeli developed his idea of a popular 'One-nation' Tory party which intended to reduce the divide between rich and poor. Despite the Thatcherite 1980s, this idea is still alive today within the modern Conservative party.

After the fall of Peel's ministry (see page 64) Disraeli was to return as chancellor of the exchequer under Lord Derby's premiership in the Conservative governments of 1852, 1858-59 and 1866-68. His greatest achievement during this period was the passing of the 1867 Reform Act which gave a further two million citizens the right to vote. Disraeli became prime minister in 1868 and declared in the Commons 'I have climbed to the top of the greasy pole'. His triumph was short-lived with the elections of the same year bringing Gladstone and the Liberals into office. It was not until 1874 that Disraeli finally became PM with sufficient power to put into practice some of his reforming ideas, by which time he was 70 years old. He continued the trend to social reform, begun by Gladstone, with important laws such as the Public Health Act (1875) and the Education Act (1876), radically changing the role of the state. His progressive domestic policy was contrasted with an aggressive foreign policy which included the annexation of the Fiji islands (1874) and the Transvaal (1877), the war against the Afghans (1878-79), and the Zulu War of 1879. Disraeli's imperial ambitions were finally realised with Queen Victoria assuming the title of Empress of India in 1876. The Liberals defeated the Conservatives in the 1880 general election and Disraeli decided to retire from politics. He died on 19th April 1881. His favourite primrose flowers are placed at his monument on the anniversary of his death.

7. Edward Stanley, 14th Earl of Derby (1799-1868)

Parliament Square, SW1
Sculptor Matthew Noble, Bronze, 1874

This bronze figure of three times prime minister Edward Stanley wearing the Garter is interesting for the bronze reliefs which depict him publicly speaking at various stages in his long career. One of the reliefs shows St Stephen's Chapel, which was the meeting place of the Commons before the present parliament was built. Stanley entered parliament as a Whig in 1820 and soon acquired a reputation as an orator; Lord Lytton described him as "the Rupert of Debate", no doubt after Prince Rupert, the head of the Cavaliers in the Civil War. Like many politicians of his day, Stanley changed parties and formed cross-party alliances when necessary. He served in Canning's government of 1827 and after a period out of office was made Secretary of State for War and the Colonies in 1837 in Peel's second ministry. In this position he took over the responsibility for the conduct and conclusion of the Opium Wars with China and concluded the Treaty of Nanking in August 1842. Although a fairly progressive young man, Edward Stanley became increasingly conservative with age and resigned from Robert Peel's government over the repeal of the Corn Laws. His three periods as prime minister were not particularly eventful and his greatest single achievement, the 1867 Reform Act, was not his work but that of Benjamin Disraeli, who succeeded him as prime minister just before his death in 1868. There is a stone bust of the Earl of Derby in Great Windmill Street, W1 (see page 30).

8. Henry Temple, 3rd Viscount Palmerston (1784-1865)

Parliament Square, SW1
Sculptor Thomas Woolner, Bronze, 1876

Palmerston was one of the giants of the late Victorian political scene, but his name is not as well known as Gladstone or Disraeli. The reason for this may well be that Harry Temple (later Lord Palmerston) was 70 when he became Prime Minister for the first time in 1855 and was a creature of the Regency period. He disliked the Victorian spirit of reform, doing all he could to prevent such changes and preserve the rights and privileges of the aristocracy.

Palmerston was a popular political figure largely because of the aggressive populism of his foreign policy which included the bombing of Canton following the Chinese seizure of a pirate boat registered under the British flag. The Chinese had a legal case for seizing the boat and Palmerston lost the vote in parliament. He fought the subsequent election on jingoistic lines and won by a landslide.

Palmerston was also popular for his jaunty and energetic character and was knicknamed 'Lord Cupid' for his many affairs. His reputation did not endear him to Queen Victoria and he was almost dismissed for attempting seduce one of the queen's ladies-in-waiting. Even at the age of 78 Palmerston was cited as co-respondent in a divorce case, which only increased his popularity. Lady Palmerston was a witty and fun-loving woman who tolerated her wayward husband. Her London parties were renowned for their grandeur as well as being occasions for political intrigue. Palmerston fell ill in October 1865, and it is said his last words were "Die, my dear doctor? That is the last thing I shall do!"

9. Field Marshal Jan Christiaan Smuts (1870-1950)

Parliament Square, SW1
Sculptor Jacob Epstein, Bronze, 1956

Jan Smuts was a South African politician and soldier of exceptional talent who received an English education, but fought against the British on his return to South Africa during the Boer War (1899-1902). There can be few monuments in London to those that fought a guerila war against the British, but Jan Smuts was to prove a loyal ally to Britain once the *Vereeniging Peace Treaty* (1902), which he helped to draft, was signed. During the First World War, Smuts fought an effective campaign against the Germans in East Africa, before joining the Imperial War Cabinet in 1917. Smuts participated in the Treaty of Versailles before returning to South Africa to play a key role in his country's politics, including many years as prime minister.

Smuts was again to prove a key ally to the British during the Second World War and was promoted to field marshal in the British army in 1941. He participated in the Paris Peace Treaty at the end of the war, making him the only politician to be involved in the conclusion of both world wars. He was a major figure in the forming of the United Nations after the war, but his anglophile position proved unpopular amongst the Afrikaners and he was to lose the 1948 election to a pro-apartheid party. Jan Smuts coined the term 'holism' and 'holistic' from his academic studies. He died in 1950 at the age of 80.

10. David Lloyd George (1863-1945)
Parliament Square, SW1
Sculptor Glynn Williams, Bronze, 2007

David Lloyd George was brought up in humble circumstances in Wales, his schoolmaster father having died when he was young. He was bright and ambitious and after qualifying as a solicitor was elected as Liberal member of parliament for Caernavon – a seat he held until his death 55 years later.

Lloyd George started as a young radical. He opposed the Boer War and his first budget as Chancellor of the Exchequer in 1909 introduced social insurance through taxation which was the precursor of the Welfare State. His budget was so controversial that the Parliament Act of 1911 was passed to override the opposition of the Lords.

Despite his earlier opposition to war, Lloyd George supported British involvement in World War I, and became minister of Munitions, then Secretary of State for War and in December 1916 replaced Asquith as Prime Minister with the support of the Conservative and Labour leaders. He proved a dynamic war leader, introducing the convoy system and unifying Allied command under General Foch (see p.288). He was also a leading figure in the Paris Peace Conference and the Treaty of Versaille.

After the war Lloyd George continued in power with the support of the Conservatives, but his firebrand days were long gone. Having secured the settlement of the Irish Free State in 1921, he was involved in a scandal involving the selling of honours which damaged is reputation. In October 1922 the Conservatives withdrew their support and Lloyd George was forced to resign as Prime Minister.

In the proceeding years Lloyd George would occasionally make a stand on a particular issue and in January 1935 presented a keynesian inspired economic paper to the cabinet which was rejected. His outspoken admiration for Hitler as the 'George Washington of Germany' was to further marginalise him from mainstream politics.

Lloyd George had a considerable reputation as a womaniser despite his long marriage and was nicknamed 'the Goat', by cabinet colleagues. The music hall song 'Lloyd Georgeg Knew My Father' is thought to be an oblique reference to his personal life. After his first wife's death in January 1941, he married his secretary and mistress at the age of 80.

On his death Churchill called him 'the greatest Welshman which that unconquerable race has produced since the age of the Tudors' and so it is a pity that this recent addition to Parliament Square is such a poor representation of the man, looking more like an enormous Telly Tubby than a great statesman.

11. Sir Winston Churchill (1874-1965)

Parliament Square, SW1
Sculptor Ivor Roberts-Jones, Bronze, 1973

There are five monuments to Winston Churchill to be found in London, but this is by far the largest and most prominent. Churchill will forever be associated with the travails of the Second World War and what he termed 'our finest hour'. British culture has remained in some way deeply attached to this image of itself as a bastion of freedom against Nazi oppression and Churchillian rhetoric is used in all kinds of circumstances including our dealings with Europe.

Churchill was half American, his mother being a New York heiress, but his father was a full-blooded English aristocrat descended from the Duke of Marlborough.

Churchill received the education of a young English gentleman at Harrow and then, due to his poor academic performance, was sent to Sandhurst before joining the army and seeing action in India and the Sudan. Winston had a way with words and sent dispatches to the papers recounting his exploits. When he left the army in 1899 he became a war reporter and was taken prisoner during the Boer War. His escape made the headlines and he wrote a book of his adventure on his return home. In 1900 he was elected as Conservative MP for Oldham, but the young Churchill soon changed sides to the Liberal party. It was as a Liberal that he first entered the cabinet in 1908 under Herbert Asquith. Promoted to home secretary after the 1910 election, Churchill passed many liberal reforms of the prison service before losing the job because of his mishandling of the miners' strike. He was moved to the Admiralty where he helped develop the Royal Naval Air Force. At the outbreak of World War One Churchill joined the War Council, but his Gallipoli campaign of 1915 led to heavy casualties. Most politicians would make excuses for such failing, but Churchill joined the army and saw action at the Western Front. He was brought back into the cabinet by David Lloyd George, but again he made some radical and wrong decisions. In Iraq, Churchill believed that British rule could be maintained with a very small number of troops through the use of the Royal Air Force. The policy was a disaster and in 1920 there was an uprising of Kurdish and Arab tribes that continued for many years and led to heavy casualties. It is interesting to note that Churchill favoured the use of chemical weapons in Iraq against "recalcitrant Arabs".

Churchill was returned as a Conservative MP in the 1924 election. As Chancellor he returned Britain to the Gold Standard (which proved a disaster) and took a hard line against the General Strike (which proved unpopular). The Conservatives were defeated in 1929, and the 1930s were to be Churchill's years of political isolation – a lone voice on the back benches warning against Hitler and condemning the policy of Appeasement. The start of the Second World War marked the end of Neville Chamberlain's policy and career and in May 1940 Churchill was appointed prime minister. The war did not initially go well and Churchill even faced a vote of no confidence in the house but he played a vital role in inspiring the country and involving both the Soviet Union and the United States in the war against Nazi Germany. After victory over Germany in 1945 Churchill lost the 1945 election to Clement Attlee's Labour party (see page 372) but was again to win power in 1951. Old and unwell he retired from politics in 1955 and died in 1965 having lived his early life under the reign of Queen Victoria and died while the Beatles were at their height. Like all great men, Churchill was a mixture of the very good and the very bad. Those that see him as one or the other are usually engaged in some form of propaganda.

12. Oliver Cromwell (1599-1658)
Westminster Hall, Parliament Square, SW1
Sculptor Sir William Hamo Thornycroft, Bronze, 1899

In 1640 Oliver Cromwell was an obscure MP for Cambridgeshire and modest country squire. Cromwell was also a devout Puritan and in 1634 had even attempted to emigrate with his family to

America to avoid the widespread persecution of Puritans by archbishop Laud with the support of the crown. It was this religious and political conflict between parliament and Charles I and the bloody civil war that followed that were to prove Oliver Cromwell's making. When the war began in the summer of 1642 Cromwell joined the parliamentary army and was a key contributor to the parliamentary victory at Marston Moor in 1644. By the battle of Naseby in the summer of 1645 Cromwell had risen to second-in-command of parliament's New Model Army. He proved as effective a politician as he was a soldier and was the dominant figure during the trial of Charles I in the winter of 1648, leading to the king's execution in January 1649. Within two years of the regicide Cromwell had subjugated both Ireland and Scotland in bloody conflict, succeeding where Charles I had singularly failed. The redistribution of land from Irish Catholics to Protestant settlers under Cromwell was to lead to centuries of bitterness. By the winter of 1653 Cromwell's domination of parliament was publicly acknowledged with his appointment as Lord Protector. The five years of Cromwell's reign were to see the establishment of religious tolerance and parliamentary civilian government in Britain.

On Cromwell's death in 1658, the republic soon fell apart and the monarchy was restored to the throne. The surviving signatories to the king's execution were themselves executed at Charing Cross (see Charles I statue page 19) and Cromwell's body was exhumed from Westminster Abbey and hung at Traitors' Gate. Despite these public displays of vengeance, Cromwell had changed the nature of British politics and the ultimate authority of parliament was never again questioned by the crown.

Cromwell remains a controversial figure in Britain's history. It took over two centuries for a statue to be erected in London to commemorate him and this was fiercely objected to by Irish Nationalist members of parliament for his brutality towards Ireland in 1649-50. It was eventually left to Lord Rosebery to personally pay for the erection of this statue, which shows Cromwell with the two great influences in his life in each hand, the sword and the bible.

13. Richard I (Coeur de Lion) (1157-1199)
Old Palace Yard, SW1
Sculptor Cast of original by Carlo Marochetti, Bronze, 1851

Richard 'the Lion Heart' is a symbol of Britain's heroic past and this bronze statue shows him in full military dress, to reinforce the national image. The monument was erected during the Great Exhibition to represent Britain to the world, but the real Richard I was very different from this myth.

Richard was more French than English having been brought up by his French mother. His first language was French and he cared far more for his continental possessions, spending only six months of his ten-year reign in England. Power and good family relations are seldom compatible and Richard fought his brothers and father on several occasions before finally making an alliance with Philip II of France to overthrow his father.

After assuming the throne Richard joined the unsuccessful third Crusade to liberate the Holy Land in 1190. On the journey home Richard was captured and imprisoned for several years by Holy Roman Emperor Henry VI and in his absence Philip II formed an alliance with his brother John. On his release in 1194 Richard defeated his brother and recaptured the land taken by Philip II, defeating Philip near Gisors in 1198. In the spring of the following year he was killed in a minor skirmish. As Richard lay dying he asked to see the archer who had fired the fatal arrow, ordering that the man be pardoned and given a sum of money, but on Richard's death his killer was flayed alive and then hanged. Richard failed to produce an heir and his crown was passed to his brother John.

14. George V (1865-1936)
Old Palace Yard, SW1
Sculptor Sir William Rein Dick, Stone, 1947

George V was born the second son of Edward VII in 1865. He was not expected to become king and began his adult life in the Royal Navy. It was only when his older brother died in 1892 that George became the heir to the throne. Despite the sudden change of circumstances George's character remained that of a middle-ranking naval officer, obsessed with punctuality, discipline and duty.

In 1910 Edward VII died in the middle of a constitutional crisis, the newly crowned George V kept his father's promise and supported the 1911 Parliament Act. The First World War was to present problems for a British Royal Family bearing the surname Saxe-Coburg-Gotha. George V took the dramatic step of changing the family name to Windsor and towards the end of the war refused refuge to his cousin, Tsar Nicholas II, fearing any such links would damage the popularity of the British royal family.

In 1924 the King recognised Ramsay MacDonald as the first Labour prime minister, and later helped lessen the severity with which the Conservative government dealt with the general strike of 1926. The formation of a coalition government in 1931 with MacDonald as prime minister owed a good deal to the political skills of the king.

George V may have been a dull man, but he showed himself to be a rather wise statesman and his ordinariness endeared him to the British people who showed their affection for him during his silver jubilee of 1935. His death from influenza the following year was the cause of considerable national mourning.

15. Emmeline Pankhurst (1858-1928)
Victoria Tower Gardens, SW1
Sculptor A. G. Walker, Bronze, 1930

Emmeline Pankhurst was active in politics as a supporter of her radical husband Richard Pankhurst who campaigned among other things for votes for women. After the death of her husband Emmeline established the Women's Social and Political Union (WSPU) in 1903 with her eldest daughter (Christabel), to fight for women's right to vote.

The WSPU adopted the rallying cry 'deeds not words' and its members were increasingly prepared to damage property and obstruct the police for their cause with many suffragettes being imprisoned for their actions. The split in the suffragette movement came when Emmeline decided to support the government during the First World War. The WSPU slogan became "We have buried the hatchet, but we know where to find it." They even went so far as to hand out white feathers to civilian men not enlisted. The hatchet was never needed – immediately after the war the vote was given to women over 30 and in 1928 women were given the same voting rights as men.

Emmeline had moved to Canada after the war and only returned in 1926 when she attempted to get elected to parliament as a member of the Conservative party. When she died in 1928 the political establishment were keen to give her credit for her actions and this monument was unveiled next to parliament by Stanley Baldwin. Her daughter Christabel has a tablet next to her mother. There is currently a campaign to commemorate the more radical Sylvia Pankhurst who became estranged from her family.

16. The Burghers of Calais
Victoria Tower Gardens, SW1
Sculptor Auguste Rodin, Bronze, 1915 (replica of an original of 1895)

This is one of several copies of Rodin's famous sculpture – the original stands outside the town hall of Calais. The monument commemorates the terrible siege of Calais which lasted for over a year and ended in 1340 when the king of France abandoned the town with his army, leaving it to the mercy of the English king, Edward III. Edward was determined upon revenge having lost many men in the siege and demanded the complete subjugation of the town. Sir Walter Manny advised the king to show mercy and it was eventually agreed that six of the town's most important burghers should surrender themselves to the king with the keys to the city. Once the burghers presented themselves to the king he immediately ordered their execution, despite many of his own knights pleading for mercy. It was the queen that persuaded Edward to show leniency. The six were fed, clothed and returned safely to the town on her instruction.

Westminster Abbey
Broad Sanctuary, SW1
Open: Mon-Fri 9.30am-3.45pm, Saturday 9.30am-1.45pm
www.westminster-abbey.org

Westminster Abbey was built around 1045-1050 by Edward the Confessor who became the first monarch to be buried on the site. Henry III (1207-1272) later continued Edward's work by rebuilding the Abbey in the Gothic style and was buried in the Confessor's Chapel in 1272 – beginning a tradition of royal burial that lasted until the internment of George II in 1760. It was during the reign of Richard II (1367-1400) that the first notable commoners were buried in the Abbey, and over the centuries hundreds of influential people have been commemorated here – many of them now forgotten.

There is a charge for visiting the Abbey, but the history of the building and the number of monuments and tombs make it well worth the expense. There are over 600 people commemorated in some way in the Abbey and below is a brief list of some of the more prominent figures still recognised by visitors today:

THE NAVE:

Anthony Ashley-Cooper, 7th Earl of Shaftesbury – reformer (see p.31)
Charles James Fox – politician (see p.235)
William Pitt the Younger – politician (see p.256)
Franklin D. Roosevelt – US President (see p.253)
Henry Fawcett – statesman (see p.127)
Lord Mountbatten – statesman (see p.50)
Robert Baden-Powell – founder of scouts (see p.303)
General Sir James Outram – soldier (see p.137)
Baron John L. Mair Lawrence – soldier (see p.94)
Major John André – soldier
George Peabody – Philanthropist (see p.202)
Robert Stephenson – engineer (see p.354)
Field Marshal Colin Campbell – soldier (see p.96)
Neville Chamberlain – politician
Michael Faraday – scientist (see p.123)
Sir Isaac Newton – scientist (see p.25 & p.354)
James Stanhope – soldier and politician (see p.83)
Major General Charles George Gordon – soldier (see p.140)
Clement Attlee – politician (see p.372)
Ernest Bevin – politician (see p.364)
John Hunter – surgeon (see p.27)

NORTH AND SOUTH CHOIR:

Charles Darwin – scientist (see p.309)
Joseph Lister – surgeon (see p.265)
Benjamin Britten – composer
Henry Purcell – composer (see p.290)
William Wilberforce – reformer
Sir Thomas Foxwell Buxton – philanthropist (see p.84)
Baron Robert Clive – colonialist (see p.48)
Sir Noel Coward – actor and playwright
John Wesley – theologian (see p.211)
William Tyndale –theologian

NORTH TRANSEPT:
Richard Cobden – politician (see p.353)
Robert Stewart, Viscount Castlereagh – politician
Henry John Temple, Viscount Palmerston – politician (see p.68)
William Pitt the Elder – politician (see p.206)
John Holles, Duke of Newcastle – politician
George Canning – **politician** (see p.59)
Benjamin Disraeli, Earl of Beaconsfield – politician (see p.65)
William Gladstone – politician (see p.165)
Sir Robert Peel – politician (see p.63)

SOUTH TRANSEPT (POETS' CORNER):
Geoffrey Chaucer – poet
W.H. Auden – poet
Robert Browning – poet
George Eliot – novelist
Dylan Thomas – poet
Henry James – novelist
George Gordon Byron – poet (see p.275)
Lewis Carroll – writer
Ben Jonson – dramatist and poet
John Milton – poet
Samuel Taylor Coleridge – poet
William Wordsworth – poet
Dr Samuel Johnson – writer and critic (see p.168)
Jane Austen – novelist
John Keats – poet
Percy Bysshe Shelley – poet
William Shakespeare – playwright and poet (see p.26)
Robert Burns – poet (see p.132)
Sir Henry Irving – actor (see p.24)
William Makepeace Thackeray – novelist
Charles Dickens – novelist (see p.46)
Thomas Hardy – novelist and poet

Sir Isaac Newton

Charles James Fox

Poet's Corner

Robert Peel

Stringer Lawrence

William Wilberforce

James Stanhope

17. Sir Thomas Fowell Buxton (1786-1845)
Victoria Tower Gardens, SW1
Sculptor S. S. Teulon, Stone (memorial fountain), 1865

Thomas Buxton was the MP for Weymouth from 1818 and spent his energies attempting to reform the cruelty of that time. He was first a prison reformer, writing an influential book based on his investigations in Newgate Prison. He then attempted to abolish the death penalty and succeeded in restricting its use to only the most severe crimes. In 1825 Buxton took over the Society for the Mitigation and Gradual Abolition of Slavery after the retirement of William Wilberforce. His efforts were rewarded with the Slavery Abolition Act of 1833, but he continued to campaign for the improved implementation of the act until his death in February 1845. This memorial fountain was erected thanks to the efforts of his son Charles Buxton MP. The fountain was originally placed on Parliament Square, but was removed in the 1950's and placed in this more obscure location in 1957. The fountain recently underwent a considerable restoration and appears now very much as it would have done at its initial unveiling, but without the original brass figures that have been stolen over the years.

THE MALL

Queen Elizabeth The Queen Mother, p.108

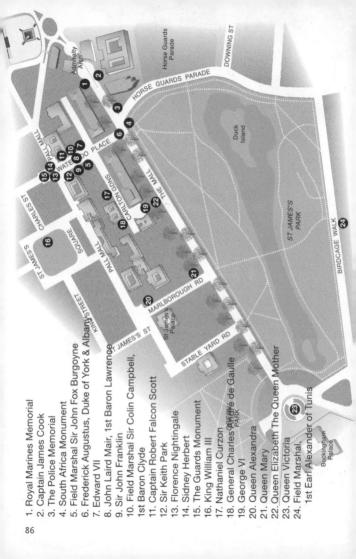

1. Royal Marines Memorial
2. Captain James Cook
3. The Police Memorial
4. South Africa Monument
5. Field Marshal Sir John Fox Burgoyne
6. Frederick Augustus, Duke of York & Albany
7. Edward VII
8. John Laird Mair, 1st Baron Lawrence
9. Sir John Franklin
10. Field Marshal Sir Colin Campbell, 1st Baron Clyde
11. Captain Robert Falcon Scott
12. Sir Keith Park
13. Florence Nightingale
14. Sidney Herbert
15. The Guards Monument
16. King William III
17. Nathaniel Curzon
18. General Charles de Gaulle
19. George VI
20. Queen Alexandra
21. Queen Mary
22. Queen Elizabeth The Queen Mother
23. Queen Victoria
24. Field Marshal, 1st Earl Alexander of Tunis

The Mall

The Mall and Pall Mall were laid out in the 1660s during the Restoration as an area for London's rich and fashionable. The French croquet-like game of 'paille maille' was played here – after which both avenues are named. Until the game fell from favour The Mall was a place for courtship and flirtation. Jonathan Swift recorded in his diary of 1711, 'When I pass the Mall in the evening it is prodigious to see the number of ladies walking there'.

When Lord Palmerston (see p.68) became prime minister in 1855 he would walk through this area on his way to Parliament passing only two monuments, to William III (1800) and the Duke of York (1833). Palmerston's leadership during the Crimean War contributed to the arrival of the Guards Monument of 1859 which commemorates that terrible conflagration. Between the death of Palmerston in 1865 and that of his successor, Disraeli, in 1881; Franklin, Campbell and Burgoyne were all to be commemorated on Waterloo Place. Baron Lawrence's monument was the last to be erected during Victoria's reign in 1882.

The Mall was redeveloped in 1903 and a new wave of memorials to the Royal Marines, the South African War, Queen Victoria and Captain Cook all found a place on the Mall. Pall Mall saw the arrival of Captain Scott and Florence Nightingale took her place next to the Guards Monument. An equestrian monument to Edward VII claimed a prime location on Waterloo Place in 1922 to be followed by an art deco fountain in memory of Queen Alexandra on Marlborough Road. The politician Lord Curzon was the last to find a place before the Second World War and since then a host of notables have joined him, the most recent being the Queen Mother in 2009.

1. Royal Marines Memorial

The Mall (near Admiralty Arch), SW1
Sculptor Adrian Jones & Sir Thomas Graham Jackson, Bronze, 1903

This memorial commemorates the marines who fell in China during the Boxer Rebellion and in the Boer War. The main statue by Adrian Jones shows a defiant marine defending his injured comrade while the bronze reliefs by Sir Thomas Jackson illustrate battle scenes from the two wars. The Chinese Boxer Rebellion and The Boer War had recently been concluded when Admiralty Arch was being constructed.

2. Captain James Cook (1728-1779)

The Mall (near Admiralty Arch), SW1
Sculptor Sir Thomas Brock. Bronze, 1914

James Cook came from humble origins in Yorkshire. As a young man he was fascinated by the sea and took up work transporting coal in large ships – called colliers – along the English coast. Having received little formal education Cook taught himself navigation, astronomy and mathematics which were to make him such a fine seaman and explorer. In 1755, on the eve of the Seven Years War, he transferred from the Merchant to the Royal Navy.

During the Seven Years War Cook's skills as a draftsman were put to good use making maps of the coast of North America and Canada. It was Cook who made the detailed maps used by General Wolfe in his attack on the Plains of Abraham (see p.340) in 1755. During the 1760's Captain Cook continued to map Newfoundland and the Antarctic Circle, his maps being of such accuracy that many were used until the 20th century. In 1768 he embarked on his first major voyage to the South Pacific on behalf of the Royal Society. In just three years he became only the second European to set foot in New Zealand, mapped the coastline and became the first European to discover the east coast of Australia. In June 1770 Cook's ship ran aground on the Great Barrier Reef where the delay allowed the botanist Joseph Banks to collect a vast array of the region's fauna and flora. During this voyage Cook prevented the spread of scurvy by forcing his crew to take malt and was instrumental in the eradication of the disease.

Cook soon embarked on his second voyage between 1772-3 during which he disproved the existence of the mythical Terra Australis, discovered South Georgia and the South Sandwich Islands and circumnavigated the globe at a high southern latitude. Cook's voyage also successfully tested John Harrison's timekeeping instruments, which at last facilitated accurate measurement of longitude. Cook was offered retirement but instead embarked on his third and last voyage in 1776. He explored and mapped the coast from California all the way to the Bering Strait, on the way discovering what came to be known as Cook Inlet in Alaska. In 1779 Cook returned to Hawaii. Ill with a stomach upset and behaving erratically, Cook mishandled a dispute with the locals and was killed in the altercation that followed. This statue was erected next to Admiralty Arch, at the time of its construction and shows Cook in nautical attire. The inscription on this monument reads 'Circumnavigator of the globe, explorer of the Pacific Ocean, he laid the foundations of the British Empire in Australia and New Zealand...'

3. The Police Memorial
Corner of The Mall and
Horse Guards Parade, SW1
Sculptor Sir Norman Foster and Per
Arnoldi, Marble and glass, 2005
Unveiled in 2005 by the Queen, this
monument commemorates British
police who have died in the course
of their duties. The monument is an
uncompromisingly modern design
consisting of a glass obelisk at the
centre of a fountain alongside a
black marble square structure which
displays a book containing the names
of 1,600 fallen officers. The memorial was conceived by the late
director Michael Winner, best known for his *Death Wish* films.

4. South Africa Monument
The Mall, SW1
Sculptor Robert Colton, Bronze and stone, 1910

This is the only monument in London
dedictated to the Boer War. The South
African War (or Second Boer War) was
fought between the British and the two
independent republics of the Orange
Free State and the Transvaal Republic.
The war was fought over access to the
gold discovered in these territories and
the rights of the British prospectors.
The British were confident of victory and
the Cape Colony governor, Sir Alfred
Milner, held the ambition of securing a
Cape-to-Cairo British Colony.

The Boers, under the leadership of Louis Botha and Jan Smuts (see p.69), confounded British expectations and although there were only 88,000 of them, they initially made considerable headway in the first months of the war, besieging the British garrisons at Ladysmith, Mafeking and Kimberley. Reinforcements arrived in 1900 and made advances against the Boers, capturing Pretoria by June 1900. The Boers reverted to guerilla tactics and the British, under Lord Kitchener (see p.51), responded with brutality, burning Boer farms and placing Boer women and children in concentration camps. The British response was widely criticised and in May 1902 the *Treaty of Vereeniging* was signed which ultimately led to self-government for the two republics in 1907. Several key figures were involved in the Second Boer War, among them Mahatma Gandhi, Robert Baden-Powell and Winston Churchill (see pages 243, 303 and 72).

5. Field Marshal Sir John Fox Burgoyne (1782-1871)

Waterloo Place, SW1
Sculptor Sir Joseph Edgar Boehm, Bronze, 1877

John Fox Burgoyne was the illegitimate son of the famous soldier and playwright General John Burgoyne and the opera singer Susan Caulfield. He fought alongside Wellington in the Pyrenees, later being posted to San Sebastian where he participated in the siege of Rosetta and later took part in the Battle of New Orleans. Burgoyne was responsible for providing relief to the starving during the Irish Potato Famine. He later played a key part in the Crimean War, participating in the siege of Sevastopol. He retired as field marshal in 1868.

6. Frederick Augustus, Duke of York and Albany (1763-1827)

Carlton Gardens, SW1
Sculptor Sir Richard Westmacott
Bronze on stone column, 1833

George III's second and favourite son was created a duke by the age of 21 having already been promoted to high rank within the army. Frederick was involved in the Napoleonic Wars, commanding at the Flanders Campaigns (1793-98) and the invasion of Holland (1799), both of which were considered disasters. The campaign in Holland inspired the nursery rhyme 'The Grand Old Duke of York' which ridiculed his indecisiveness. Frederick's position was never questioned and despite his many failings he became Commander-in-Chief of the army in 1795. As a strategist and reformer the Duke proved a success, but in 1809 he was to lose this position because of a scandal. Frederick had an expensive mistress named Mary Anne Clarke but because of his debts was often not able to pay her allowance. In 1809 it was discovered that his mistress had received money from soldiers and civil servants in return for promotion by the Duke. Frederick renounced his mistress, but she threatened to publish his letters and in return received a generous pension. Clarke spent the rest of her life in France; her great-granddaughter was the author Daphne du Maurier who wrote her life story. Frederick briefly resigned while the scandal raged but was reinstated as Commander-in-Chief in 1811 and served in that position until his death in 1827. The grandeur of this monument can be explained by Frederick's close relationship with his equally profligate older brother, George IV (see p.13) – it was funded by stopping one day's wages from every soldier in the British army.

7. Edward VII (1841-1910)

Waterloo Place, SW1
Sculptor Sir Bertram Mackennal, Bronze, 1922

Edward was to have a difficult relationship with his parents whose seriousness and sense of propriety he did not share. He spent most of his adult life waiting to inherit the throne and dedicated this time to pleasure. His affair with an actress became a public scandal just before Prince Albert fell ill and his mother unreasonably blamed Edward for Albert's death. Edward married the beautiful Alexandra, eldest daughter of King Kristian IX of Denmark, in 1863 and they moved to Marlborough House. Edward's happy marriage did not calm his appetites and he was involved in several public scandals, including the Mordant divorce case of 1870 and the Tranby Croft case of 1891.

The British public enjoyed reading about Edward's antics and these scandals increased his popularity. He certainly had a more deft touch with public relations than his mother, making friends with business people and helping the social rise of many wealthy Jewish families. Against his mother's wishes he cultivated a friendship with Gladstone that helped the royal family's popularity.

Edward's influence on government policy was limited but he had some role in the Anglo-French *Entente Cordiale* and in the cooling of relations with Germany, partly because of his dislike for his cousin, Kaiser Wilhelm II. Edward's nine years as King were a time of pomp and ceremony which helped to strengthen the constitutional role of the monarchy. His death in 1910 was deeply mourned with an estimated two million people lining the streets for his funeral. This monument bears very little resemblance to the real King, who was fat and only encountered horses at the races.

8. John Laird Mair, 1st Baron Lawrence (1811-1879)

Waterloo Place, SW1

Sculptor Sir Joseph Edgar Boehm, Bronze, 1882

Lawrence spent his early years in Northern Ireland before travelling to India in 1829 with his older brother, Sir Henry Montgomery Lawrence, to serve as a colonial administrator. During the First Sikh War he organised the supply of British troops in the Punjab and later served under his brother as commissioner in the Jullundur district. In 1849, after the Second Sikh War, Lawrence worked as a member of the Punjab Board of Administration which carried through many significant reforms and helped limit the spread of mutiny in the region while it raged in other parts of India. As chief commissioner to the province, Lawrence became famous for his command of an army which recaptured Delhi after its fall to insurgents. For his actions he earned the subriquet 'Saviour of India'. After a brief return to England, Lawrence was sent back to India to serve as Viceroy between 1863 and 1869 where he acquired a reputation as a cautious administrator willing to make reform but determined to avoid involvement in the problems of neighbouring Afghanistan and Persia. He returned to England in 1869 and was raised to the peerage for his services. This statue is a replacement for a more bellicose original which depicted the administrator with a pen in one hand and a sword in the other bearing the inscription 'Will you be governed by the pen or the sword?'. After much criticism, Boehm replaced it with the more neutral work which stands in Waterloo Place today.

9. Sir John Franklin (1786-1847)

Waterloo Place, SW1
Sculptor Matthew Noble, Bronze, 1866

Like Captain Scott, Sir John Franklin was an explorer in the heroic British tradition and one best known for his disastrous last voyage. Franklin joined the navy at 14 and fought at Copenhagen and Trafalgar. After leaving the service in 1815, Franklin was given command of his first Arctic expedition in 1819 which reached the Arctic coast in 1821 and successfully mapped over 500 miles of uncharted territory. The expedition encountered many problems and ten members of the crew died; the rest only survived because of the help of native Inuit people. The second Arctic expedition in 1825 was easier and mapped a further 500 miles of territory. Franklin returned home a hero and was knighted for his services in 1829.

Franklin embarked on his last voyage to find the Northwest Passage in May 1845 with two ships and a crew of 134. They were never seen again. As many as 40 ships searched for Franklin and his crew between 1848 and 1859 and over the years more men died in the search than were lost in the expedition itself. A monument to Joseph Bellot's expedition can be found in Greenwich (see page 329).

In recent years enough wreckage, notes and bodies have been found to establish that Franklin's ships were trapped in the ice for two years and the crew died on board ship or attempting to make their escape. It is also thought that the canned provisions on board gave the crew lead poisoning. Much of the expedition still remains in the Arctic and expeditions continue to this day to find wreckage of the two fateful ships. Some of the remnants can be seen at the National Maritime Museum.

10. Field Marshal Sir Colin Campbell, 1st Baron Clyde (1792-1863)

Waterloo Place, SW1

Sculptor Carlo Marochetti, Bronze, 1867

Campbell's father was a humble carpenter and he assumed his mother's maiden name when joining the army at the age of 16. Campbell soon saw action during the Napoleonic wars and was wounded several times, forcing his return to Britain where he was rewarded with promotion. So began his long career in the British army which included the quelling of the Demerara Insurrection (1823), the Chinese War (1842), and the Sikh War (1848-49). His role in the victory at Gujrat brought him considerable praise and he was made a KCB in 1849.

During the Crimean War Campbell accepted the command of the Highland Brigade, who distinguished themselves at the Battle of Alma and fought off the Russian attack at Balaklava. After the end of hostilities in the Crimea, Campbell had little time to rest on his laurels for he was sent by Lord Palmerston to quell the Indian Mutiny in July 1857, which he succeeded in doing with the capture of Lucknow in March 1858. On his return to England he was raised to the peerage and awarded a substantial pension and on his death buried in Westminster Abbey. His native town of Glasgow also has a statue in his honour.

11. Captain Robert Falcon Scott (1868-1912)
Waterloo Place, SW1
Sculptor Lady Scott, Bronze, 1915

Captain Scott became famous for his first expedition to the South Pole on the ship *Discovery* with Ernest Shackleton (see p.307) which got within 530 miles of the Pole. This monument is the work of Scott's widow and commemorates his last disastrous expedition to the South Pole which embarked in 1910. Scott was beaten to the Pole by a Norwegian expedition led by Roald Amundsen, and his team were to die on their homeward journey. The bodies of Scott and two of his five fellow explorers were found in November 1912 along with Scott's journal which states 'These rough notes and our dead bodies must tell the tale.' Lady Scott was protective of her husband's reputation and edited his writings to present a more heroic image of the expedition. The reality was one of serious disagreements within the team and a lack of survival experience in Arctic conditions – Amundsen's men had gained weight during their expedition, Scott's men starved. The monument shows Scott in his full Arctic dress, but is intended as a memorial to all those that lost their lives on the fateful expedition.

12. Sir Keith Park (1892-1975)
Waterloo Place, SW1
Sculptor Leslie Johnson, Bronze, September 2010

Sir Keith Park was a New Zealander who played a major part in the Second World War and was known by the German's as 'the defender of London'.

Park began his career as a soldier seeing action at Gallipoli and the Somme before transferring to the British Flying Corps and earning a Military Cross for his distinguished action in Northern France.

During the Battle of Britain, Park took command of No.11 Group RAF who were responsible for defending London and the Southeast. Park's strategic planning and careful management of scarce resources were vital to Britain's success during those early years of the war, and he personally commanded forces on key days of the battle. Despite his success his disagreement with Air Vice Marshal Trafford Leigh-Mallory of 12 Group led to him loosing command of no.11 Group. He was soon playing a vital role in Egypt and Malta and ended the war as Allied Air Commander in South East Asia. The promotions did not lessen Park's sense that he had been ill treated long after his retirement in 1946.

Park returned to New Zealand after the war and took up successful civilian roles before his death in 1975 at the age of 82. Park's contemporaries began a campaign in March 2008 to recognise his importance which culminated in the this monument taking its place alongside Scott and Franklin with 14 survivors of the Battle of Britain witnessing the unveiling.

13. Florence Nightingale (1820-1910)

Waterloo Place, SW1
Sculptor Arthur Walker, Bronze, 1915

Florence Nightingale proved an able student particularly gifted at mathematics and, against her wealthy parent's wishes, continued her studies to a very advanced level. In her late 20s, she determined to become a nurse, an occupation which had a very low status and no formal training in this country. Her wealth allowed her to travel widely and acquire nursing experience in Egypt and Germany.

When the Crimean War began in March 1854 reports soon came back of the poor medical care. The Secretary for War, Sir Sidney Herbert (see p.100), was a friend of the Nightingale family and recruited Florence as a nursing administrator to improve the situation.

When Nightingale arrived at the Scutari hospital in November 1854 injured soldiers were seven times more likely to die from disease in hospital than on the battlefield. She immediately improved the sanitary conditions and greatly increased the life expectancy of casualties. Using statistics that proved the need for better hygiene, Nightingale campaigned for reform on her return to London and largely due to her efforts a Royal Commission was set up in 1857. Nightingale became the first female Fellow of the Royal Statistical Society in 1858. Her work was to have a major effect upon health care and was instrumental in improving the training and status of nurses. Nightingale outlived Queen Victoria and died at the age of 90.

14. Sidney Herbert, 1st Baron Herbert of Lea (1810-1861)
Waterloo Place, SW1
Sculptor John Foley, Bronze, 1857

This statue first stood on Pall Mall, but was moved to Waterloo Place in 1915. Herbert served as a minister under Peel. His mistress leaked Peel's change of mind over the Corn Laws and so led to Peel's resignation. Despite this indiscretion, Herbert went on to serve as Secretary of War and appointed his friend Florence Nightingale to improve the medical situation in the Crimean. Herbert's health suffered from the pressures of work – he resigned in July 1861 and died just a month later. His death removed one of the key advocates for military reform.

15. The Guards Monument
Waterloo Place, SW1
Sculptor John Bell, Bronze 1859

The Crimean War was the most important and costly war of the Victorian era. This vast monument stands in commemoration of the 22,162 guardsmen who lost their lives in the conflict. The granite pedestal has three bronze figures of a Grenadier, a Fusilier and a Coldstream Guard. Upon a smaller block of granite at the back stand the actual broken Russian guns from Sevastopol. At the top of the monument is a bronze figure of Honour, with arms extended. The entire island is dedicated to the Crimean war, with statues of Florence Nightingale and Sidney Herbert standing either side of the main Guards Monument.

The war started in March 1854 when France and Britain declared war on Russia to defend the Ottoman Empire against Russian aggression. The Russians claimed to be acting to protect the Orthodox Christians living under Ottoman rule, but the long-term cause of the conflict was the evident decline of the Ottoman Empire. It was fear of Russian dominance in Eastern Europe that led Britain and France to go to the aid of the Turks.

In September 1854 Allied troops invaded the Crimea and began the siege of Sevastopol which was the main port for the Russian fleet. The Russians maintained a stiff resistance, sinking their own ships and using the guns on land to beat off Allied attack. While the siege continued, several major battles were fought as the Russians attempted to liberate Sevastopol, including the Battles of Balaclava (October 1854) and Inkerman (November 1854). The British public had expected an easy victory, but the war proved costly with more troops dying from disease and starvation than from battle. The Crimean was the first war to be influenced by the new medium of war reportage, with William Russell's articles for the *London Times* shocking the public with accounts of the conditions and casualties.

After two years of bloody and inconclusive war, Sevastopol finally fell to the Allied troops on 8th September 1855. The new Russian Emperor, Alexander II, agreed to sign a peace treaty at the Congress of Paris in 1856. The ultimate futility of the war was made evident in 1870 when Napoleon III fell from power and the new French Republic declined to uphold the Paris Treaty. The Russians were therefore able to establish a naval presence in the Mediterranean, the prevention of which had been the main achievement of the Paris Treaty. Key figures that fought in the Crimea include Sir Colin Campbell (see p.96) and the 2nd Duke of Cambridge (see p.38).

16. King William III (1650-1702)
St James's Square, SW1
Sculptor John Bacon the Younger, Bronze, 1800

In 1688 the Dutch aristocrat William III deposed his father-in-law,
James II (see p.8), in what has become known as the Glorious
Revolution. The coup established Britain as a Protestant kingdom
and ended James's often harsh attempt to catholicise his realm.
After a brief interregnum the parliaments of England and Scotland
recognised James's eldest daughter Mary and her husband and
cousin William as joint monarchs – although it was William
that was to wield power. It was a compromise that divided the
country's ruling class and in so doing created a two-party system of

government, with Whigs supporting the monarchy and a sceptical Tory party introducing clauses to prevent William's heirs – should he re-marry – from claiming the throne.

William was less interested in establishing a royal dynasty than pursuing political power to confront the ambitions of France. His reign was entirely devoted to war with expansionist France, who had overrun his home country of Holland. To raise money to fund these wars William established the Bank of England and the National Debt and accepted regular parliaments to authorise further military funds. The Jacobite struggle to reclaim the throne also led to considerable bloodshed and bitterness, with the Battle of the Boyne still celebrated by the Protestants of Northern Ireland today (see William Duke of Cumberland on page 258).

One consequence of William's reign was a considerable increase in the importation of Dutch Gin which was to have such a deleterious effect upon the poor of London as depicted in the pictures of Hogarth (see p.28). When later attempts were made to restrict the sale of gin there were riots. The loveless marriage of William and Mary produced no heir and after Mary's death in 1694 William reigned alone. His controversial rule ended in 1702 when he fell from his horse and caught a chill. It is said that the horse tripped on a molehill – Jacobites used to offer a toast to 'the little gentleman in the black velvet waistcoat' in thanks to the subterranean mammal's role in history.

This fine equestrian monument was funded from the 1724 will of Samuel Travers, but was not erected for 80 years, the will having been lost. A grand monument to William also stands in the Bank of England, but this is not accessible to the public. There is another monument to William in the grounds of his former home at Kensington Palace (see p.300). He was succeeded by his sister-in-law, Anne, who became the last of the Stuart line (see p.218), her death ushering in the Hanoverian dynasty in 1714.

17. George Nathaniel, 1st Marquess Curzon of Kedleston (1859-1925)

Carlton Terrace, SW1

Sculptor Sir Bertram Mackennal, Bronze, 1931

George Nathaniel Curzon lived for some time at number 1 Carlton Terrace, just across from where his statue stands today. He was an aristocrat and a brilliant scholar, which helps explain his legendary conceit. His fellow students at Balliol College wrote of the young Curzon;

My name is George Nathaniel Curzon
I am a most superior person.
My face is pink, my hair is sleek,
I dine at Blenheim once a week.

After his studies, Curzon travelled widely in the Middle-East and Asia and became a successful travel writer before entering politics as a Conservative MP and later as Viceroy of India (1899-1905). Curzon resigned as Viceroy after a dispute with Lord Kitchener (see p.51) and returned to England where he took his seat in the Lords and used his talents to fight against the suffragette movement and resist any reform of the second house. During the First World War, Curzon held a minor cabinet position but was promoted to Foreign Secretary in 1919 and held the post until 1924. His key achievement was the Treaty of Lausanne, negotiated with Turkey. Curzon was bitterly disappointed when passed over for the position of Prime Minister in 1924 in favour of Stanley Baldwin. He died in March 1925 having recently lost his job as Foreign Secretary. He was married twice and had three daughters, one of whom married the British fascist leader Oswald Mosley. His second daughter and his second wife were also to have affairs with Mosley.

18. General Charles André de Gaulle (1890-1970)

Carlton Terrace, SW1
Sculptor Angela Conner, Bronze, 1994

Charles de Gaulle began his career as a soldier and was decorated during the First World War and for his defence of the Polish nation against the Soviets just after the war. He spent the interwar years campaigning for modernisation of the French army but his considerable height, arrogance and forceful personality made him many enemies and he was still only a colonel in 1939.

De Gaulle was soon promoted to brigadier general, but the defeat of France was to mark the end of his military career and re-birth as a politician and figurehead of French resistance. The headquarters of the Free French was established on Carlton Terrace and de Gaulle gave his famous 'Appeal of June 18th' to the French people on BBC Radio. He moved his headquarters to Algiers in May 1943 and flew into Paris when France fell to the Allies to proclaim the continuation of the Third Republic. He was soon disillusioned with peacetime France and withdrew from politics in 1947. The collapse of the Fourth Republic under the pressure of the Algerian question saw de Gaulle's return. He became President in January 1959 and over the next ten years supervised the Independence of Algeria, established the Fifth Republic, withdrew from Nato and vetoed Britain joining the European Economic Union. De Gaulle's conservatism was increasingly against the spirit of the time, with the student riots of 1968 marking the effective end of his presidency. He resigned in 1969 and died suddenly in 1970. Unlike so many politicians who manage to enrich themselves while in office, de Gaulle died with considerable debts.

19. George VI (1895-1952)
Carlton Gardens, SW1
Sculptor William Macmillan, Stone, 1955

The second son of George V was a sickly youth neglected by his parents. The future George VI grew up in the shadow of his older and more glamorous brother and was never expected to take the throne. The prince served in the Royal Navy during the First World War and was made Duke of York in 1920. In the inter-war years he proved a conscientious member of the Royal family competing in the men's doubles at Wimbledon in 1926, visiting factories and mines and establishing the Duke of York's Camps which were a kind of summer camp for children of all classes.

In all his work he was assisted by his young wife, Elizabeth Bowes-Lyon (see page 108), with whom he had two daughters. Their happy life together was brought to an end with the abdication of Edward VIII and the Duke's unexpected coronation as George VI in December 1936. The new King was awkward and suffered from a stutter, so emphasis was placed on the 'family on the throne' which involved the Queen and the young princesses. George was in favour of Neville Chamberlain and his policy of Appeasement, and even offered to visit Hitler, Mussolini and Emperor Hirohito to try to avoid war. During the war George's political influence was limited but he and his family did serve a symbolic role for the country. The king's health had never been robust and in 1952 he died at the age of 56, ushering in the current reign of his daughter Queen Elizabeth. This statue shows the King in the uniform of Admiral of the Fleet and Garter robes.

20. Queen Alexandra (1844-1925)
Marlborough Road, SW1
Sculptor Sir Alfred Gilbert, Bronze, 1926

This art nouveau memorial stands in the wall of Marlborough House where Queen Alexandra lived as consort to Edward VII. The marriage was generally a happy one producing six children, but the beautiful Alexandra could not stop Edward's philandering. After a period of estrangement she came to accept her husband's infidelities and his lover, Alice Koppel, was even allowed a place at Edward's deathbed. Alexandra remained a popular member of the Royal family until her death in 1925.

21. Queen Mary (1867-1953)
Marlborough Road, SW1
Sculptor Sir William Reid Dick
Slate Medallion, 1967

Mary Victoria of Treck was a German aristocrat who married the future George V in 1893, having been previously engaged to the Duke of Clarence until his sudden death in 1892. She became the Queen consort in 1910, but avoided public attention. Queen Mary was known for her conservative dress sense and her interest in antiques.

22. Queen Elizabeth The Queen Mother (1900-2002)
The Mall, SW1
Sculptor Philip Jackson, Stone reliefs: Paul Day, Bronze, 2009

Elizabeth Bowes-Lyon was born into an aristocratic family, her father inheriting an Earldom in 1904. She came to national attention when marrying Albert, Duke of York, in 1923. At the time there was little prospect of her awkward husband assuming the throne over his charismatic brother.

In 1936 this changed with Edward VIII's abdication to marry the America divorcee Wallis Simpson. Elizabeth was now the Queen consort of King George VI and together they did much to shore up the fragile reputation of the Royal Family and act as national figureheads during the Second World War. The Royal visits to the East End were not always popular, but Churchill had received similar hostility when visiting bomb victims. When Buckingham Palace was hit during the Blitz she is famously reported to have said 'I can (now) look the East End in the face'.

Her life was to change again in 1952 with the death of her husband and the ascension of her daughter Elizabeth to the throne. She then assumed the role of Queen Mother which she held for the remaining 50 years of her long life. She is said to have enjoyed horse racing, was an enthusiastic drinker and privately held very conservative political views. It is perhaps because of, rather than despite, these traits that she was a popular public figure. She also shared the nation's enthusiasm for easy credit having accumulated a multi-million pound overdraft at Coutts Bank.

This monument shows the Queen Mother at the time of her husband's death and has reliefs depicting scenes from her life. It stands in front of the monument to her husband erected in 1955.

23. Queen Victoria (1819-1901)

The Mall, SW1

Sculptor Sir Thomas Brock, Sir Aston Webb (design); Marble, 1911

Princess Victoria of Kent was born to the Duke of Kent and Princess Victoria of Saxe-Coburge-Saalfield in May 1819, although there are some doubts about the Duke's involvement (see p.266). Following the death of William IV in June 1837, Victoria ascended to the thrown at the age of 18.

Queen Victoria's reign became synonymous with Britain's dominance and prosperity but the monarchy was by this time far less powerful than during the reign of her grandfather, George III (see p.6). Prime Minister Lord Melbourne taught the young queen to question government policy but leave the final decision to politicians. She followed this advice throughout her long reign – even after her marriage to Prince Albert (see p.301) in 1840. The royal couple had little influence on government policy and were ignored on important issues such as the Crimean War, when they favoured an alliance with Russia.

Following Prince Albert's death from typhoid in 1861, Victoria withdrew from public life and spent the rest of her reign in mourning, although forming strong attachments to several of her male servants – most famously John Brown. Victoria was very susceptible to flattery and in the rivalry between Gladstone and Disraeli it was the later who won the Queen's favour by 'laying it on with a trowel'. Disraeli ingratiated himself further when he made Victoria Empress of India in 1876. Victoria died in 1901 having become Britain's longest serving monarch and establishing the form of modern British monarchy which survives to this day.

24. Field Marshal,
1st Earl Alexander of Tunis (1891-1969)

Guards Museum, Birdcage Walk, SW1
Sculptor James Butler, Bronze, 1985

Harold Alexander was the third son of the 4th Earl of Caledon and educated at Harrow and Sandhurst. He was commissioned into the Irish Guards in 1911 and as part of the British Expeditionary Force (BEF) distinguished himself during the First World War, receiving the Military Cross in 1915, and becoming a Brigadier in 1918.

By the start of the Second World War Alexander was a Major-General. He led the withdrawal from Dunkirk and was the last British soldier to leave. Alexander was then sent to command the withdrawal from Burma (see Field Marshal Slim page 42) and was made Commander-in-Chief in North Africa in August 1942, working with General Montgomery (see p.44) to secure the victory at El Alamein. In January 1943 Alexander became deputy to Eisenhower and was put in command of the Allied Armies in Italy where he received the German surrender in April 1945.

After the war, Alexander was created Viscount of Tunis for his command in Italy and North Africa and from 1946 to 1952 was a successful and popular Governor-General of Canada. His time as Minister of Defence in Churchill's government was less successful and he resigned from the position and from politics in 1954. This monument shows Alexander in full military dress, binoculars in hand, and stands within the courtyard of the Guards Museum.

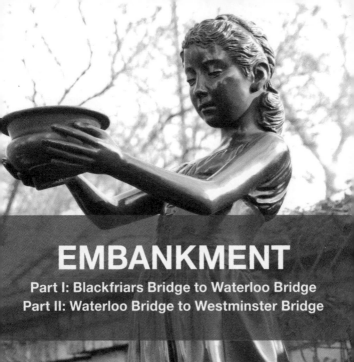

EMBANKMENT

Part I: Blackfriars Bridge to Waterloo Bridge
Part II: Waterloo Bridge to Westminster Bridge

Lady Henry Somerset, p.118

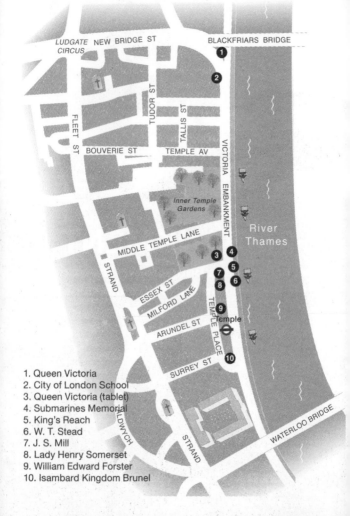

1. Queen Victoria
2. City of London School
3. Queen Victoria (tablet)
4. Submarines Memorial
5. King's Reach
6. W. T. Stead
7. J. S. Mill
8. Lady Henry Somerset
9. William Edward Forster
10. Isambard Kingdom Brunel

Embankment Part I:
Blackfriars to Waterloo

It is fitting that Queen Victoria's monument is the first to be encountered on the journey west from Blackfriar's to Waterloo Bridge, because the roads, pathways and gardens along the route were all created during her reign. It was Joseph Bazelgette (see p.135) who was given the task of improving London's decaying sewer system and as part of his plan built the Victoria, Albert and Chelsea Embankments between 1865 and 1870 under which vast sewer pipes carry the effluence of London out to sea. The inventive Victorians made good use of the reclaimed land to create wide roads, boulevards and several beautiful gardens.

The City of London School has Victorian statues to several great English men of former times – Bacon, Shakespeare, Milton and Newton – no doubt to inspire their young scholars. The other monuments in this area commemorate figures of the 18th and early 19th centuries, with the philosopher J. S. Mill and the engineer Brunel the only names that will be recognised by most people today. The tablet to W. T. Stead declares his virtues as a pioneering journalist, but in reality he was one of the first tabloid hacks who was imprisoned for fabricating a salacious story. There are several worthy but lesser figures commemorated here, including William Forster, who introduced state education and the philanthropist Lady Somerset. The Submarine Memorial, with its detailed reliefs and mosaic of anchors, is the most interesting of the monuments to be found on this stretch of the Embankment.

1. Queen Victoria (1819-1901)

New Bridge Street, EC4

Sculptor C. B. Birch, Bronze, 1896

This monument was erected towards
the end of Victoria's reign, but depicts
her in her regal prime with sceptre
and orb. The monument is located
at the start of the embankment which
bears her name. A little further
along the Embankment is a tablet
commemorating the last visit of the
Queen to the City of London in 1900
(see p.109 for further details about
Queen Victoria).

2. City of London School

Victoria Embankment, EC4

Sculptor J. Daymond and Son, Stone, 1882

The City of London School has four monuments, to Francis Bacon
(see p.187), William Shakespeare (see p.26), John Milton and Isaac
Newton (see p.25) on the second floor of their grand Victorian
building overlooking Blackfriars Bridge.

3. Victoria Tablet
Victoria Embankment, EC4
Sculptor C. H. Mabey
Marble Medallion, 1902
This stone was erected to
commemorate Queen Victoria's last
visit to the City of London in 1900. For
a biography of Victoria see p.109.

4. Submarines Memorial
River Parapet,
Victoria Embankment, WC2
Sculptor F. Brook Hatch &
A. H. Ryan Tenison, Bronze, 1922
This monument was originally erected
to commemorate those who lost their
lives in Royal Navy submarines during
the First World War. After 1945 further
additions were made to recognise the
sacrifice of submarine crews in the
Second World War. The bronze relief
lists the submarines lost in both wars
and is flanked by the figures of Truth
and Justice.

5. King's Reach
River Parapet,
Victoria Embankment, WC2
Bronze plaque, 1935
This plaque was erected to
commemorate the 25th anniversary of
the accession to the throne of George
V. For further information about
George V see p.77.

6. W. T. Stead (1849-1912)
River Parapet, Victoria Embankment, WC2
Sculptor Sir George Frampton, Bronze plaque, 1920

Journalism was considered in the Victorian era to be a means of providing information, it was William Thomas Stead who identified the power of the press to shape public opinion and in so doing became the first truly modern journalist. As the son of a congregationalist minister, Stead was the first to realise that the moral indignation of the pulpit could be applied to the writing of newspaper copy, a practice that was most effective when combined with a good degree of sensationalism.

In 1876, as editor of The Northern Echo, the young Stead was to employ his skills to engender righteous indignation against the Ottoman Turks for their brutality in Bulgaria. The long-term situation in Bulgaria was far from Stead's mind by the time he had become editor of the influential Pall Mall Gazette in 1883. It was in this position that Stead performed his most famous exploit – calling for the return of General Gordon (see p.140) to right the problems of the Sudan. His campaign helped persuaded Gladstone to appoint Gordon to a role for which he was unsuited and it was the disaster of this policy that led to the defeat of Gladstone's government in 1885.

Stead eventually served three months in prison for publishing an entirely fictitious account of child prostitution which involved the actual kidnapping of a child in order to provide convincing pictures to accompany the story. On the anniversary of his imprisonment Stead would walk to work across Waterloo bridge in prison garb. He died on board the Titanic in 1912.

7. J. S. Mill (1806-1873)
Victoria Embankment – Temple Section, WC2
Sculptor Thomas Woolner, Bronze, 1878

John Stuart Mill received a rigorous education from his philosopher and historian father James Mill. By the age of 12 he had mastered Latin and Greek and was familiar with the works of classical philosophy. Jeremy Bentham, founder of Utilitarian philosophy, was Mill's godfather and it was under the influence of his writings that the young J. S. Mill became an enthusiastic advocate of the new science of morality, whose most popular principle was 'The greatest happiness for the greatest number'.

The harsh rationalism of Mill's education was to launch him on a successful career as a thinker, essayist and reformer but had serious consequences for his emotional well-being. At the age of 21 Mill suffered a serious breakdown which he attributed to his upbringing and led to a change of mind and a more critical approach to the Utilitarian School. In the course of the next 50 years Mill was to write all manner of radical liberal works beginning with A *System of Logic* (1843) and ending with *The Subjection of Women* (1869). Mill's work *On Liberty* (1859) is probably the most famous and widely read of his books, setting out the liberal argument for limited state intervention in people's actions unless those actions are harmful to others. As well as a philosopher, Mill briefly became a radical MP for Westminster between 1865 and 1868, in which position he campaigned with Henry Fawcett (see p.127) for women's suffrage. Mill became the godfather of another famous philosopher, Bertrand Russell (see p.188).

8. Lady Henry Somerset (1851-1921)

Victoria Embankment, WC2; Bronze birdbath, 1897

This drinking fountain and birdbath is in memory of Methodist, Lady Henry Somerset who was a key figure in the Temperance movement.

9. William Edward Forster (1818-1886)

Victoria Embankment, Temple Section, WC2

Sculptor H. R. Pinker, Bronze, 1890

William Edward Forster was a Victorian philanthropist, reformer and politician. Forster received a Quaker education and as a young man was an anti-slavery campaigner while training to be a lawyer. Forster took to business rather than law and made his fortune in the Bradford wool trade. He was expelled from the Quaker church when he married outside the religion in 1850 and then devoted much of his energy to the local Liberal Party. He became MP for Bradford in 1861 and was soon appointed to Gladstone's cabinet, doing much to carry the 1870 Education Act which ensured universal elementary education. Forster had a great interest in Irish politics and was appointed Chief Secretary for Ireland in 1880. He was a fierce supporter of the union and there were several assassination plots against him. When Gladstone changed his mind on home rule Forster resigned from office and became one of his most determined critics. This monument commemorates his role as educational reformer.

10. Isambard Kingdom Brunel (1806-1859)

Victoria Embankment, Temple Section, WC2
Sculptor Baron Carlo Marochetti,
pedestal & surround Norman Shaw, Bronze, 1877

Isambard Kingdom Brunel was born with engineering in his blood, being the son of the famous French emigré engineer Marc Isambard Brunel. After a thorough scientific education, Isambard began work with his father on the ambitious Wapping to Rotherhithe Tunnel which encountered many problems and was only completed in 1843. Isambard won the competition to design the Clifton Suspension Bridge and soon after was appointed the chief engineer of the Great Western Railway, revolutionising rail travel with viaducts, bridges and wider gauge track which greatly increased the speed of rail travel. At the London end of the Western line he was given the task of designing a new station to rival that of Euston. Brunel's work can still be seen today in the vast glass edifice of Paddington Station.

Among his other achievements were the design of a prefabricated 1,000 bed hospital for the Crimea and the design and building of three ships between 1837 and 1859, each larger and more revolutionary than the last. The construction of the last ship – The Great Eastern – on the banks of the Thames was fraught with financial and technical risks and the stress involved contributed to Brunel's fatal stroke on the ship's deck within days of its launch. Brunel's engineering achievements are some of the greatest of the Victorian era, the most impressive being the Clifton Suspension Bridge which was completed to Brunel's design after his death.

1. Sir Walter Besant
2. Michael Faraday
3. Sir Arthur Seymour Sullivan
4. Herbert Francis Eaton, 3rd Baron Cheylesmore
5. Robert Raikes
6. Henry Fawcett
7. Belgium War Monument

8. Cleopatra's Needle
9. Sir Wilfrid Lawson, 2nd Baronet
10. Camel Corps
11. Robert Burns
12. York Watergate
13. William Schwenck Gilbert
14. Sir Joseph W. Bazalgette
15. Samuel Plimsoll
16. General Sir James Outram
17. Sir Henry Edward Bartle Frere
18. William Tyndale
19. General Charles G. Gordon
20. Lord Charles Portal
21. Fleet Air Arm Monument
22. Royal Air Force Memorial
23. Battle of Britain
24. Viscount Hugh Montague Trenchard
25. Chindit Special Force Memorial
26. Richard Norman Shaw
27. Queen Boudicca

120

Embankment Part II:
Waterloo Bridge to Westminster Bridge

It is impossible to feature the many monuments between Waterloo and Westminster Bridges without giving mention to the three Embankment gardens in and around which they stand. In the case of the Embankment Main Garden, monuments to Arthur Sullivan, Robert Raikes, Wilfred Lawson, Robert Burns and many others are randomly dotted about the garden with no discernible theme. Whitehall Garden is a more ordered affair, with only three monuments to General Outram, the colonial administrator Bartle Frere and the theologian William Tyndale taking central positions among the symmetrical flower beds. Whitehall Garden is the plainest and least attractive of the gardens, but its location behind the Ministry of Defence has given it a martial theme. General Gordon is the only 19th century military man to feature here, with Hugh Trenchard and Sir Charles Portal both playing a major role in the establishment of the Royal Air Force in the 20th century. Complementing these two men are monuments for The Royal Air Force and The Fleet Air Arm as well as one to the Chindit Special Forces which operated behind enemy lines in Burma during World War Two.

There are quite a number of monuments which stand outside the gardens and form a more direct route from Waterloo to Westminster Bridge. This more direct route begins with the now forgotten Victorian writer Sir Walter Besant and takes in Cleopatra's Needle, William Schwenck Gilbert (of Gilbert and Sullivan fame), the creator of the Embankment Sir Joseph Bazelgette, a modest tablet to the architect Richard Norman Shaw and culminates with the enormous figure of Queen Boudicca astride her chariot and accompanied by her scantily clad daughters.

1. Sir Walter Besant (1836-1901)

Victoria Embankment, under Waterloo Bridge, WC2
Sculptor Sir George Frampton, Bronze bust, 1902

Sir Walter Besant is one of the famous names of the late-Victorian period now consigned to the dustbin of history and these days his bestselling books are only to be found in antiquarian bookshops. His early books were written with James Rice and were of a florid and romantic style with titles such as *The Golden Butterfly* (1876). After Rice's death in 1882, Besant continued to write books, but of a more serious nature, tackling social problems with titles such as *All Sorts* and *Conditions of Men* (1882) and *Children of Gideon* (1886) — which dealt with the evils of child labour.

Besant was also a scholarly historian who wrote many books about London's history, including the unfinished *A Survey of London*. He was an able campaigner who helped realise Barber Beaumont's dream of building a People's Palace on Mile End Road. The building was a great success as a leisure and educational centre for London's poor, but was burnt down in 1931. Besant was also instrumental in improving copyright law and was one of the founders of the Society of Authors in 1884. In 1895 he was knighted. The original of this bust was commissioned and erected in St Paul's Cathedral soon after Besant's death in 1901.

2. Michael Faraday (1791-1867)

Corner of Savoy Place, WC2

Sculptor John Foley, Bronze copy of a marble original, 1988

Michael Faraday was the son of a blacksmith who became the foremost scientist of his generation and discovered the principles of electro-magnetism. Faraday received very little formal education and became an apprentice bookbinder in London. The young Faraday attended the lectures of the chemist Humphry Davy and using his bookbinding skills bound the copied-out text into a fine volume which he sent to Davy along with a request for employment.

Faraday's efforts were successful and in 1813 he was employed as Davy's assistant. In this position Faraday travelled Europe, meeting many of the continent's leading scientists and returned in 1815 as a superintendent of the laboratories and mineral collection. He published his first work on electromagnetic motors in 1821, but was unjustly accused of plagiarism which damaged his reputation.

It was only after the death of Davy in 1829 that Faraday continued the work on electromagnetism that was to seal his reputation as the foremost scientist of his day. It was Faraday that established the principles behind electric motors, batteries, generators and transformers and created the words ion, cathode and anode which are still used today. At the time of his discoveries, people – including Gladstone – could not imagine what use could be made of electricity and yet within a few years of Faraday's death in 1867 the first electric lighting was being installed on London's streets. The bronze monument that stands outside the Institute of Electrical Engineers looking towards the Thames is a copy of John Foley's marble original.

3. Sir Arthur Seymour Sullivan (1842-1900)

Embankment Gardens, WC2

Sculptor Sir William Goscombe John, Bronze bust, 1903

Arthur S. Sullivan's father was the bandmaster at the Royal Military College. Young Arthur won several musical scholarships and attended the Royal Academy of Music, finishing his studies in Leipzig. He returned to England in 1861 and began his musical career which included composing *Onward Christian Soldiers* (1871) – his music was the first to be made into a phonograph record in England. Sullivan is best known for his 24 year partnership with librettist William S. Gilbert (see p.134) with whom he wrote 14 comic operettas.

Many of the operettas were performed nearby at the Savoy Theatre – built by the impresario Richard D'Oyly Carte. Relations between Gilbert and Sullivan were always fraught – Sullivan had grander ambitions than comic opera, ambitions that were bolstered by his knighthood in 1883. In this difficult atmosphere the two men produced some of their most popular works including *The Mikado* (1885) and *The Yeoman of the Guard* (1888), but in 1890 they separated acrimoniously. They reformed and produced three further operettas before Sullivan's premature death at the age of 58. Against his wishes he was buried in St Paul's Cathedral. The words of Gilbert from *The Yeoman of the Guard* are inscribed on Sullivan's bust;

> *"Is life a boon?*
> *If so, it must befall that Death,*
> *when e'er he call,*
> *must call too soon".*

4. Herbert Francis Eaton, 3rd Baron Cheylesmore (1848-1925)

Embankment Gardens, WC2

Sculptor Sir Edwin Lutyens, Stone, 1930

Herbert Francis Eaton became the 3rd Baron Cheylesmore on the death of his brother in 1902. Herbert was educated at Eton and rose to the rank of major-general in the British Army. Although appearing a member of the establishment, his father – Henry William Eaton – was a humble omnibus driver who prospered after being offered a job in the city by one of his regular passengers impressed by his elegant appearance and manner. Henry Eaton's rise was spectacular, enabling him to acquire a fortune, an aristocratic title and his sons the requisite education of English aristocrats. It is said that after Henry Eaton's membership for White's Club was rejected he bought the club, increased the fees and still refused to become a member – a policy adopted by both his sons. Herbert Francis served on several committees concerning military reform and briefly as chairman of London County Council (1912-13). During the First World War he presided over several military courts one of which condemned the German spy Karl Loder to death. Herbert died in a motorcycle accident in 1925, becoming the first peer to die in such a manner.

5. Robert Raikes (1735-1811)
Embankment Gardens, WC2
Sculptor Sir Thomas Brock, Bronze, 1880

Robert Raikes inherited the Gloucester Journal from his father who had founded the paper in 1757. The young Raikes improved the paper and used his position as editor to pioneer the Sunday School movement in the 1780s. Raikes started his first Sunday School in Gloucester in 1780 and his reports of its progress helped the spread of the schools. In 1785 the Sunday School Society was established. At a time when there was very little education for the working-class, Sunday schools played an important educational role. Forty years after Raike's death, three-quarters of working-class children were attending Sunday School.

6. Henry Fawcett (1833-1884)

Embankment Gardens, WC2
Sculptor Mary Grant, Bronze medallion, 1886

Henry Fawcett was a draper's son who managed through his abilities to get a place at Cambridge University. The young Henry came under the influence of the radical political and economic thought of Jeremy Bentham and John Stuart Mill, but his plans for a political career received a blow when he was blinded by his father in a hunting accident.

Henry Fawcett refused to be hindered by his disability and at the age of 30 he was appointed Professor of Political Economy at Cambridge. In 1865 he became the Liberal MP for Brighton, joining a radical group of MP's (including J.S.Mill) campaigning for the vote for women. Fawcett had a romance with a prominent suffragette, Elizabeth Garrett, and went on to marry her sister Millicent in 1867.

Henry Fawcett was appointed Post Master General in 1880 by William Gladstone and it is in this capacity that he really made his mark, introducing the parcel post, postal orders, the sixpenny telegram and promoting the employment of women within the Post Office. Fawcett became ill in 1882 and after a brief recovery succumbed to pleurisy in 1884. Through the work of his wife, the name of Fawcett is commemorated in the eponymous women's library and archive.

7. Belgium War Monument

Embankment, WC2

Sculptor Sir Reginald Blomfield & Victor Rousseau, Bronze, 1920

This monument was a gift from the Belgium government in thanks for Britain's help during the First World War. At the start of the war about 250,000 Belgians fled to this country.

8. Cleopatra's Needle

Embankment, WC2
Sculptor Bronze Sphinxes by G. J. Vulliamy, Pink granite, 1878

Many visitors assume Cleopatra's Needle is a Victorian copy, but it is in fact a genuine 68-foot high, 186 ton Egyptian obelisk dating from 1475 BC. The vast edifice was originally erected in Heliopolis for Pharaoh Thutmosis III, but was later moved to Alexandria. In 1819 the Turkish Viceroy of Egypt presented the now recumbent obelisk to the British.

It remained in Alexandria for a further 58 years before a British engineer named John Dixon designed a huge iron pontoon to carry it by sea to England. The obelisk was envisaged as a monument to the British victory over Napoleon and money was raised by public subscription to fund the project.

During the obelisk's transportation a storm off the Bay of Biscay cost the lives of six sailors but the Needle eventually reached its destination on the Thames Embankment in 1878 to be greeted by vast crowds. A plaque commemorating the sailors that drowned during its transportation can be found at the base of the Needle along with two very fine Victorian bronze sphinxes on either side. Cleopatra's Needle is one of a trio of Egyptian obelisks that travelled to the west, the others can be found in Paris and New York.

9. Sir Wilfrid Lawson, 2nd Baronet (1829-1906)
Embankment Gardens, WC2
Sculptor David McGill, Bronze, 1886

The expression 'falling off the wagon' derives from the temperance wagons that would travel through the towns and cities of Britain advocating Christian sobriety. The politician Sir Wilfrid Lawson was one of the key figures in the temperance movement and spent much of his energies in parliament trying to pass a law that would allow residents to veto the granting of liquor licenses if they achieved a two-thirds majority. The law was never passed but Lawson's campaign helped to highlight the dangers of heavy alcohol consumption which were blighting many poor families.

Anti-drug campaigns these days are largely run by those on the right of the political spectrum; Lawson was however a radical politician who believed in the disestablishment of the Church of England, abolition of the House of Lords and disarmament. In 1900 he lost his seat because of his determined opposition to the Boer War, only to return to parliament in 1903. Wilfrid Lawson died in 1906 having served over 40 years in parliament. The figures of Temperance, Peace, Charity and Fortitude that once adorned this monument were stolen in 1979.

10. Camel Corps
Embankment Main Gardens, WC2
Sculptor Major Cecil Brown, Bronze, 1921

This monument commemorates the short-lived Imperial Camel
Corps who fought in Egypt, Sinai and Palestine between 1916
and 1918. The Camel Corps contained troops from many
Commonwealth nations including Australia, New Zealand, Britain
and India. On the side of the plinth is listed the many battles the
Camel Corps were engaged in; 346 of their number died in the
course of World War One. The sculptor of this monument was one
of the corps surviving members.

11. Robert Burns (1759-1796)
Embankment Gardens, WC2
Sculptor Sir John Steel, Bronze, 1884

Burns was the first of seven children of a poor Ayrshire farmer who became the Bard of Scotland and whose birthday of 25th January is celebrated with haggis, whisky and one of Burn's most famous poems 'Address to a haggis'.

Burns worked on his father's farm from childhood, but his father paid for a tutor to provide some education for his children and young Robert showed promise. When his father died in 1784, Robert and his brother took over the running of the farm. A hard life at the plough was not suited to his nature and after a number of affairs the handsome young Robert was planning to flee to the West Indies. It was the success of his first book of poetry that dissuaded him from his plans and led to a life roaming Scotland performing his poetry. Burns did not earn enough as a poet and was forced to work as a tax collector to support his young wife and growing family while continuing to write in the evenings. Burns became an increasingly troubled figure as his fame increased. His radical politics, including open support for the French Revolution, alienated many of his less radical literary friends and his hedonistic habits began to seriously affect his health. When Burns suddenly died of heart disease at the age of 37 over 10,000 people attended his funeral. The monument that stands in Embankment Gardens was a gift from fellow Scott, John Gordon Crawford, and shows Burns in his romantic prime.

12. York Watergate

Embankment Gardens, WC2
Sculptor Inigo Jones, Stone, 1625

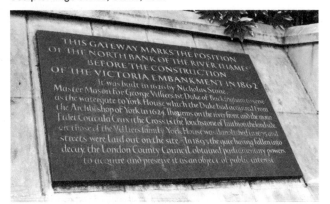

THIS GATEWAY MARKS THE POSITION
OF THE NORTH BANK OF THE RIVER THAMES
BEFORE THE CONSTRUCTION
OF THE VICTORIA EMBANKMENT IN 1862

It was built in 1626 by Nicholas Stone, Master Mason for George Villiers 1st Duke of Buckingham to serve as the watergate to York House which the Duke had acquired from the Archbishop of York in 1624. The arms on the river front and the motto Fidei Coticula Crux (the Cross is the Touchstone of Faith) on the landside are those of the Villiers family. York House was demolished in 1675 and streets were laid out on the site. In 1893 the gate having fallen into decay, the London County Council obtained parliamentary powers to acquire and preserve it as an object of public interest

This stone tablet is all that remains of York House and marks the
bank of the Thames before Joseph Bazelgette (see p.135) built
the Embankment in the 1860s. York House was built in the early
17th century for the favourite and lover of James I, the 1st Duke of
Buckingham – York Watergate still bears the Buckingham family
arms. Buckingham continued to wield great power and influence
after the death of James and the ascension to the throne of Charles
I, but his charm at court was not matched by any political or military
skill. Buckingham's clumsy diplomacy helped precipitate war with
France and his leadership of the British fleet at La Rochelle in 1627
was to prove a disaster. He was assassinated by an infuriated former
naval officer while reviewing the fleet in Portsmouth in 1728. The
portrait of the Duke is one of the most impressive pictures in the
National Portrait Gallery. York House was never fully completed and
the Duke's son, George Villiers, sold it to developers on the condition
that the new streets were named after him; hence Villiers, Duke,
Buckingham and George Street.

13. William Schwenck Gilbert (1836-1911)

Embankment, WC2

Sculptor Sir George Frampton, Bronze plaque, 1914

William S. Gilbert began his professional career as a barrister, but supplemented his income with poetry published in a popular magazine. Gilbert began to acquire a reputation for his comic re-working of popular operas and became increasingly involved in the production of his work. He was a meticulous producer who changed the trend in British theatre by insisting that his actors follow his instructions and not play to the crowd.

It was as a librettist with Arthur Sullivan (see p.124) and the producer Richard D'Oyly Carte that Gilbert achieved greatest success. The relationship between the two men was a difficult one with numerous rows about whose work should take precedence. Sullivan's higher social status was further emphasized by his knighthood in 1883 which made their conflicts worse. It was only in 1907 – long after Sullivan's death – that Gilbert finally achieved equity when he was knighted for his work. Gilbert drowned after a heart attack in May 1911. It is worth noting that the difference between Gilbert and Sullivan's social status continued after their deaths – Sullivan, commemorated with a bust, while Gilbert has this modest plaque.

14. Sir Joseph W. Bazalgette (1819-1891)

Northumberland Avenue, WC2

Sculptor George Simonds, Bronze bust, 1899

Joseph Bazalgette was one of the great Victorian engineers who transformed the landscape of London and eradicated the scourge of cholera with the building of a vast sewer system. Like his friend Brunel (see p.119), Bazalgette came from French stock and had an appetite for hard work. In 1856 he became the Chief Engineer of the Metropolitan Board of Works given the task of improving London's ramshackle sewer system. Between 1848 and 1854 over 30,000 Londoners died from cholera, but it was only when the raw effluent flowing into the Thames caused the 'Great Stink' of 1858, which affected Parliament, that improvements were demanded. Bazalgette proved equal to the task, devising 82 miles of main sewers running along the Thames connected to over a thousand miles of smaller street sewers.

Bazalgette simultaneously made London a more attractive city – reclaiming vast tracts of land from the Thames to create the Victoria, Albert and Chelsea embankments below which run the main sewer pipes as well as new tube lines. The York Watergate (see p.133) marks the north bank of the Thames before the embankment was constructed. Many of the streets surrounding this bust are the work of Bazalgette including Northumberland Avenue and Charing Cross Road. Bazalgette was knighted for his work in 1875 having eradicated cholera from London. One of Joseph's great-great-grandsons is Peter Bazalgette, responsible for reality TV programmes such as Big Brother – pumping back into homes what his great-great-grandfather successfully removed.

15. Samuel Plimsoll (1824-1898)
Outside gates of Whitehall Gardens, SW1
Sculptor Ferdinand V. Blundstone, 1929

Samuel Plimsoll came from a working-class family and received only a rudimentary education. As a young man he worked in the coal industry, but failed in his business ventures and experienced several years of destitution. Plimsoll never forgot the suffering he endured in his youth and when he became MP for Derby in 1868, he embarked on a campaign to improve conditions for merchant seamen.

The term 'coffin ships' was widely used at the time to describe unseaworthy vessels, overloaded with cargo. Plimsoll wrote a book entitled *Our Seamen* in 1873 outlining the injustice of a practice which benefited the heavily insured shipping companies but killed over 1,000 seamen every year. What Plimsoll lacked in his oratory and literary style he compensated for with passion and determination – he was even censured by parliament for using offensive language when Disraeli withdrew his promised bill of reform under pressure from the shipping companies. Public opinion was on Plimsoll's side and in 1875 the government was forced to pass the 'Unseaworthy Vessels Bill' and make amendments to existing law to improve the lot of merchant seamen. This monument was erected by the National Union of Seamen and the markings on the bow of ships to prevent overloading is called the Plimsoll Line in his memory.

16. General Sir James Outram, (1803-1863)
Whitehall Gardens, WC2
Sculptor Matthew Noble, Bronze, 1871

James Outram was one of the great Victorian soldiers and spent most of his life in far flung parts of the British Empire. He departed for India as a skinny teenager in 1819 but soon acquired a reputation as a skilled and courageous wild game hunter and a natural leader of men. In 1838 he fought with distinction in the First Afghan war and the following year was promoted to Major and sent to the Indian province of Sind to serve under General Charles Napier (see p.20).

Outram strongly disagreed with Napier's heavy-handed approach but fought valiantly when the policy led to bloody conflict. This was not to be Outram's last conflict with authority and in 1856 he was removed from his responsibilities for too efficiently uncovering corruption in the Bombay Army. Outram was such a skilled soldier that within a year he was called back into service to assist Havelock (see p.16) in the relief of Lucknow. He again performed his duties with bravery and successfully held the city until the second relief force arrived.

In 1858 Outram was made a baron and received the thanks of parliament. He returned to England in 1860, but his health was weakened by the rigors of war and he died in 1863. Outram gained the respect of all those who worked with him and acquired the nickname The Bayard of India after the medieval French knight renowned for his courage and honour.

17. Sir Henry Edward Bartle Frere (1815-1884)

Victoria Embankment Gardens, SW1
Sculptor Sir Thomas Brock, Bronze, 1887

Henry Frere was a colonial administrator who began his career in the Indian civil service in 1834. By 1850 Frere was appointed Chief Commissioner of the troubled Sind Province and in 1857 played a key role in suppressing the First War of Indian Independence – sending troops to Multan and the Punjab to prevent them being overrun. Frere was given a knighthood for his services and a place on the Viceroy Council in Calcutta.

During the 1860s Frere adopted a paternalistic policy towards India – building colleges to educate the Indian elite and reversing the corrupt practices of the East India Company as First Governor of Bombay. Frere received considerable public criticism after the collapse of the Bombay Bank which hastened his returned to England in 1867. He maintained the trust of the crown and was appointed High Commissioner of South Africa in 1877. British rule in South Africa was facing difficulties and Frere made the situation worse – abandoning the enlightened policies of his time in India and confronting the Zulu tribes of Natal with brutal force. This heavy-handed approach was unpopular and Gladstone dismissed Frere as soon as he came into office in 1880. Frere came back to England and spent the last years of his life justifying his actions against critics which included Anthony Trollope. Frere is buried in St Paul's Cathedral and there is a mountain in Australia which bears his name.

18. William Tyndale (1484-1536)

Victoria Embankment Gardens, WC2
Sculptor Sir Joseph Edgar Boehm, Bronze, 1884

William Tyndale was a 16th-century priest and scholar who was the first person to translate the Bible from Latin and Hebrew into the English of his day. As a student at Cambridge, Tyndale was strongly influenced by the teachings of Erasmus and became an advocate of the Reformation which questioned the teachings and practices of the Catholic Church.

Tyndale's preaching soon caused controversy and in 1522 he was forced to flee Cambridge for London having been accused of heresy. He was by this stage convinced of the need for an English translation of the Bible so that it could be understood even by 'a boy that driveth the plough'. In London, Tyndale began his work but was soon forced to flee to Germany to evade his persecutors. It was in Cologne and later the town of Worms that Tyndale used the new process of printing to publish his work in 1525. Tyndale wrote commentaries on all aspects of scripture and it was his opposition to Henry VIII's divorce, and not his translation, that led the King to seek his arrest and return to England. Tynsdale was arrested in Antwerp, tried on the charge of heresy in 1536 and promptly executed.

Within a year his translation was published in England with the encouragement of the King. Tyndale's work was the basis for the later King James Bible and has made a considerable contribution to the English language – introducing words such as 'scapegoat', 'atonement' and 'passover', and phrases such as 'the powers that be', 'my brother's keeper' and 'the salt of the earth'.

19. General Charles G. Gordon (1833-1885)

Whitehall Extension, SW1
Sculptor Sir Hamo Thornycroft, Bronze, 1887 (Trafalgar Square)
removed 1943, moved here 1953

Charles G. Gordon was a career soldier who saw action in the Crimea and China during the Second Opium War where he participated in the destruction of the Summer Palace. In May 1862 he was assigned to strengthen Shanghai and did much with his native army to prevent the Taiping Rebellion. He returned to England in 1865 to great public acclaim and acquired the nick-name 'Chinese Gordon'. Britain was becoming increasingly involved in the political situation in Egypt and the Sudan and Gordon was appointed governor of the Sudanese province of Equatoria and did much to tackle the local slave trade and map the upper Nile. He returned to England in 1880 due to ill health, but was soon travelling in India, China and South Africa on colonial duties. Gordon was about to take an appointment as governor of the Congo on behalf of the Belgian government when events in Egypt and the Sudan reached crisis in 1884. Gordon's appointment owed much to the populist campaign of W. T. Stead (see p.116) and the indecisiveness of Gladstone's government. General Gordon returned to the Sudanese capital of Khartoum in February 1884 with a moral mission but no army to hold the Sudanese rebels at bay. He allowed the city to fall under siege rather than withdraw, as was his instruction. The siege lasted a year and ended with the overrunning of the city and the death of Gordon in January 1885, just two days before relief forces arrived. Gordon's death turned him into a national hero and contributed greatly to the defeat of Gladstone's government in the election of the same year.

20. Lord Charles Portal,
1st Viscount Portal of Hungerford (1893-1971)

Whitehall Extension, SW1
Sculptor Oscar Nemon, Bronze, 1975

Charles Portal was one of the key military figures of the Second World War but one largely forgotten by the British public. Portal studied at Oxford before joining the Royal Engineers in August 1914. He flew many missions for the Flying Corps and after the war joined the newly established Royal Air Force. Portal was Air Vice-Marshal by the start of World War Two, but his intelligence and clear thinking were soon to win him a place at Churchill's side and promotion to Commander-in-Chief of Bomber Command by April 1940.

It was Portal who adopted the policy of strategic bombing developed by Trenchard (see p.144). This involved the bombing of German cities and towns without any specific military target, with the intention of demoralising the enemy and limiting their ability to wage war. The British bombing of Berlin on the 25th August 1940 was the first step in the policy of 'Total War' which led to Germany's brutal retaliation of the London Blitz in September 1940. Portal's determination to win the war at any cost gained him promotion to Chief of Air Staff and a knighthood. By early 1944 he wanted to reduce the role of heavy bombing but was opposed by Arthur Harris (see p.164), and Churchill supported the continuation of a policy which culminated in the bombing of Dresden, Berlin and other major cities in early 1945. At the end of the war, Portal was rewarded with a baronetcy and worked as head of Atomic Energy and later the British Aircraft Corporation. This monument by Oscar Nemon stands close to his wartime offices.

21. Fleet Air Arm Monument
Victoria Embankment, SW1
Sculptor James Butler, Bronze, 2000
The Fleet Air Arm is that part of the Air Force which operates
from aircraft carriers. During the Second World War it became
the most important and effective part of the Royal Navy. This
monument commemorates those who gave their lives in service
of the Fleet Air Arm.

22. Royal Air Force Memorial
Victoria Embankment, SW1
Sculptor Sir Reginald Blomfield and Sir William Reid Dick
Bronze Eagle on stone column, 1923
This monument stands on the embankment and commemorates
those that fought in the First World War in the Royal Flying Corps
and the Royal Naval Air Service which amalgamated to become the
Royal Air Force in 1918. The monument stands close to those for
Trenchard and Portal, both associated with the foundation of the
modern Royal Air Force.

23. Battle of Britain

Victoria Embankment, SW1
Sculptor Paul Day, Granite and Bronze, 2005

This elaborate 25-metre-long monument is dedicated to the 2,936 airmen from 15 countries who fought to defend Britain from German air attack in what became known as the Battle of Britain. The battle is particularly important in British history because it represents a time when Britain stood alone against Germany after the fall of France in June 1940. On 10th July the battle began when the Luftwaffe launched 'Operation Eagle' with the intention of destroying Britain's air defences in preparation for a land invasion.

The campaign started with attacks upon ports and convoys, but in August attention was turned to radar stations, airfields and aircraft factories in the south of England. The defence of Britain was directed by Sir Hugh Dowding (see p.167) who managed his limited resources with considerable care and economy – never committing more that half his aircraft to the defence of the south at any one time. By the end of August 1940 Dowding felt that the RAF were close to defeat and a serious disagreement broke out within Fighter Command as Sholto Douglas and Trafford Leigh-Mallory advocated more aggressive tactics. In the end the greatest ally of the British proved the erratic judgement of Hitler who, on the verge of victory, ordered the Luftwaffe to switch its attention to the bombing of civilian targets in retaliation for Charles Portal's bombing of Berlin. The start of the Blitz (see p.221) marked the effective end of the Battle of Britain. The words of Churchill are inscribed on this monument, 'Never in the field of human conflict was so much owed by so many to so few'.

24. Viscount Hugh Montague Trenchard (1873-1956)
Whitehall Extension, SW1
Sculptor William Macmillan, Bronze, 1961

Like his successor Charles Portal, Hugh Trenchard joined the army and only later transferred to the Flying Corps during the First World War. He was a straightforward character who acquired the nick name 'Boom' Trenchard because of his loud voice. He became the first Chief of Staff of the Royal Air Force and was instrumental in its formation, in April 1918, from the disparate squadrons that existed at the time.

Trenchard was one of the first to realise the importance of the Air Force in future conflicts and in the 1920s enthusiastically employed mustard gas dropped from aircraft to suppress Kurdish rebellion in Iraq and in Somaliland. Although some British soldiers and pilots were unhappy about the policy, one advocate was the young Arthur 'Bomber' Harris (see p.164). Trenchard was emboldened to devise the idea of 'strategic bombing', which justified the bombing of civilian areas to demoralise the enemy. Trenchard wrote a document advocating this policy and even suggesting that such a tactic could be used to suppress domestic industrial disputes. Churchill was alarmed by Trenchard's ideas and asked him never to put them in writing again. He resigned his position in 1929 and later become the Metropolitan Police Commissioner between 1931 and 1936 – thankfully avoiding the use of aircraft to deal with the capital's crime problem. Trenchard was too old to play any part in the Second World War, but lived to see many of his ideas put into practice by his successors.

25. Chindit Special Force Memorial

Whitehall Extension, SW1

Sculptor David Price, Frank Forster, Bronze, 1990

This monument commemorates those
special forces that fought the Japanese
in Burma (1943-44) under General Orde
Wingate (1904-44). The bronze figure is
the eponymous Burmese mythological
dragon. Wingate used his experience
of guerilla warfare in Palestine and
Ethiopia and applied it to his special
forces campaign in Burma. Chindit
expeditions cost many lives and there is
some argument as to their effectiveness

compared with the broader war fought in Burma under General
Slim (see p.42). There is no doubt, however, that the campaign
gave a moral boost to the Allied war effort. The unit disbanded after
Wingate's death in a plane crash in April 1944. He is venerated in
Israel for his efforts to form a Jewish state in the 1930s and wreaths
from Jewish veteran groups are often found at the monument.

26. Richard Norman Shaw (1831-1912)

Norman Shaw Building, Embankment, W1

Sculptor W. R. Lethaby, portrait relief Sir W. H. Thornycroft,
Bronze, 1914

This tablet to the architect Richard
Norman Shaw is on one of his few
major London buildings – the former
offices of New Scotland Yard. Now
parliamentary offices and inaccessible
to the public, the building is still
visible from the Embankment. Shaw
also designed the headquarters of The
Royal Geographical Society (see Sir
Clement Markham p.305).

27. Queen Boudicca

Victoria Embankment, SW1
Sculptor Thomas Thornycroft, Bronze, 1902

Victoria Embankment begins on New Bridge Street with a monument of Queen Victoria and ends with an impressive statue to Boudicca with whom the 19th-century monarch was compared. Boudicca was the wife of Prasutagus – king of the Iceni Celtic tribe of Norfolk and Suffolk. When the Romans, under emperor Claudius, occupied Britain in AD43, Prastagus co-operated with them and prospered under the patronage of Rome. When Prasutagus died the Romans took the opportunity to overrun the Iceni – thrashing their queen and raping her daughters. She was not the sort of woman to accept such abuse and rallied the Iceni and Trinovantian tribes to fight the Roman occupiers. Boudicca and her army succeeded initially as the greater part of the Roman army was away fighting the pagans in North Wales. The Roman settlements of St Albans, Colchester and London were razed to the ground by the Celtic army who slaughtered their inhabitants. The Ninth Legion, who came to their defence, were routed and the Britons briefly seemed in the ascendancy. Their success was short-lived, as the main Roman legions returned from Wales under the command of Suetonius Paullinus and crushed the Celtic army in battle. Boudicca killed herself to prevent being captured. The story of Boudicca is known through the writings of Roman historian Tacitus who is surprisingly even-handed in his account. Boudicca became a symbol of British strength during Victoria's reign and this monument was erected within a year of her death.

SOUTHBANK

Coade Stone Lion, p.154

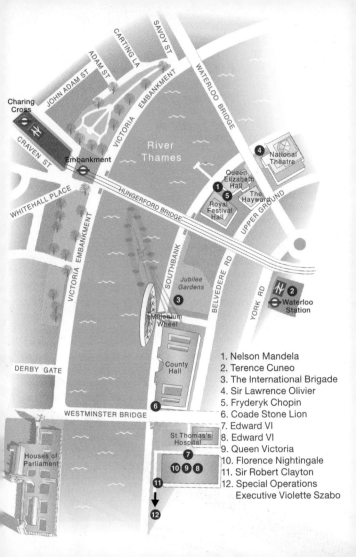

1. Nelson Mandela
2. Terence Cuneo
3. The International Brigade
4. Sir Lawrence Olivier
5. Fryderyk Chopin
6. Coade Stone Lion
7. Edward VI
8. Edward VI
9. Queen Victoria
10. Florence Nightingale
11. Sir Robert Clayton
12. Special Operations
    Executive Violette Szabo

South Bank

The south bank of the Thames from Waterloo Bridge to St Thomas's Hospital is one of the most attractive and popular pedestrian thoroughfares in London. This area was largely one of manufacturing and warehousing before the war but after heavy bombing many buildings, such as the old Lion Brewery, were demolished. The Royal Festival Hall was part of the postwar regeneration of the area and having been recently refurbished, stands here today amid the cafés, shops, galleries and arts institutions that now define the area.

The bust of Nelson Mandela has moved to the side entrance of the Festival Hall building. The work is by Ian Walters and is well worth taking the steps to see. Further along, next to the old County Hall building is another monument by Walters to the International Brigade. The two monuments were both unveiled in 1985 as a last defiant gesture by the Greater London Council before being abolished by the Conservative government. Further along is the Coade Stone Lion which once stood on the ramparts of the old Lion Brewery. Made in a long-closed factory close by, it is a last symbol of the area's industrial past. Sir Lawrence Olivier and Fryderyk Chopin are both recent additions to the area.

The other monuments on this part of the south bank are concentrated in the grounds and buildings of St Thomas's Hospital and all those commemorated have some link with the place. Edward VI re-founded the hospital in 1552 and is remembered by two monuments in his honour. Robert Clayton funded the rebuilding of the hospital in the late 17th century, but his fine Grinling Gibbons statue now stands forgotten outside a disused building in the hospital grounds. Queen Victoria and Florence Nightingale were both patrons of St Thomas's and their monuments now stand in the modern surroundings of the hospital's central hall. The walk ends outside the Garden Museum with a newly erected monument to The Special Operations Executive (SOE).

1. Nelson Mandela (1918-)
Riverside Walk close to the Royal Festival Hall, SE1
Sculptor Ian Walters, Bronze, 1985

Nelson Mandela is one of the few men to make the journey from terrorist/freedom fighter to respected elder statesman. He began his political career when a student at Fort Hare University from where he was expelled for his political activities; later he joined the African National Congress (ANC) while studying law in Johannesburg. He was further radicalised when the Afrikaaner-dominated National Party came to power in 1948 and introduced a system of racial discrimination known as Apartheid.

Mandela at first sought non-violent means to fight for black rights and with his friend Oliver Tambo provided legal aid to those suffering at the hands of the government. The authorities did not tolerate such interference and Mandela and his ANC colleagues were charged with treason and subjected to a long trial resulting in their acquittal in 1961. The pressures of the trial combined with the killing of protesters in what became known as the Sharpeville Massacre in 1960, persuaded Mandela that non-violent means would not bring an end to apartheid. From this point onwards he organised sabotage attacks upon military and government targets in which people were killed, and he continued to advocate such tactics after his arrest and imprisonment in August 1962.

Mandela came to represent the struggle against South Africa's apartheid system and became a hero to those who fought against it in the west – boycotting the country's products, disrupting sports events and protesting outside the South African Embassy in London. The political pressure continued to mount and in the spirit of change that also witnessed the demise of the Soviet Union, South Africa's

President F.W. de Klerk unconditionally released Mandela in February 1990. The system of apartheid was later abolished in a referendum in March 1992. Mandela was awarded the Nobel Peace Prize (with de Klerk) in 1993 and became the country's first black president in a government of national unity in 1994. He retired from politics in 1999 but remains a respected international figure.

This imposing 8ft-high bust of Mandela is the work of the committed socialist sculptor Ian Walters, who is also responsible for the monuments to the International Brigade and Fenner Brockway (see pages 152 and 189). It was unveiled in October 1985 while Mandela was still serving the life sentence imposed on him in June 1964. At the time, Margaret Thatcher's Conservative government regarded Mandela as a terrorist and this monument was one of the last defiant gestures of the Labour-controlled Greater London Council (GLC), run by Ken Livingstone before its abolition in March 1986. These days Mandela is regarded as a world statesman and a second monument to him now stands in Parliament Square (see p.62).

2. Terence Cuneo (1907-96)
Waterloo Station, SE1
Philip Jackson, Bronze, 2004

Terrence Cuneo was a popular artist, painting in a representational style whose most notable subjects were grand public events. Cuneo's paintings always included a small mouse and this monument has two, one at the artists feet and the other at the base of the plinth.

3. The International Brigade

Jubilee Gardens, SE1
Sculptor Ian Walters, Bronze, 1985

The Spanish Civil War that raged between July 1936 and April 1939 captured the interest of the world and divided opinion between those of the left and right. The war was between Spain's elected Republican government and the Nationalist forces of General Franco who were supported by Fascist Italy and Nazi Germany. Western governments did not come to the Republic's defence and it was left to the Soviet Union to establish the International Brigade. The Brigade attracted nearly 60,000 volunteers from 55 countries to fight for the Republican cause including around 2,000 British volunteers. They experienced physical hardship, but fought bravely alongside the Republican army against the better equipped Nationalist forces.

The Brigade initially enjoyed some success with the defence of Madrid in November 1936. Divisions soon, however, emerged within the Brigade, as Nationalist forces continued their advance. In September 1938 the International Brigade was disbanded by Spain's Republican government in an attempt to win the support of western democracies. The attempt failed and in April 1939, just five months before the start of the Second World War, Franco declared victory.

This monument is in memory of the British men and women who volunteered for the International Brigade, of whom 526 gave their lives in the struggle. The monument is a wonderful figurative piece by Ian Walters, who also made the bust of Mandela further along the south bank (see p.150). Many participants in the Spanish Civil War regarded it as part of the wider struggle against fascism and went on to fight bravely in the world war that followed.

4. Sir Lawrence Olivier (1907-89)

Outside Royal National Theatre, SE1
Sculptor Angela Conner, 2007

Lawrence Olivier was arguably the greatest actor of his day whose performances of Hamlet, Othello and Richard III were to make his name. He was the first stage actor to become a screen idol with his 1948 film of *Hamlet* winning him two Oscars. In the 1960's he transformed his career, embracing darker contemporary works, most notably playing Archie Rice in *The Entertainer*. Olivier was the first director of the National Theatre. This diminutive monument does little to convey the glamour and physical appeal of one of this country's great actors.

5. Fryderyk Chopin (1810-49)

Royal Festival Hall, SE1
Sculptor Bronislaw Kubica, 2011

This unusual abstract monument commemorates Fryderyk Chopin, the Polish virtuoso pianist and composer. He gave few large concerts and made his living performing in the salons of Paris, teaching and selling his music. Chopin's work was to have a profound influence on piano music. The end of his ten-year relationship with the author George Sand (Amandine Dupin) and his worsening health led to a rapid decline. Chopin died of tuberculosis in Paris in October 1949, aged just 39.

6. Coade Stone Lion

Westminster Bridge, SE1

Sculptor W. F. Woodington, Coade stone, 1837 (moved here 1966)

This is one of two lions that once stood upon the roof of the old Lion Brewery that was located next to Waterloo Bridge. The brewery was demolished in 1948 to make way for the concrete edifice of the Royal Festival Hall. The lion was a feature of the Festival of Britain in 1951 but was unveiled on this site, next to County Hall, in 1966.

The lion derives its name from the hard wearing artificial stone from which it is made. Coade stone was the invention of Mrs Eleanor Coade (1733-1821) who established her stone factory in Lambeth in 1769.

The stone was a form of kiln-fired ceramic which proved very popular in public buildings such as Somerset House and the Royal Opera House. Mrs Coade had several untrustworthy business partners during her career and kept the exact formula and process for making her stone a closely guarded secret. She took the secret to her grave in 1821 and her factory, which stood remarkably close to where this lion stands today, subsequently closed in 1833. There have been several attempts to rediscover the exact Coade stone manufacturing process, but none have succeeded.

The lion wore a coat of red paint when it was a symbol of the Lion Brewery, but this has long ago been removed to reveal the wonderful and mysterious stone that lies beneath. The Coade stone lion has a prominent position looking across the Thames towards parliament, but the lion's genitals were considered too large and distracting and were reduced in size to keep the traffic flowing. The lion's more virile sibling now stands in Twickenham Rugby ground.

7. Edward VI (1537-1553)
St Thomas's Hospital, SE1
Sculptor Thomas Cartwright
Stone, 1681

St Thomas's Hospital was established
long before the reign of Edward VI,
being founded on Borough High Street
in 1215 by the Bishop of Winchester. The
hospital was run under ecclesiastical
governance and was therefore closed
when Henry VIII confiscated monastic
property during the English Reformation
(1538-41). It was left to his son and
heir, the young Edward VI, to refound
the hospital in 1551 and provide it with a royal charter the following
year. The young king was stirred into helping St Thomas's after a
sermon by the Bishop of London, his action being part of a broader
royal initiative which included the founding of Christ's and Bridewell
hospitals. Edward VI succeeded to the throne at the age of ten and
largely relied on Edward Seymour and later John Dudley to carry out
the business of government. The founding of St Thomas's was one of
the few things that bore the mark of the
young king's capacity to rule and it is
fitting that two monuments to Edward
are to be found here.

8. Edward VI (1537-1553)
St Thomas's Hospital, SE1
Sculptor Peter Scheemakers
Bronze, 1737

This later monument to Edward VI
stands by the entrance to the hospital he
founded.

9. Queen Victoria (1819-1901)

St Thomas's Hospital, SE1
Sculptor Matthew Noble, Marble, 1873 (presented to hospital 1898)

Following St Thomas's move from Borough High Street, Queen Victoria laid the foundation stone of this building in 1868 and opened the hospital in 1871. The president of the hospital at the time, Sir John Musgrove, presented this monument to Victoria in 1873 and it was later given to the hospital by the company of Mercers on the 60th anniversary of the Queen's reign in 1898. There are several monuments to Victoria in London (see pages 109, 290 and 299).

10. Florence Nightingale (1820-1910)

St Thomas's Hospital, SE1
Sculptor Frederick Mancini, Metal composite, 1958

Florence Nightingale became involved with St Thomas's in 1859 and established her famous nursing school here a year later.

The Florence Nightingale Museum is situated on the hospital site and contains many artefacts relating to her nursing career and time in the Crimea. The original bronze statue was unveiled in 1958 but was stolen in 1970. This replica is made of a less valuable composite metal and has recently been moved from the hospital entrance. It now stands within the main atrium of the hospital. The most prominent monument to Nightingale stands in Waterloo Place next to the Guards Monument (see p.99).

11. Sir Robert Clayton (1629-1707)

St Thomas's Hospital, SE1
Sculptor Grinling Gibbons, Stone, 1702 (moved here 1976)

Robert Clayton was born in Nottingham, but came to London as an apprentice scrivener to his uncle. Scriveners were employed to transcribe legal and financial documents and were an essential part of London's commerce. It was while learning his trade that Clayton became friends with his fellow apprentice John Morris and the two men soon formed a business partnership which became the bank Clayton & Morris Co. Robert Clayton quickly made his fortune and in 1769 was awarded a baronetcy and in the same year had his portrait painted by Gainsborough. Clayton served as Lord Mayor in 1679 and as MP for the City of London from 1678 to 1681 and later allied himself to the Whig cause and the Hanoverian dynasty. He used his considerable fortune to advance many causes and one of his properties was the first meeting place for the London Institution for the Advancement of Literature. Clayton was also a patron of St Thomas's Hospital and largely paid for the hospital's rebuilding between 1693 and 1709.

This rare example of a Grinling Gibbons statue was commissioned in 1702 and placed at the front of the hospital while Clayton was still alive. In the subsequent centuries the monument has moved several times and suffered wartime fire damage which turned the marble pink and destroyed both the statue's hands. Alabaster replacements were fitted during restoration work carried out in 1955, but these have since fallen off. Today Clayton's statue languishes outside an abandoned building at the back of the modern St Thomas's, unnoticed by most visitors to the hospital, but with newly attached replacement hands.

12. Special Operations Executive
Violette Szabo (1921-45)
Lambeth Palace Road, SE1
Sculptor Karen Newman, 2009

This monument commemorates the Special Operations Executive (SOE) responsible for espionage and sabotage behind enemy lines in occupied Europe. The SOE was established in July 1940 under the instruction of Winston Churchill to 'set Europe ablaze'. The SOE worked with the French Resistance delaying German tank reenforcements during the D-Day landings. The monument explains that of the 470 SOE agents operating in France, 117 were killed. The handsome bust that looks out across the Thames represent the youngest and most beautiful of the operatives to loose their lives in SOE operations – Violette Szabo.

Szabo was Anglo-French and was working behind a perfume counter in a Brixton department store when war began. It was the death of her husband in Oct 1942 having never seen their baby daughter which inspired Violette Szabo to join the SOE. Her first mission in France in April 1944 to reorganise a Resistance network was a great success. Following D-Day In June 1944, Szabo returned to France but was soon captured and suffered interrogation and torture at the hands of the SS. She was shot at Ravensbrück concentration camp on 5th February 1945. Szabo became famous with the publication of R J Minney's book *Carve her Name with Pride*.

There is a further plaque on the monument commemorating the Heroes of Telemark. This was a small group of Norwegian resistance commandoes sponsored by the SOE who sabotaged the Norsk Hydro Plant and so disrupted German H-Bomb preparations.

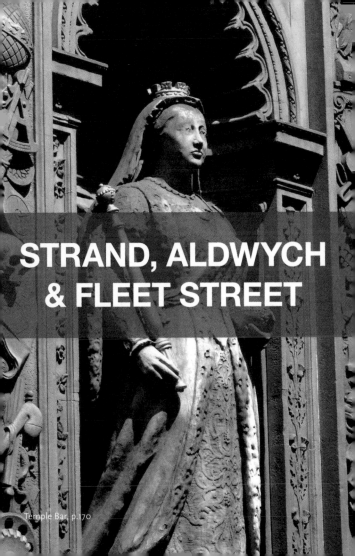

STRAND, ALDWYCH
& FLEET STREET

Temple Bar, p.170

1. Count Peter of Savoy
2. George III
3. Jawaharlal Nehru
4. Arthur (Bomber. Harris
5. William Ewart Gladstone
6. Hugh Dowding, Air Chief Marshal
7. Dr Samuel Johnson
8. Robert Devereux, 2nd Earl of Essex
9. Temple Bar
10. King Lud
11. Alfred Harmsworth, Lord Northcliffe
12. Queen Elizabeth I
13. John Wilkes
14. Mary, Queen of Scots
15. Robert Waithman
16. Thomas Power O'Connor
17. Edgar Wallace

Strand, Aldwych & Fleet Street

The walk from Strand through Aldwych to Fleet Street is less than a mile in length but the monuments that stand along this ancient thoroughfare encompass almost 800 years of London's history. The monument to Count Peter of Savoy commemorates an ally of Henry III who, in 1263, built a grand palace on what is now the Strand. On Aldwych stand monuments to the first prime minister of India, Jewaharlal Nehru and two important figures from the Second World War; Hugh Dowding and Arthur 'Bomber' Harris. On a vast marble pillar towering above these two airmen stands one of the giants of the Victorian era – William Gladstone. Probably the greatest English man of letters, Samuel Johnson, can be found just behind St Clement Danes church, where he once worshipped. Robert Devereux was a favourite of Queen Elizabeth I who fell from favour and was eventually executed for treason.

Within the boundaries of the old City of London, marked by Temple Bar, stands a monument to the queen that signed Devereux's death warrant and further along is a monument to her cousin – Mary Queen of Scots – who met the same fate as Devereux. The monument to Elizabeth I is perhaps the oldest outdoor monument in London, dating from 1586 – although King Alfred's monument in Borough may be older (see p.367). Fleet Street was the birthplace of the printed word and all the monuments in this area have some association with newspapers. The press baron Lord Northcliffe has a bust alongside Queen Elizabeth at the entrance to St Dunstan's church, and further east is a monument to John Wilkes, who campaigned for press freedom. Robert Waithman was a Whig politician who, like Wilkes, fought for greater representation and press freedom and has a stone obelisk in his memory just off Fleet Street. The last two monuments in this area commemorate two of the 20th century's most famous journalists; T. P. O'Connor and Edgar Wallace.

1. Count Peter of Savoy (1203-1268)

The Savoy Hotel, Fleet Street, WC2
Sculptor Frank Lynn Jenkins, Bronze, 1904

The name of Savoy has been associated with this part of the Strand since 1241. Henry III married Eleanor of Provence in 1236 and her uncle, Peter of Savoy, was given land in this area and became an ally to the King in his battles with the barons led by Simon de Montfort. Peter assumed the title of Count of Savoy in 1263 and in that same year built the Savoy Palace on the Strand. His palace was burnt down by Wat Tyler's men during the Peasant's Revolt of 1381 (see p.183). The Savoy hotel was built in 1889 on the former site of the palace. During the hotel's expansion in 1903 this gilt bronze statue of Count Peter was placed on the hotel's canopy.

2. George III (1738-1820)

Somerset House, WC2
Sculptor John Bacon the Elder
Bronze, 1780

This fine monument has a maritime theme with George III in classical attire with a ship in the background and Father Thames sitting below. See p.6 for more details of George III's reign.

3. Jawaharlal Nehru (1889-1964)

India Place, WC2
Sculptor Lati Kalcatt, Bronze bust, 1990

Jewaharlal Nehru was an English-educated lawyer who practised in India before dedicating himself to Indian independence after the Amritsar Massacre of 1919. Nehru became a follower and ally of Mahatma Gandhi (see p.243) and was elected President of the Congress Party in 1929 under Gandhi's leadership. In 1930 Nehru declared Indian Independence as the party's aspiration and spent many of the inter-war years in jail for his campaigns against British rule. When the Second World War started Nehru broke with Gandhi and advocated support for the British in return for independence. The offer was rejected and Nehru joined Gandhi's *Quit India* campaign which led to his arrest and imprisonment for the last two years of the war. The war's end saw Nehru's release and his ascendancy to the presidency of the Congress Party as Gandhi withdrew from direct participation in Indian politics. Nehru became Prime Minister during the difficult first years of Indian independence and presided over the country's partition, its first war with Pakistan (1947-9) and the military integration of the princely states. Nehru provided stability for the fledgling Indian state after Gandhi's assassination and remained Prime Minister until his death from a heart attack in May 1964. He established a dynasty which was to see his formidable daughter, Indira Gandhi, become his successor and his grandson also led India. This bust stands just outside the High Commission of India.

4. Arthur Travers (Bomber) Harris (1892-1984)
Strand (west of St Clement Danes), WC2
Sculptor Faith Winter, Bronze, 1992

Arthur Travers Harris joined the Royal Flying Corps in 1915 and became a pilot in the First World War at the head of 44 Squadron. In 1919 he was made a squadron leader in the newly formed Royal Air Force and saw action in India, Iraq and Iran. In Iraq Harris showed his preference for brutality when bombing villages to quell a rebellion. Air Commodore Lionel Charlton resigned in protest after witnessing the casualties. Harris had no doubts about his policy and wrote of his actions, 'The Arab and Kurd now know what real bombing means, within 45 minutes a full-sized village can be practically wiped out'.

His advocacy of a policy of strategic bombing, developed by Hugh Trenchard (see p.144), and his lack of scruples was to earn Harris the nickname 'Bomber' or 'Butcher' within the RAF and the position of Air Vice Marshal by the start of World War Two. Harris served under Charles Portal (see p.141) as head of Bomber Command and worked hard to cripple Germany's morale through strategic bombing of its major cities. As Allied victory became more certain, it was Harris who successfully appealed to Churchill for the policy of strategic bombing to continue, culminating in the bombing of Dresden and other cities in February 1945. After the war Harris continued to defend his actions, but spent most of the post-war years living in South Africa. This monument was unveiled by the Queen Mother in 1992 amid controversy, with a crowd booing and throwing eggs in protest at the celebration of someone they considered a war criminal.

5. William Ewart Gladstone (1809-1898)
Strand (West of St Clement Danes), WC2
Sculptor Sir Hamo Thornycroft, Bronze, 1905

William Gladstone was one of the great statesmen of the Victorian era and certainly the greatest reformer of the late-19th century. He was not born into radicalism, his father being a self-made Liverpool merchant and MP, whose influence allowed his young son to enter parliament under the patronage of the Duke of Newcastle and to serve in the Conservative administration of Robert Peel (see p.63). The Repeal of the Corn Laws in 1846 divided the party, with

Gladstone committed to free trade and Benjamin Disraeli (see p.65) in favour of protectionism. Gladstone never forgave Disraeli for his betrayal of Peel and the genuine enmity between the two men was to shape the political landscape as these two great political figures rose to prominence. Gladstone became more radical with age and by 1859 he was Chancellor of the Exchequer in Palmerston's Liberal administration. Palmerston was against parliamentary reform, but when he died in 1865 Gladstone became the driving force for a second reform bill which would extend the franchise and give more seats to urban areas. The bill that was passed in 1867 owed a great deal to Disraeli's change of heart on the matter, but the electorate realised it was the work of Gladstone and voted him into office in 1868.

Gladstone's first administration was to make many of the institutional changes necessary to accommodate the new democratic age, its greatest achievement being the 1870 Education Act (see William Forster page 118) and the introduction of the secret ballot. Gladstone was to lose power to his arch-rival Disraeli in 1874, but was to lead three further administrations, all of them continuing the process of parliamentary and social reform. Gladstone's moral crusading on domestic issues was always sure-footed, but the same approach to foreign policy was often to lead him into difficulties. His dispatch of General Gordon (see p.140) to Khartoum was to prove a disaster which ended his second administration, while his moral stand against the Turks and their treatment of Bulgarians was popular, but wrong-headed. Gladstone's career came to an end in March 1894 when his repeated attempts to introduce Home Rule for Ireland were defeated. He died in retirement four years later having established his reputation as one of the great political figures of his age. Like many moral and decent people, Gladstone had a reputation for being rather dull. He did spend his free time looking for prostitutes, but his only motive was to help them reform their ways. There is also a bronze monument to Gladstone in Bow Churchyard, erected in 1882 (see p.374).

6. Hugh Dowding, Air Chief Marshal (1882-1970)

Strand (west of St Clement Danes), WC2
Sculptor Faith Winter, Bronze, 1988

Hugh Dowding started his career in the army but transferred to the Royal Flying Corps in 1913 and saw action in the First World War. During the war Dowding argued with General Hugh Trenchard over the issue of rest for pilots and was sent home, playing no further part in the conflict. Between the wars Dowding pursued his career in the newly formed Royal Air Force rising to the rank of Air-Marshal in 1933 and playing a key role in the development of the Spitfire and Hurricane fighter planes. He was also instrumental in promoting the use of radar systems which were to prove vital during the Second World War.

When the war started it was Dowding's controversial decision to limit the use of fighter planes during the evacuation of Dunkirk in May 1940, that enabled the RAF to emerge victorious from the Battle of Britain (see p.143). Dowding's command during this key period of the war was vital in deterring Hitler from launching any further direct attack upon British soil, but Air Chief Marshal Portal (see p.141) was more critical of his decisions and Dowding was replaced in November 1941 by Vice-Marshal Sholto Douglas.

Dowding retired from the RAF in July 1942 and was awarded a baronetcy in 1943. In his long years of retirement Dowding pursued rather unusual interests for a former Air Chief Marshal – writing books about spiritualism and fighting for the rights of animals. A lone Spitfire flew overhead when this monument was unveiled by the Queen Mother in October 1988.

7. Dr Samuel Johnson (1709-1784)

St Clement Danes, Strand, WC2
Sculptor Percy Fitzgerald, Stonebust, 1910

Samuel Johnson's father was a Lichfield bookseller and his son was to continue this fascination with words and books despite an early illness which caused the loss of one eye. As a young man Johnson attended Oxford University but could not afford to continue his studies. After some time as a teacher Johnson left for London in 1837 to make his fortune and found work as a writer of thinly disguised accounts of parliament (see John Wilkes on p.173), and other commissioned books. The work did not pay well and at one stage Johnson and his friend John Savage walked around St James's Square all night because they could not afford lodgings. Despite poverty, Johnson thrived in London society, embarking on a happy marriage with an older woman and enjoying some literary success. His greatest achievement was the compilation of the first comprehensive and detailed English language dictionary in 1755, which employed six scribes and took seven years to produce. Johnson was by then a widower and the most successful stage of his life was spent as a bachelor – working, drinking and socialising. He had a talent for friendship which is well documented by his friend and biographer James Boswell, who immortalised many of Johnson's most famous sayings. This monument was a gift from the sculptor and stands by St Clement Danes where Johnson worshipped. The inscription reads, 'Critic. Essayist. Philologist. Biographer. Wit. Poet. Moralist. Dramatist. Political Writer. Talker'. Dr Johnson's house – where he compiled his dictionary – is now a museum and is close by in Gough Square.

8. Robert Devereux, 2nd Earl of Essex (1566-1601)

Devereux Inn, Devereux Court, WC2
Sculptor Anonymous, Stone bust, 1676

The Earl of Essex was one of the favourites of Queen Elizabeth and a patron of Francis Bacon (see p.187). Following the death of his father in 1576 his mother married the influential Earl of Leicester and it was he who arranged young Robert's education and his introduction at court. The handsome and tall young Devereux quickly became a favourite of Queen Elizabeth (see p.172) and established his reputation as a daring soldier on the battlefield against the French. Devereux could be a charming courtier and brave soldier but he lacked diplomacy and was prone to quarrels with his rivals which made enemies of Raleigh (see p.328), Blout and the Cecil family.

Devereux's fall from grace began with his marriage to Sir Philip Sidney's widow, which displeased the Queen, and was completed with his disastrous expedition to Ireland in 1599. When Devereux and his army landed in Ireland he avoided battle with the Catholic rebellion and against orders made peace with the Earl of Tyron. Devereux was exiled from court in 1600 for his failure and embarked on a rash conspiracy with James VI of Scotland to overthrow the Queen. When arrested it was not his obvious enemies that worked for his conviction and execution, but his former friend Francis Bacon. Partly due to the efforts of Bacon, the 2nd Earl of Essex was executed for treason in February 1601. This bust is located in the area where the Earl's grand house once stood and in streets and courts which bare the family name.

9. Temple Bar

Fleet Street, EC4
Sculptor Horace Jones (memorial),
Sir Joseph Boehm (Edward VII and
other panels), Marble, 1880

Temple Bar marks the boundary of the
City of London and it is here that the
Lord Mayor has greeted the monarch
when visiting the City since the time
of Elizabeth I. Traitors' heads were
displayed here and this was also the
site of a pillory where dissenters such
as Titus Oates and Daniel Defoe
were publicly humiliated. Several
gates have stood on the site, the grandest being of Portland stone
was erected in 1672. The gate was dismantled in 1878 and this
memorial by Horace Jones was placed on the site, with a statue
to Edward VII and bronze reliefs by Sir Joseph Boehm added later.
The gate of 1672 now stands in Paternoster Square (see p.220).

10. King Lud (1100-1155) and his sons

St Dunstan-in-the-West, Fleet St, EC4
Sculptor NA, 1586

According to pagan legend King Lud
originally founded a settlement that
later became London in around 66BC.
The King gave his name to the area
of Ludgate and it is here that he is
believed to be buried. These stone
figures originally stood on a Tudor
reconstruction of the gate but have
moved several times before being
placed in this quiet alcove in 1935.

11. Alfred Harmsworth, Lord Northcliffe (1865-1922)
St Dunstan-in-the-West, Fleet Street, EC4
Sculptor Lady Scott, Bronze bust, 1930

Alfred Harmsworth began his career as a writer for *Cycling News*, but soon went into newspaper publishing – launching a publication called *Answers to Correspondents* which proved a great success. Harmsworth changed British newspapers forever by introducing banner headlines, human interest stories, more photography and adopting an outraged populist style of writing. The formula was an instant success, transforming the *Evening News* within two years of buying the paper in 1894. In 1896 he launched the *Daily Mail* as a cheap condensed read based on US papers.

He described his papers as standing 'for the power, the supremacy and the greatness of the British Empire' and this was best demonstrated in the build-up to the First World War. As early as 1897 the *Daily Mail* published a series of articles entitled 'Under the Iron Heel' which portrayed Germany as the great threat and campaigned for war. A rival paper wrote 'Next to the Kaiser, Lord Northcliffe has done more than any living man to bring about the war'. When the war started he used his papers to chastise those he considered responsible for the Allied casualties. Lord Kitchener (see p.51) was the main recipient of his criticism. Northcliffe was offered a place in cabinet by Lloyd George, but he declined the poisoned chalice. Harmsworth was made Lord Northcliffe in 1918 and his final campaign was against what he regarded as a Zionist plot within the British establishment. Suffering from stress, anxiety and paranoia he had a breakdown in 1922 and died in the same year.

12. Queen Elizabeth I (1533-1603)
St Dunstan-in-the-West, Fleet Street, EC4
Sculptor William Kerwin, Stone, 1586

Queen Elizabeth I was the last of the Tudor monarchs. She claimed the throne after the death of her half-sister Mary in 1558 and reigned for almost 45 years. Unlike Mary, Elizabeth had been brought up a Protestant and with the Act of Uniformity and Bill of Supremacy of 1559, effectively established the Protestant nature of her realm. This may explain the location of her monument in puritan London, originally located above Ludgate at the very entrance to the City. In the North of England there was considerable Catholic support and Elizabeth was to face what became known as the Northern Rebellion in 1569. Elizabeth's faith had consequences for her foreign policy leading to war with Catholic Spain in 1585. The defeat of the Spanish Armada and Elizabeth's speech to the troops at Tilbury became a landmark in English history, but the war continued against Spain and France for many more years. Relations with Ireland were also very difficult, with several rebellions leading to the eventual bloody suppression by Baron Mountjoy in 1601.

There were inevitable failings during Elizabeth's reign, particularly in the matter of state financing where Elizabeth resorted to the selling of monopolies to raise money, but her greatest achievement was to provide a stable commonwealth which allowed Britain's art and commerce to flourish. She died in February 1603 and the crown passed to her cousin James I. This small stone figure is considered the oldest outdoor monument in London and considerably pre-dates the church upon which it stands.

13. John Wilkes (1727-1797)
Fetter Lane, EC4
Sculptor James Butler, Bronze, 1988

John Wilkes was one of the most influential radicals of his time and, as his monument proclaims, 'A champion of English Freedom'. As a young man he acquired the reputation as a rake but at the age of 30 became interested in politics and moderated his excesses, becoming a member of Parliament for Aylesbury in 1757. In April 1763, Wilkes wrote an article which criticised George III's speech to parliament and the Treaty of Paris which it endorsed, claiming it was the work of the Earl of Bute. Wilkes was arrested for seditious libel and imprisoned for a week – being released because of public protest. In November he was shot and wounded in a duel with a friend of the King and fled to France in 1764 where he remained for four years. On Wilkes' return he gained the seat for Middlesex, but was imprisoned, which caused rioting on the streets of London. In the following years he was elected to several positions, including Lord Mayor of London, and was eventually permitted to sit in Parliament. Wilkes also successfully campaigned to report parliamentary speeches verbatim, which was then prohibited. He continued to campaign on radical issues such as representative government and freedom of the press, but lost public sympathy when he headed the suppression of the Gordon Riots. He died in 1797 having withdrawn from politics for some years. Wilkes once wrote 'The liberty of the press is the birthright of a Briton'. This monument stands close to Fleet Street in recognition of his role in securing this birthright.

14. Mary, Queen of Scots (1542-87)

Fleet Street, EC4
Sculptor Not Known, Stone, 1905

Mary became Queen of the Scots when only six days old. Her claim to the English crown and relations between the two kingdoms were to shape the young Queen's life and ultimately lead to her death.

She was initially betrothed to Henry VIII's son, but Catholic's opposed the plan and held her at Stirling Castle, precipitating Henry's military incursions into Scotland which became known as 'The Rough Wooing'. Henry failed in his tactics and in April 1558 the tall, graceful Mary married the French Dauphin Francis and for a brief period was Queen of France and Scotland before the death of her husband in 1560. She returned to Scotland in August 1561 and the first years of her reign were peaceful. It was marriage to her second cousin, Lord Darnley, in 1565 that was to introduce a dark period of political intrigue amongst the Scottish nobles. Darnley murdered her secretary within a year of marriage only to be murdered himself outside the walls of Edinburgh in February 1567.

Mary's rapid marriage to the Earl of Bothwell – who was believed to be involved in he husband's murder – was the last straw for the Protestant lords of Scotland and they rose up to depose her in June 1567. Mary fled to England and the protection of her cousin Queen Elizabeth. She spent the next 19 years in captivity before being charge with treason and executed in February 1587. She was only 44 years old. This first storey monument was privately funded and is just a few hundred meters from that of her cousin who signed her death warrant.

15. Robert Waithman (1764-1833)

Salisbury Square, EC4
Stone, 1833

At 14 Robert Waithman came to London to be an apprentice draper and by the age of 22 he had his own draper's shop on Fleet Street and proceeded to make his fortune. He took a keen interest in politics and was an advocate for reform and served as MP for the City on several occasions and Mayor of London. He was an ally of Major John Cartwright (see p.240) and promoted the cause of reform which resulted in the Parliamentary Reform Act passed just before Waithman's death in 1833. This stone obelisk was erected close to his shop. He is buried nearby in St Bride's Church.

16. Thomas Power O'Connor (1848-1929)

72 Fleet Street, EC4
Sculptor F. Doyle-Jones, Bronze bust, 1934

From a modest Irish family, O'Connor gained a scholarship to Queen's College, Galway before embarking on a career in journalism and politics. As a fluent speaker of French and German he was offered a job at the *Telegraph* when the Franco-Prussian War broke out in 1870. O'Connor – or T.P. as he was commonly known – became a popular figure on Fleet Street, but did not lose his interest in politics and the cause of Irish nationalism. In 1880 he was elected MP for Galway as a representative of Parnell's Home Rule League and in 1885 won a Liverpool seat. O'Connor remained an MP for nearly 50 years and continued his career in journalism throughout his time in parliament, founding the then radical papers *The Star* (1887) and *The Sun* (1893) and *T.P's Weekly* (1902). In later years he returned to the *Telegraph* where he was a noted obituary writer and, as the longest serving MP, became Father of the House – a position he held until his own obituary was printed in November 1929. This bust stands opposite the Telegraph building where he worked.

17. Edgar Wallace (1875-1932)
Ludgate Circus at the junction with Fleet Street, EC4
Sculptor F. Doyle-Jones, Bronze medallion, 1934

Edgar Wallace tried many jobs before enlisting in the army to escape his mounting debts and unhappy engagement. He was sent to South Africa during the Second Boer War but left to become a war correspondent for the *Daily Mail* in 1898 and later the editor of the *Rand Daily Mail*. He returned to England and was given a job at the *Daily Mail* by Alfred Harmsworth (see p.171).

While reporting the Russo-Japanese War Wallace began his first thriller *The Four Just Men*. The book was a great success but owing to a reckless competition which Wallace devised he lost money on the venture. He went on to write all kinds of popular page-turners but divorce and his reckless lifestyle left him always in debt. He moved to Hollywood to become a screenwriter, but died soon after his arrival. Wallace's writing is now largely forgotten, but during the 1960s his racy plots and sharp dialogue were adapted for television and he is still a household name in Germany, where many of these programmes were made.

HOLBORN

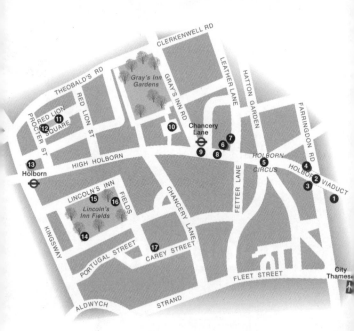

1. Sir Thomas Gresham
2. Holborn Viaduct Statues
3. Henry Fitz Eylwin
4. Sir William Walworth
5. Prince Albert
6. Charles Dickens
7. Prudential Assurance
   War Memorial
8. Royal Fusiliers,
   City of London Regiment
9. Holborn Bars

10. Francis Bacon,
    Viscount St Albans
11. Bertrand Russell,
    3rd Earl Russell
12. Fenner Brockway
13. John Bunyan
14. John Hunter
15. Margaret Ethel MacDonald
16. William Fredrick Danvers Smith
17. Sir Thomas More

Holborn

Contemporary Holborn consists largely of offices and shops with very few residents, but until the 17th century this area was dominated by the Holborn Road – an important thoroughfare into the City of London with an established resident population. Holborn Bars (see p.186) marks the entrance to the City of London where all visiting tradesmen were obliged to pay a toll before entering the City to sell their goods. Holborn was often busy with live cattle on their way for slaughter at Smithfield Market until the New Road (now Marylebone and Euston Roads) was built in 1756 to by-pass the inner city areas. The coaching inns of Holborn such as the Dagger, the Bull and Gate and Furnival's Inn were famous in their day but disappeared with the arrival of the railways which saw the end of the stagecoach. The gates and tolls that once protected the guilds of London have long disappeared, but the division between the old established City and the areas that were consumed by London's expansion, are still in some way marked by the area's monuments.

Within the bounds of the City can be found two war memorials (see pages 185 and 186), an equestrian statue to Prince Albert (see page 184), several statues of former Lord Mayors and one to the financier Sir Thomas Gresham. Charles Dickens is the only radical to be commemorated within the boundary of the old City in Holborn and this is because he lived for a time at Furnival's Inn which once stood on the site of his memorial. The area features heavily in *Great Expectations* and in *Nicholas Nickleby* the eponymous hero leaves London via the stage coach at nearby Snow Hill. It is outside the City that more controversial figures such as the pacifist philosopher Bertrand Russell, the left-wing politician Fenner Brockway and the non-conformist preacher and writer John Bunyan are to be found.

1. Sir Thomas Gresham (1519-1579)
Gresham House, Holborn Viaduct, EC1
Sculptor Henry Bursill, Bronze, 1868

Thomas Gresham was born into a family of wealthy Norfolk merchants. Through family connections Gresham became a royal financial agent in Antwerp in 1551 and soon made a personal fortune and a reputation for financial acumen. It was Gresham that managed to raise the value of the Pound on the Antwerp market after its collapse in 1551 and so relieve many of Edward VI's debts.

He became particularly important as financial advisor to Elizabeth I and spent some time as ambassador to Palma while maintaining his business interests in Antwerp. In 1567 Gresham moved to London to avoid the political instability in Holland prior to the Dutch Revolt and remained in the city until his sudden death in 1579. As he had no heir, he devoted his great fortune to public works such as Gresham College (founded by his uncle) and the Royal Exchange. He is credited with having established Gresham's Law which states 'Bad money drives out good money'. The law applies to counterfeit or inferior coinage which will remain in circulations while good coinage is withdrawn by hoarders. It is certain that Gresham did not invent this law but merely adopted it. A further monument to Gresham stands in a niche of the Royal Exchange where it was placed in 1845.

2. Holborn Viaduct Statues

Holborn Viaduct, EC1

Sculptor Henry Bursill, Farmer and Brindley, Bronze, 1868

There are four bronze statues on Holborn Viaduct that were commissioned at the time of the viaduct's construction. Statues by Farmer and Brindley representing Commerce and Agriculture are on the north side, while on the south are two statues by Henry Bursill representing Fine Art and Science.

Agriculture

Fine Art

Science

3. Henry Fitz Eylwin (d.1212)
Holborn Viaduct, EC1
Sculptor Henry Bursill, Stone, 1868

Henry Fitz Eylwin was a successful London draper who became the first Lord Mayor of London in 1192 and held the post until his death in 1212. Although Fitz Eylwin has drifted into the margins of history, his appointment as the first mayor of the City of London does mark an important change in the status of the City. The granting to the City of a mayor, with special rights and authority only superseded by the Crown, was a major concession by Richard I to the powerful merchants of the capital, upon whom the king was dependent for revenue. Fitz Eylwin introduced the first building ordinances which specified the materials to be used and set building standards to minimise the spread of fire; prospective builders were obliged to present their plans for approval to the 'Fitzailwyn Assize'. Fitz Eylwin built his own city mansion in an area now occupied by Salters Hall Court and Oxford Court, near the Bank of England. It is said that he continued to trade as a draper while Lord Mayor and gave over several rooms within his house to the running of his business. Not long after Fitz Eylwin's death and partly due to his good governance, London was given further privileges under the City Charter of 1215 and a month later London's 'ancient liberties and free customs' were confirmed in the Magna Carta. This monument is a mid-Victorian creation and depicts Fitz Eylwin as a medieval knight, holding a vast battle axe, while in reality he was a prosperous draper more familiar with needle, thread and making money than with the weapons of medieval battle.

4. Sir William Walworth (d.1385)

Holborn Viaduct, EC1
Sculptor Anonymous, Stone, 1868

His family was from Durham but Sir William Walworth moved to London to follow the fishmonger trade and rose through the Fishmongers' Guild to become Sheriff of London in 1370 and Lord Mayor in 1374. Walworth became famous for his actions during the Peasant's Revolt of 1381 when he raised a City bodyguard to defend London Bridge as the peasant armies of Kent and Essex marched on London with Wat Tyler as their leader. Walworth was forced to abandon the defence of the bridge when Tyler threatened to burn it down and as prisons were emptied and London's poor joined the rebel army the 14-year old King Richard was forced to give concessions to the rebels at Mile End. Some of the rebels dispersed having achieved what they wanted, but Tyler and his army remained in London settling old scores and waiting for further concessions. The armies met again at Smithfield when Walworth was so enraged by Tyler's arrogance towards the king that he pulled him from his horse and killed him with a dagger while Tyler's army looked on. Walworth was awarded a knighthood for his services and his actions have gone down in history. His dagger is kept at Fishmongers' Hall and at the east end of Mansion House there is a stained glass window depicting Tyler's killing. After serving two terms as Lord Mayor, Walworth died in 1385 and was buried in St Michael's Church, Crooked Lane. He was immortalised in verse by Richard Jonson in his 'Nine Worthies of London' published in 1392 and for some time remained a popular nursery rhyme hero in the same vein as Dick Whittington.

5. Prince Albert (1819-61)

Holborn Circus, EC1
Sculptor Charles Bacon, Bronze, 1874

This equestrian monument was presented to the City of London by Charles Oppenheim. It shows Prince Albert in field-marshal uniform and stands on an oblong plinth with plaques showing Britannia and the prince. He is kept company by bronze figures representing Commerce and Peace. The grandest monuments to Prince Albert are to be found either side of the Royal Albert Hall (see p.301).

6. Charles Dickens (1812-70)

Prudential Assurance Co., 142 Holborn Bars, EC1
Sculptor Percy Fitzgerald, Cupronised plaster, 1907

This bust stands on the site of the rooms Dickens lived in when he started his career as a writer. The area was the site of Furnival's Inn which was popular with young lawyers and it is here that Dickens began one of his great works, *Pickwick Papers*. Dickens said in his will; 'I conjure my friends on no account to make me the subject of any monument, memorial, or testimonial whatever. I rest my claims to the remembrance of my country upon my published works'. There is also a bust of Dickens just off Parliament Square (see p.46).

7. Prudential Assurance War Memorial

Prudential Assurance Co., 142 Holborn Bars, EC1
Sculptor F. V. Blunderstone, Bronze, 1922

This fine monument was erected just after World War One
to commemorate the 794 Prudential staff who lost their
lives in the conflict. The main figures depict a fallen soldier
being carried by two angels while four female figures at each
corner of the pedestal hold symbols of the conflict; one holds
a Howitzer machine gun, another a bi-plane. Close to the
main monument are large bronze panels listing the names of
the dead. The Prudential Company moved out of its Alfred
Waterhouse-designed offices in the 1990s.

8. Royal Fusiliers, City of London Regiment
Holborn, EC1
Sculptor Alfred Toft, Stone, 1922

The Royal Fusiliers served in the First World War at Le Cateau, Mons, Marne, Aisne, Ypres, Somme, Arras, Passchendaele, Cambrai and Gallipoli. Members of the regiment became the first two soldiers to receive the Victoria Cross during the war. The regiment was amalgamated in April 1968 with three others to form the Royal Regiment of Fusiliers that has served in recent conflicts and took part in the invasion of Iraq in 2003. The Royal Fusiliers Museum is located in the Tower of London and gives a full account of the regiment's history.

9. Holborn Bars
The bottom of Gray's Inn Road, EC1
Stone

Holborn Bars mark the entrance to the City of London where tolls were paid to enter the city with goods to trade. These gates to the city were originally established around 1130. The stone obelisks surmounted by silver griffins are a Victorian creation.

10. Francis Bacon, Viscount St Albans (1561-1626)
South Square, Gray's Inn, WC1
Sculptor F. W. Pomeroy, Coade Stone, 1912

Francis Bacon's reputation rests upon his achievements as a philosopher who advocated the use of scientific methods, observation and deduction to determine knowledge and truth. He argued against the abstract reasoning of Aristotle and in this way helped establish the philosophical ground upon which men such as Newton (see p.25) and Faraday (see p.123) could prosper. Bacon's life did not match the clarity and purity of his writings. His father was a successful member of the legal establishment and Francis was born within walking distance of this statue, but when his father died in 1579 his estate was divided between his five sons. Francis had extravagant tastes and despite becoming a barrister and member of court he was imprisoned briefly for debt in 1598. Ambition and lack of money led him to betray his friend and patron, the 2nd Earl of Essex (see p.169), in order to gain a position in court and even helped in the prosecution which led to the hapless earl's execution in 1601. Bacon became a favourite of James I and was made Lord Chancellor in 1618, but was dismissed for corruption in 1621. He was barred from office and spent the last years of his life writing. In 1626, while attempting to preserve the carcass of a chicken using snow – pre-empting Birdseye by several centuries – he contracted pneumonia and died. Gardening was another of Bacon's interests and he did much work in the garden surrounding this monument, including, it is claimed, the planting of the Catalpa Tree which can still be found here today. There is a smaller monument to Bacon on the 2nd floor of City of London School, Victoria Embankment.

11. Bertrand Russell, 3rd Earl Russell (1872-1970)
Red Lion Square, WC1
Sculptor Marcelle Quinton, Bronze, 1980

Bertrand Russell was a philosopher, logician, essayist and political campaigner who is considered – along with his colleague G.E. Moore – the founder of analytic philosophy. Russell's philosophy concerned itself with logic and reasoning and avoided the metaphysical concerns of continental philosophers such as Hegel and Nietzsche. As well as writing complicated philosophical texts, Russell also led a fascinating public and private life.

He was a life-long pacifist who was dismissed from Trinity College in 1916 for his anti-war protests and imprisoned under the Defence of the Realm Act in 1918. He was also interested in education and, with his second wife, opened an experimental school in 1927, based on his unconventional libertarian ideas. In 1929 he wrote 'Marriage and Morals' which advocated sex before marriage, contraception and open marriages – his second marriage ended as both he and his wife put these ideas into practice. Despite a post being withheld from him in America because of his views, Russell continued to lecture and write and in 1950 won the Nobel prize for literature. He continued to campaign for peace and was the founding president of the Campaign for Nuclear Disarmament in 1958. Russell was imprisoned again for an illegal anti-nuclear protest in 1961 at the age of nearly 90 and continued to campaign against the Vietnam War throughout the final years of his life. He died in 1970 having been born in the middle of Victoria's reign and lived to see the end of the swinging 60s. This modest bust is close to Conway Hall where Russell often lectured.

12. Fenner Brockway, Baron Brockway (1888-1988)
Red Lion Square, WC1
Sculptor Ian Walters, Bronze, 1985

Fenner Brockway was a left-wing journalist and politician who started his political life as a liberal but became a socialist after interviewing Labour leader Keir Hardie. Like Bertrand Russell, Brockway was a pacifist who campaigned against the First World War and spent much of that time in prison. After the war Brockway became one of the founders of the India League, which campaigned for independence for India, and continued to write for left-wing publications as well as briefly becoming Labour MP for East Leyton.

During the 1930s Brockway reconsidered his pacifist position and supported the International Brigade in the Spanish Civil War and Britain's involvement in the Second World War. After the war Brockway rejoined the Labour Party having spent many years as a member of the more left-wing Independent Labour Party. He won the seat of Eton and Slough in 1950 for Labour, but always remained on the left of the party, campaigning for independence for Britain's colonies, supporting CND and founding the charity War on Want. Brockway lost his seat in 1964 and accepted a life peerage from which position he offered critical support to the various Labour governments of the time. Brockway was 97 years old when this charming and animated monument was unveiled by Michael Foot.

13. John Bunyan (1628-1688)

Baptist Church House, Southampton Row, WC1
Sculptor Richard Garbe, Stone, 1903

John Bunyan was born into a tinker family in Bedfordshire at the high point of English puritanism. Bunyan was an extremely imaginative boy, who despite having very little formal education, transformed the religious fervour of the time into his own tales of fantasy. As a young man his fertile imagination and sensitivity were to lead him close to insanity. He fought in the parliamentary army during the English Civil War (1642-6), but his troubled mental state and religious visions continued. In 1653 he joined the Baptist Church and focused his imagination within an organised religion, proving himself to be a charismatic and powerful preacher. Charles II had ambitions to return Britain to the Catholic faith and Bunyan was prosecuted by the authorities in 1660 for preaching without a licence. He refused to renounce preaching and so spent 12 years in Bedford prison from where he started writing his famous religious allegorical tale *Pilgrim's Progress*. After a second period of imprisonment the book was completed and published to great acclaim. Bunyan's fame was to prevent his further prosecution by the authorities and he went on to write many more religious books and preach to vast audiences. Having contracted a cold on the way to London he died in 1688 and was buried at the non-conformist Bunhill Fields cemetery. This monument stands on the first floor of a Baptist Church and shows Bunyan holding a copy of his famous book.

14. John Hunter (1728-93)
Lincoln's Inn Fields, WC2
Sculptor N. F. Boonham, Bronze, 1977
See review on page 27.

15. Margaret Ethel MacDonald (1870-1911)
Lincoln's Inn Fields, WC2
Sculptor Richard Goulden, Bronze, 1914
This monument commemorates the life of Margaret MacDonald, wife of the British Prime Minister Ramsey MacDonald. Margaret was the daughter of a doctor who became a socialist at the age of 20 and began working for various organisations concerned with improving the lot of the working-class and particularly women. She met Ramsey MacDonald in 1895 and they married in 1896. She bore six children but continued her work helping to establish trade schools for women and campaigning for women's suffrage. She died prematurely from blood poisoning in 1911 and this monument with the inscription 'She brought joy to those with whom she lived and worked' was erected soon after.

16. William F D Smith, 2nd Viscount of Hambleden (1868-1928)

Lincoln's Inn Fields, WC2
Sculptor Plinth with bust removed, Stone

William Smith inherited the newspaper and bookselling business known as W.H. Smith and Son. This plinth is close to where the business once had its offices. The bust which sat on this stone plinth and the entrepreneurial spirit which once drove the company have both disappeared.

17. Sir Thomas More (1478-1535)

Carey Street, WC2
Sculptor Robert Smith, Stone, 1866
See review on page 319.

18. Pocahontas (1595-1617)

Formerly in Red Lion Square
Sculptor David B. McFall, 1955, Bronze

The statue of the native American princess Pocahontas was a feature of Red Lion Square for many years. It was commissioned by the map publisher Cassell's in 1955, who were based in a former inn where Pocahontas had stayed in 1616. The reclining figure of the princess was their logo. The sculpture was removed when Cassell's moved and in 1996 it was sold at Christie's. For more information about Pocahontas see John Smith's monument in the City (see p.207).

THE CITY

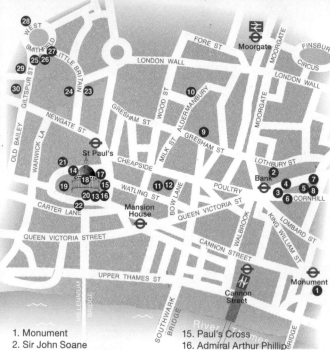

1. Monument
2. Sir John Soane
3. Field Marshal Arthur Wellesley,
   1st Duke of Wellington
4. War Memorial to London Troops
5. Abraham Lincoln
6. James Henry Greathead
7. George Peabody
8. Paul Julius Reuter
9. Guildhall: William Beckford
   & William Pitt the Elder
10. John Heminge & Henry Cordell
11. Captain John Smith
12. Admiral Arthur Phillip
13. John Donne
14. St Andrew

15. Paul's Cross
16. Admiral Arthur Phillip
17. John Wesley
18. Sir Christopher Wren
19. Queen Anne
20. St Thomas Becket
21. Temple Bar
22. Blitz / Firefighters' Memorial
23. Postman's Park
24. Sir Rowland Hill
25. Henry VIII
26. Sir William Wallace
27. Protestant Martyrs
28. Smithfield War Memorial
29. Golden Boy
30. Charles Lamb

The City

Between Wren's monument to the Great Fire and the Golden Boy on Giltspur Street, where it is said the fire was extinguished, there are many monuments to admire. Bank is largely dominated by Victorian architecture and the monuments here are all dedicated to great Victorians – Wellington, Abraham Lincoln, James Greathead, George Peabody and Paul Reuter. The only exception is the architect Sir John Soane who was an old man when Victoria came to the throne in 1837.

Further west towards St Paul's there are some fine monuments in the Guildhall and in and around the Church of St-Mary-le-Bow where the explorers Captain John Smith and Admiral Arthur Phillip are to be found. St Paul's Cathedral dominates the skyline and has around it monuments to the religious figures John Wesley, Thomas Becket and St Andrew. Queen Anne, whose reign witnessed the completion of the cathedral, takes pride of place at the Cathedral's entrance. The bust of John Donne is a recent addition to the area. It is appropriate that the memorial to the Blitz stands just opposite St Paul's, whose survival came to symbolise the City's defiance during the Blitz. Wren's Temple Bar, has recently been returned to the capital and now serves as a grand entrance to the modern shops and offices of Paternoster Square.

The inventor of the postage stamp, Rowland Hill, stands outside the old Post Office building and looks over Postman's Park. The park has a wall of painted tiles commemorating fatal acts of heroism by members of the public and was the inspiration of the sculptor George Watts.

Both William Wallace and the Protestant Martyrs are commemorated with tablets in the wall of St Bartholomew's Hospital close to where they were executed; the founder of the hospital, Henry VIII, has a monument above the entrance. On Giltspur Street can be found the Golden Boy statue and a bust of the Georgian writer and essayist Charles Lamb.

1. Monument

Monument Street and Fish Street Hill, EC2
Sculptor Christopher Wren and Robert Hooke, reliefs by Caius
Gabriel Cibber, Stone, 1677

The Monument commemorates the Great Fire of London which started on the 2nd September 1666 and raged for four days, destroying two thirds of the City. The act of parliament which provided for the rebuilding of London also contained provision for a monument 'the better to preserve the memory of this dreadful Visitation'. The result was the work of Christopher Wren and Robert Hooke and consisted of a Doric order column made of Portland stone with a viewing tower. The tower is 202 feet tall, which is the distance from the base of the monument to the shop on Pudding Lane where the fire started. There are panels at the base, the grandest being the West bas-relief by Cibber, which gives an allegorical account of the City's reconstruction, with Charles II at its centre.

A French Catholic called Robert Hubert was quickly arrested, made to confess and hung at Tyburn and in 1681 the following words were added to the monument; 'But Popish frenzy, which wrought such horrors, is not yet quenched'. The inscription was removed in 1830 once the accidental nature of the fire was established. Another dark aspect of the monument's history was its use as a place of suicide. A baker threw himself from the viewing tower in 1788 and a further six people followed his bloody example before the balcony was enclosed in an iron cage in 1842. The Monument is still open to the public and the exhausting climb is worth it for the spectacular views of the City (tel: 020 7626 2717 for further details).

2. Sir John Soane (1753-1837)
The Bank of England, Corner of Lothbury, EC2
Sculptor Sir William Reid Dick
Stone, 1937

Sir John Soane, the son of a bricklayer, was christened John Swan and became one of the most prominent neo-classical architects of his generation. Swan changed his name to Soane when he came to London to study at the Royal Academy in 1771. After studying in Italy for three years, he returned to England in 1780 and inherited a considerable fortune when he married in 1784.

Soane's big break came when he became Surveyor of the Bank of England in 1788. He redesigned the Bank over many years and put his name to Dulwich College (1812), the Church of St Peter in Walworth (1823-25) and Holy Trinity on Marylebone Road (1828) in the proceeding 40 years. Unfortunately much of his work has been lost and his greatest masterpiece, The Bank of England, was completely redeveloped by Sir Herbert Baker between 1921 and 1937. Some idea of Soane's original interior can be found at the Bank of England Museum where his Stock Office has been faithfully recreated. Sir John Soane is now best known for the museum bearing his name which is located in his former home at 12 Lincoln's Inn Fields and contains his huge collection of art and artifacts. One of the prize exhibits is the sarcophagus of Pharaoh Seti I. Soane held a three-day party when it arrived in 1825, with guests who included Samuel Taylor Coleridge. Soane donated his house and collection to the nation, partly to spite his surviving son whom he disliked.

3. Field Marshal Arthur Wellesley, 1st Duke of Wellington (1769-1852)

Royal Exchange, EC2
Sculptor Chantrey, Bronze, 1844

The Duke of Wellington was born Arthur Wellesley, the fifth son of the 1st Earl of Mornington, who was a member of the Protestant squirearchy of Ireland. The young Arthur did not show any promise as a student at Eton and was without vocation until he was enlisted in the army. He spent several years as a dissolute young officer, but having been rejected in marriage he reformed his ways and began to seriously study military strategy. Wellesley first showed his talent in India during the Fourth Anglo-Mysore War (1799) and the Second Mahratta War (1803) and he returned to England in 1805 having become a Major-General and a Knight of the Bath. Wellesley's family was wealthy and he was able to buy a seat in Parliament and serve as Chief Secretary for Ireland before events on the continent forced his return to the battlefield against Napoleon's army.

Wellesley left Britain to command an expeditionary force against the French army in 1808 and spent the next six years fighting a series of key battles and sieges that drove the French army from the Iberian peninsular and culminated in the Battle of Toulouse in 1814 (see Cadiz Memorial on page 52). By this time Wellesley had been awarded the title the Duke of Wellington and was appointed to attend the Congress of Vienna after Bonaparte's surrender. The negotiations were cut short by Napoleon's escape and it was Wellington who led the allied forces to victory at Waterloo in June 1815.

Wellington returned to Britain as a hero and continued his career in politics, joining Lord Liverpool's government in 1819 and eventually becoming Prime Minister in 1828. Wellington arrived at Downing Street on his faithful horse Copenhagen but his wartime popularity was rapidly fading. He passed a Catholic Emancipation Act and Catholic Relief Act with the help of the Whigs and even fought a duel with Lord Winchilsea when accused of treachery. Despite such reforms Wellington was at heart a reactionary and refused to consider Parliamentary reform. The Duke became so reviled that his London home, Apsley House, was regularly stoned by angry mobs – he earned the epithet 'The Iron Duke' because of the iron shutters he installed rather than for the strength of his character. His Tory administration fell in 1830 and Earl Grey's Whigs passed the 1832 Parliamentary Reform Act in the face of Wellington's vehement opposition. Wellington continued in politics but was gradually superseded as leader by Robert Peel (see p.63) and retired from politics in 1846. He briefly returned to public life at nearly 80 to organise an army to prevent insurrection during the revolutions of 1848. Wellington was loved and hated in equal measure by his countrymen but is certainly one of Britain's most celebrated figures with this statue and the one in Hyde Park Corner both erected within a few years of each other (see p.278). On his death in 1852, Wellington received a state funeral and was placed in a sarcophagus next to Nelson's in St Paul's Cathedral. He is credited with the phrase 'publish and be damned', which was his response to the threat by the courtesan Harriette Wilson to reveal secrets of their affair. Wilson's memoir was a bestseller and revealed the Duke to be a jealous and boorish lover.

4. War Memorial to London Troops
Royal Exchange, EC2
Sculptor Sir Aston Webb and Alfred Drury, Bronze, 1920

This grand memorial was funded by public subscription and was initially intended to commemorate the many London soldiers that fell in the First World War. When the 'war to end all wars' failed to prevent a further World conflagration a plaque was added to commemorate those that lost their lives between 1939 and 1945.

5. Abraham Lincoln (1809-1865)
Inside Royal Exchange, EC2
Sculptor Andrew O'Connor, Stone bust, 1930

Located in the entrance to the Exchange shopping complex, this fine bust of Abraham Lincoln is easily missed. For more details of the 16th President of the United States see p.61.

6. James Henry Greathead (1844-1896)

Royal Exchange, EC2
Sculptor James Butler RA, Bronze, 1994

James Henry Greathead was one of the great Victorian engineers whose pioneering methods of tunnel construction enabled London's underground tube system to be built. Greathead was born in South Africa but came to England to study engineering. He began his career in 1864 working with engineer Peter W. Barlow and spent a brief period as assistant engineer on the Midland Railway. In 1869 Greathead and Barlow were appointed to engineer a train tunnel under the Thames from Tower Hill in the north to Vine Lane on the south bank. Greathead adapted the methods developed by Marc Brunel, involving a series of moving metal shields behind which the walls of the tunnel could be built. He employed hydraulic jacks and compressed air to greatly increase the rate of progress and the Tower Subway was opened in August 1870. The tunnel proved uneconomic and soon closed, but Greathead's skill as a tunnel engineer was widely recognised. He was appointed as the Chief Engineer responsible for building an underground railway line from Stockwell to the City of London which is now part of the Northern line. The underground was opened in 1890, by which time Greathead was already busy engineering the Central Line. He was only 52 and at the height of his powers when he died suddenly from stomach cancer. This monument was erected 98 years after Greathead's death and stands upon an air duct for the tube system which he did so much to build.

7. George Peabody (1795-1869)
Behind Royal Exchange, EC2
Sculptor W. S. Story, Bronze, 1869

George Peabody was born to a modest family in Massachusetts and left school at the age of 11 to help support his six siblings. Peabody fought against the British in the war of 1812 and afterwards established a wholesale business that made him a small fortune. He travelled to England in 1827 and over the next ten years built a successful banking business trading in currencies and American securities. In 1838 he intervened to stabilise US state bonds during a crisis. The states made good on their loans and Peabody's bonds made him a further fortune. In 1851 he profited from promoting American goods during the Great Exhibition and made further fortunes investing in US railways and trans-Atlantic cables.

Peabody was now a trusted figure and he came to the public's attention when he funded the search for the missing explorer Sir John Franklin (see p.95) in 1852. He was troubled by the poverty he saw and following the advice of Lord Shaftesbury (see p.31) the Peabody Donation Fund was established to build good cheap housing for the poor. The first Peabody estate was built on Commercial Street, Spitalfields, in 1863 and the fund went on to build many more estates. In the last years of his life Peabody spent an estimated £8 million in his philanthropic work to improve housing and education in both America and his adopted home. This monument was unveiled by the Prince of Wales in July 1869, just a few months before Peabody's death. He was briefly laid to rest in Westminster Abbey before being returned with full honours to the United States.

8. Paul Julius Reuter (1816-1899)

Behind Royal Exchange, EC2
Sculptor Michael Black, Stone, 1976

The founder of Reuters News Agency was born in Germany, the son of a rabbi. He went to work as a clerk in his uncle's bank in Goettingen and soon became interested in the new technology of telegraphs to rapidly communicate important market information.

While living in London in October 1845 he converted to Christianity, changed his name and later married the daughter of a business colleague, Ida Magnus. Reuter and his wife established their first news agency in 1850 using carrier pigeons to bridge gaps in the telegram network and so provide information about the Paris stock market faster than by rail. Reuter's first London office was established close to this memorial in 1851.

Reuter's business maxim was 'follow the cable', meaning that wherever the cable network terminated a Reuters office was established to send and receive news. English papers were reluctant to use the service, but in 1858 *The Times* used a Reuters report of a speech by Napoleon III and Reuters became a recognised news source. It was Reuters that broke the news of Lincoln's assassination several hours before the ship carrying the news docked. In 1870 Reuter signed agreements with other agencies to provide the first worldwide news network, beginning his career using pigeons only 25 years before. In 1878, having been awarded a baronetcy, Reuter retired, leaving the business to his son. He died at his villa in the South of France at the turn of a century in which the company he founded was to become the world's largest news agency.

Horatio Nelson

Sir Winston Churchill

William Beckford

Wellington

Pitt the Younger

Royal Fusiliers

Pitt the Elder

9. Guildhall EC2
Gresham Street, EC2
Open: Monday-Friday 9.30am-4pm

The Guildhall is first mentioned in a property inventory of St Paul's in 1128. It was the venue for famous trials such as those of Anne Askew (1546), Archbishop Cranmer (1563) and Henry Garnet (1605).

The Guildhall has not been without its own trials and tribulations. The Great Fire of 1666 destroyed the medieval roof and windows, but with the stone walls intact the building was quickly rebuilt, probably under the supervision of Wren. The roof and windows of the Guildhall were again destroyed in December 1940. Again the building's structure remained intact and after the war Sir Giles Gilbert Scott sympathetically reconstructed the damaged hall and built the surrounding modern buildings which stand here today.

If Bloomsbury can be regarded as a suitable place for the great Whig politician Charles James Fox, it is not surprising that the Guildhall is the site for monuments to conservative heros – Pitt the Elder and Younger, Horatio Nelson, Winston Churchill, the Duke of Wellington and a tablet to the City of London Royal Fusiliers who lost their lives in the Second South African War. Two of the great men featured here merit special attention as they are not featured anywhere else in the capital:

• William Beckford (1709-1770)
Sculptor Francis J. Moore, Stone, 1772

Beckford was born in Jamaica into a plantation-owning family and furthered their fortunes in the sugar trade. He came to London and enjoyed further success in ship-building and money-lending ventures. Beckford became a significant figure in the City of London and served as Lord Mayor twice as well as being an important ally of William Pitt the Elder in Parliament. His son, also called William, became a famous novelist and architect but managed to dissipate a great deal of the family fortune.

• William Pitt the Elder (1708-1778)

Sculptor John Bacon, Stone, 1782,

William Pitt the Elder dominated British politics for a generation, deriving his power and influence not from the crown but from the support of the people. Pitt entered politics in 1735 and formed a group of young Whigs, known as the 'Patriots', who were enemies of Sir Robert Walpole. Pitt did not gain office until he was appointed Paymaster General in 1746, establishing a reputation for honesty and probity. He advocated war as a means of securing the country's economic interests and it was his sound leadership that secured Britain's victory during the Seven Years War (1754, 1756-1763). He resigned in protest when the Treaty of Paris was signed and, although he became prime minister again in 1766, he was never able to impose himself in peacetime as he had during a time of war. Pitt collapsed in the Lords in 1778 and died four days later. He created a legacy of aggressive foreign policy which was to be followed by his son (see p.256) and by later politicians such as Lord Palmerston.

10. John Heminge (1566-1630) & Henry Cordell (1576-1627)

Garden off Love Lane

Sculptor Charles J. Allen, Bronze, 1896

This unusual monument features a bust of Shakespeare but commemorates the two actors who were friends of Shakespeare and published the first folio of his collected works. The two men's selfless efforts probably helped preserve many of Shakespeare's plays. The monument was the idea of Shakespeare enthusiast and wealthy industrialist, Charles C. Walker. The great Victorian actor Henry Irving gave a speech at the monument's unveiling.

11. Captain John Smith (1580-1631)

Outside St Mary-le-Bow Church, Cheapside, EC2
Sculptor Charles Rennick, Bronze, 1960

John Smith went to sea at 16 and fought as a mercenary against Spanish and Ottoman armies before escaping Turkish capture and travelling across Europe and North Africa. After his return to England, Smith was recruited by the Virginia Company and set sail from Blackwall in December 1606 with three ships to found a colony in America. Smith fell out with the captain and crew so badly during the voyage that he was imprisoned and destined to be executed. A letter from the Virginia Company appointing him one of the members of the colony's council saved his life.

The founding of Jamestown proved difficult and Smith was captured by one of the native tribes and only saved by the pleading of the chief's daughter, Pocahontas. Relations with the tribes and between the settlers soon deteriorated further and Smith returned to England in 1609, having been injured and fearful that some of the settlers were plotting to kill him. In 1614 he embarked on another voyage to America, sailing further north and producing detailed maps of the area he named New England. After a last unsuccessful voyage he settled in London and spent the rest of his life writing florid and self-serving accounts of his adventures. The interest in his stories was greatly increased when Pocahontas visited England in 1616. This statue is a copy of one that stands in Virginia and is close to St Sepulchre-without-Newgate, where he was laid to rest in 1631. The church has a plaque which reads 'Here lyes one conquered, that hath conquered Kings, Subdu'd large Territories, and done Things Which to the world impossible would seem'.

12. Admiral Arthur Phillip (1738-1814)

Inside St Mary-le-Bow Church, Cheapside, EC2
Sculptor Charles Hartwell, Bronze, 1992

Arthur Phillip joined the merchant navy at the age of 15 and was promoted to lieutenant during the Seven Years War. After intermittent commissions his appointment as captain of *HMS Sirius*, with responsibility for establishing a penal colony in New South Wales, was to make his name. He planned the expedition for over a year, but his requests for experienced farmers and craftsmen were refused and most of those who sailed from Portsmouth in May 1787 were convicts. The 11 ships followed Captain Cook's route (see p.88) and landed in Botany Bay in January 1788 before settling in a place they named Sydney Cove.

Phillip began a process of convict emancipation in return for hard work, saying 'In a new country there will be no slavery and hence no slaves'. He also attempted to treat the Aborigines fairly, although small pox brought by the settlers killed many of them.

Phillip proved himself as an administrator and by 1792 the colony had a small but growing farming community and a busy port. He left the colony in December 1792 due to ill health but recovered sufficiently to hold a series of commands during the Napoleonic Wars. This bust of the Admiral was first unveiled at St Mildred's Church, in 1932 and was retrieved from the rubble when the church was destroyed during the Second World War. It spent time on the Bank of America building facing St Paul's before being restored and placed here in St Mary-le-Bow Church to commemorate the Australian Bicentenary in January 1998. A replica of this bust stands next of St Paul's (see page 210).

13. John Donne (1572-1631)

Outside St Paul's Cathedral, EC2
Sculptor Nigel Boonham, Bronze, 2012

The inscriptions at the base of this monument give clues as to the life of the metaphysical poet John Donne. One reads 'birthplace Bread Street'. It was here that Donne was born into a large Catholic family when the rights of Catholics were severely restricted. As a young man Donne was unable to graduate because of his faith.

The monument also states that he was a 'reader Lincoln's Inn' where, aged 20, he studied law. Following his brother's imprisonment and death, Donne joined the Anglican Church and embarked upon a brief naval career fighting against the Spanish fleet and travelling on the continent.

The monument states 'married Anne More of Losely'. Anne was only 16 and the niece of his employer, Sir Thomas Egerton. The family disapproved and Donne was dismissed and briefly imprisoned. There followed years of hardship, but Donne's poems testify to a happy marriage only ended with Anne's death in childbirth.

Donne tried to gain favour with the new King James I and in 1615 was made Royal Chaplin and later, as the monument tells us, 'dean St Paul's Cathedral'. He died in 1631 having left behind a vast body of work. His tomb is still to be seen in St Paul's and is one of the few to have survived The Great Fire.

Donne's complicated poetry of subtle argument and extended metaphor is full of the contradictions and tensions involved in the living of a rich and full life and is still read today.

14. St Andrew
North side of St Paul's Churchyard, EC4
Sculptor Francis Bird, Portland Stone, 1724
This worn stone bust of St Andrew was originally placed upon
the south pediment and was part of a complete statue that stood
12ft high. Due to the ravages of time this part of the statue was
replaced in 1923 and it now sits upon a stone block only visible
through gates to the north of the Cathedral. St Andrew was Christ's
first disciple. He is the patron saint of Scotland but also of Greece,
Romania, Barbados and Russia and his patronage is equally broad
encompassing fishmongers, singers, spinsters, old maids and
sufferers of gout and sore throats.

15. Paul's Cross
North-east corner of St Paul's Church Yard, EC4
Sculptor Reginald Blomfield, Portland Stone, 1910
The old St Paul's had an open-air pulpit which was destroyed by
the Puritans. In 1874 the foundations of the pulpit were uncovered
and this fine Portland stone column was later erected on the site.
The monument was funded from the will of MP Henry Charles
Richards and there is a plaque on the columns base in memory of
his family. The monument's designer, Reginald Blomfield, is the
grandson of Bishop Charles Blomfield, who lies in a very fine tomb
within the Cathedral.

16. Admiral Arthur Phillip (1738-1814)
Watling Street, EC4
Sculptor C. L. Hartwell, Resin copy, 1932, placed here 2000
The original of this monument first stood at the Church of
St Mildred, but after the church's destruction in the Blitz it
was relocated to Gateway House in 1968. When this site was
redeveloped the original bust was placed in St Mary-le-Bow in 1998
(see p.208). This resin copy was erected here, amid the fine city
gardens surrounding St Pauls, in 2000.

17. John Wesley (1703-1791)
North side of St Paul's Churchyard, EC4
Sculptor Samuel Manning and Son, Bronze, 1988
(based on marble original of 1839)

Raised in a pious Protestant household, John Wesley was one of 19 children of the rector of Epworth. It was at Oxford that Wesley formed a group of like-minded theologians called the 'Holy Club' which became known as the 'Methodists' for their adherence to a methodical religious life. Wesley defined a Methodist as 'one who loves the Lord his God with all his heart, and with all his soul' and avoided scriptural disagreements with the Church of England.

John Wesley failed to find a place within the church and left for the new colony of Georgia with his brother Charles in 1735. His preaching was not liked or fully understood by the settlers and, after an unhappy love affair, Wesley returned to England. He became certain of the injustice of slavery during the voyage and campaigned against it when he returned to Britain. Failing yet again to find a church, Wesley gave his first open-air sermon in April 1739. His call to challenge the evils of poverty and injustice drew large crowds and from 1739 a network of Methodist Societies sprang up around the country. In 1777 the City Road Methodist Chapel was built, by which time the society had become so accepted that George III gave navy timber to assist in the chapel's construction. Wesley spent the rest of his life leading the Methodist movement. He died at the age of 88 and was buried in the churchyard of the City Road Chapel where another monument to him stands (see p.351). Methodism, Pentecostalism and the Christian Movement are all based upon Wesley's teachings and are still active today.

18. Sir Christopher Wren (1632-1723)
St Paul's Cathedral, Ludgate Hill, EC4
Architect: Sir Christopher Wren; Stone, 1675-1708

St Paul's Cathedral is Christopher Wren's greatest masterpiece
and – unlike many of his smaller churches – rooted in the Baroque
and Renaissance tradition. A tablet near Wren's tomb within
the Cathedral has inscribed the words, 'Reader, if you seek his
monument, look around you.' It is surprising that a statue of Wren
does not exist in London, but as a statement of Wren's genius, St
Paul's is perhaps the greatest of all London monuments.

Christopher Wren was born into an established clerical family – his father was the Dean of Windsor and his uncle the Bishop of Norwich. He excelled at school and proved himself a brilliant student of the natural sciences at Wadham College, Oxford. He was appointed professor of astronomy at Gresham College in 1657 and conducted several experiments that influenced Isaac Newton's theory of gravity (see p.25).

Wren was one of the founding members of the Royal Academy in 1662, but at the age of 30 he had studied many subjects without finding one to occupy his attentions fully. It was architecture that was to capture his imagination and after designing the Sheldonian Theatre in Oxford, he studied architecture in earnest and travelled to Italy and France to educate himself in the classical styles.

After the Great Fire of London in September 1666 Wren became a key figure in planning the new city and was appointed Surveyor of Works responsible for the city's reconstruction in 1669. This herculean task was to occupy the rest of his professional life and create many buildings that are still standing today, including the Royal Exchange, the Royal Naval College, Drury Lane Theatre, Chelsea Hospital and the Monument to the Great Fire (see p.196). St Paul's Cathedral was the centre piece of the new City and from the laying of the foundation stone in 1675 it took Wren 35 years to complete his design which was finished in 1710. It is said that when Wren was too old to climb the 530 steps to the Golden Gallery he was carried up in a basket to survey the works.

Wren's achievements were never without difficulty and criticism, and in his later years a younger generation resented his dominance and questioned his taste. He gradually lost control of the Fifty New Churches Commission established in 1711, and was dismissed from his post in 1718 in favour of William Benson, who proved a poor successor. When Wren died in 1723 he was the first person to be buried in St Paul's, followed by many of the country's most prominent men, some of whom are listed in the proceeding pages.

St Paul's Cathedral

St Paul's is not only a monument to the genius of Christopher Wren but also a place of national worship, celebration, mourning and on occasion protest. In the last 300 years the cathedral has acquired a vast collection of tombs, tablets and monuments for many of Britain's most famous figures. There are enough monuments in St Paul's to fill a book dedicated to the subject but below is a list of some of the most important. As well as some very fine monuments, visitors can also see the wood carving of Grinling Gibbons and Jonathan Maine, fine ironwork in the North Quire Aisle by Jean Tijou and a font by the hand of Francis Bird.

IN NORTH ISLE:
General Charles Gordon – soldier (see page 140)
Lord Melbourne – politician
Duke of Wellington – soldier and politician (see page 198)

IN SOUTH ISLE:
Bishop Middleton – theologian
Captain Westcott – soldier

SOUTH QUIRE ISLE:
John Donne – poet (see page 209)
Bishop Charles Blomfield – theologian (see opposite)

AT THE CROSSING:
Joshua Reynolds – painter (see page 30)
John Howard – Prison reformer
Sir William Jones – Jurist and Orientalist
Dr Johnson – Lexicographer, essayist (see page 168)

John Donne

Duke of Wellington

Bishop Charles Blomfield

Joshua Reynolds

Cuthbert Collingwood

Thomas Dundas

JMW Turner

Arthur Sullivan

Horatio Nelson

NORTH TRANSCEPT:
General Daniel Houghton – soldier
General Thomas Picton – soldier
(Around these two monuments a great many of Wellington's
General Staff and Officers stand)
Major-General Thomas Dundas – soldier

SOUTH TRANSCEPT:
Wellington's staff and many Admirals
Admiral Horatio Nelson – naval hero (see page 17)
General Charles Cornwallis – soldier
Admiral Cuthbert Collingwood – naval hero
Sir John Moore – soldier
Bishop Heber – theologian
JMW Turner –painter
Robert Falcon Scott and Companions – explorers (see page 97)

THE CRYPT:
Christopher Wren's Tomb – architect (see page 212)
George Cruikshank –cartoonist
Holman Hunt – painter
Sir John Millais – painter (see page 360)
Joshua Reynolds – painter (see page 30)
JMW Turner – painter
William Huggins (1824-1920) – astronomer
Sir John Goss – cathedral choir master
Nelson's Tomb – naval hero (see page 17)
George Dance – architect
Wellington's Tomb – soldier and politician (see page 198)
Alexander Fleming – scientist
Henry Moore – sculptor
Arthur Sullivan –composer (see page 124)

19. Queen Anne (1665-1714)
Entrance to St Paul's Cathedral, EC4
Sculptor Richard Belt
(copy of original by Francis Bird erected in 1712), Stone, 1886

Queen Anne was the second daughter of James Duke of York, later James II (see p.8). Anne was brought up as a strict Protestant and her faith was to become a major point of difference with her father, who publicly converted to Catholicism in 1673 and ascended to the throne in 1685. James II proved a despotic and unpopular King who was easily overthrown by his elder daughter Mary and her husband. Anne played no direct part in the events of 1688, but certainly knew of the plot and did nothing to prevent it. Anne soon fell out with the royal couple and following the banning of her friends, the Churchills, from court for corresponding with the exiled King, she never spoke to her sister again. Anne's marriage to George of Denmark failed to produce an heir and she suffered 18 miscarriages, bearing only three children who died in childhood.

Anne was ill with gout and rheumatism and dependent on laudanum and alcohol when she was carried to her coronation in 1702. She spent her reign as an invalid and took no part in politics. The original monument by Francis Bird was erected in 1712 to commemorate the completion of St Paul's, but the marble deteriorated over the years and was replaced by this Victorian copy in 1886. The original was saved by the writer Augustus Hare and now stands in St Leonard's-on-Sea. There is another monument to Queen Anne in Queen Anne's Gate (see p.59).

20. St Thomas Becket (1118-1170)
South side of St Paul's Cathedral, EC4
Sculptor E. Bainbridge Copnall
Stone, 1973

Thomas Becket received a sound clerical education before joining the staff of Theobald, the Archbishop of Canterbury. When Henry II came to the throne in 1155, determined to exert royal authority, Becket was appointed his Lord Chancellor. The two men became close friends and Becket proved himself a conscientious and able Chancellor. While serving the King, Becket lived luxuriously and travelled with a vast retinue that rivalled that of his master. He is known to have led troops into battle against the French and was mentor to Henry's son.

Becket's relations with the King changed when he was appointed Archbishop of Canterbury in 1162. The King was soon angered by Becket's change of allegiance when his attempts to control clerical courts were rejected by Becket. Their differences came to a head at Clarendon Palace in January 1164 when Becket refused to accept the King's reforms and was forced to flee to France to avoid the monarch's wrath. He remained in exile for six years until a compromise was reached which allowed his return to Canterbury in December 1170. Becket soon disturbed the fragile peace by excommunicating several of the King's allies. Henry's words 'who will rid me of this meddlesome priest', were not a command for Becket's murder, but were enough to encourage four knights to slay Becket just a few weeks after his return to Canterbury. Becket was quickly canonized by Pope Alexander and his tomb became a popular place of pilgrimage until its destruction by Henry VIII. This modern sculpture outside St Paul's depicts Becket in the last moments before his martyrdom.

21. Temple Bar (old)

Paternoster Square, EC4
Sculptor John Bushnell, recent additions by Tim Crawley
(design by Christopher Wren), Portland stone, 1672

This Portland stone gate by Christopher Wren was originally erected in 1672 at one of the medieval entrances to the City of London. Temple Bar was intended as a symbol of royal authority but also used as a place to display the remains of executed traitors. The body parts of Sir Thomas Armstrong were displayed here in 1684, as were the heads of the Rye House Plotters. The last head to be displayed was that of Jacobite, Francis Towneley in 1746. The dissenters Titus Oates and Daniel Defoe were also publicly chastised in stocks by Temple Bar.

Temple Bar was considered too narrow for the efficient flow of traffic by the unsentimental Victorians, who dismantled Wren's work in 1878 and replaced it with the more modest Temple Bar Memorial in 1880 (see p.170). The carefully dismantled parts of the old Temple Bar would have stayed in storage for many years were it not for the social ambitions of the former barmaid, Lady Henry Meux. She persuaded her husband to buy Temple Bar and unveil it at a grand party in the grounds of their country estate in Hertfordshire – Lady Meux is said to have dined with the future Edward VII inside the monument. Long after the Meux fortune had been spent, Temple Bar remained neglected and forgotten in Theobalds Park. In 1974, efforts were begun to restore and return Temple Bar to the City of London. The process took over 30 years and cost £3 million, but the renovated Temple Bar was finally unveiled at the entrance to Paternoster Square in 2004.

22. Blitz / Firefighters' Memorial
Old Change Court, opposite St Paul's Cathedral, EC4
Sculptor John W. Mills, Bronze, 1991 (Blitz Memorial),
re-dedicated to Firefighters 2003

This bronze sculpture was first unveiled in 1991 as a memorial to the Blitz. The bombing of London and other British cities began on the September 7th 1940 and inflicted enormous death and destruction on a population that was ill-prepared for the attack. In the first few months of the campaign the Luftwaffe dropped over 13,000 tons of bombs on the capital both day and night while suffering few casualties themselves. From November 1940 until February 1941 Germany concentrated on industrial cities and ports, including London, which suffered a devastating night of bombing on 29th December. The photograph of St Paul's rising from the smoke of the incendiary bombs on the following morning has become one of the iconic images of London's resistance to the Blitz. The bombing continued into 1941, but there were only seven attacks directed at the capital. The most devastating raid was launched on 10th May 1941. It proved a last vicious gesture before Hitler turned his attention to the invasion of the Soviet Union. In the last year of the war, Hermann Goering launched a 'Little Blitz' against London, but Germany was close to defeat and the attacks proved much less effective. It is estimated that during the Blitz 43,000 people were killed and over a million homes destroyed. This monument was re-dedicated in 2003 to the 1,192 firefighters who have died in active service. For further background concerning wartime bombing see the monuments to Hugh Trenchard, Lord Portal and Arthur 'Bomber' Harris (pages 144, 141 and 164).

23. Postman's Park
Between King Edward Street & Aldersgate Street, EC1
Open: Daily 8am-dusk

This park's unique feature is a wall of ceramic tiles commemorating acts of heroism. The wall was the idea of the painter and sculptor George Watts. Watts had become an established artist but, coming from humble origins, had a considerable dislike of the upper classes. He was a colourful character who married the beautiful 16-year-old actress Ellen Terry in 1864 when he was in his 40s. The marriage lasted only a year and Terry eloped with her lover.

In 1887 Watts petitioned *The Times* newspaper to create a wall commemorating ordinary heroic men and women who had lost their lives while saving others. The paper remained unmoved by the idea and Watts was forced to take up the scheme himself, creating a 50-foot-long Heroes' Wall within the former churchyard. The stories of selfless courage are told on hand-lettered ceramic tiles with decorative borders. The tales of heroism are recounted in florid Victorian prose which seem rather melodramatic today. One inscription reads, 'Sarah Smith, pantomime artiste. At Prince's Theatre died of terrible injuries received when attempting in her flammable dress to extinguish the flames which had enveloped her companion. January 24 1863'. The people commemorated are all everyday heroes who gave their lives to save others and rightly deserve to be remembered. Watts only established 13 tablets before his death. His second wife continued the work with a further 34 tablets. Upon her death the wall was left unaltered as a late Victorian creation commemorating heroes and heroines of that period. It remains a popular attraction to this day.

24. Sir Rowland Hill (1795-1879)

King Edward Street, EC1

Sculptor Onslow Ford, Granite, 1881, moved here in 1923

Sir Rowland Hill is best known for his reform of the Post Office but he was also an influential educationalist and thinker. His father was a teacher and friend of the radical and scientist Joseph Priestley (see p.237). Priestley's liberal educational ideas were applied with great success to Rowland's education and as a young man he established his own school to further Priestley's methods. Hill made his first impact on public thinking with a pamphlet on liberal education, but in 1833 he left teaching and took up a post as secretary in the South Australian Colonization Commission.

In 1837, while still working for the Commission, Hill wrote a paper suggesting reform of the complicated postal system and the introduction of postage stamps paid by the sender with charges based on weight rather than distance. Such clear thinking was not welcomed by the politicians but the business community campaigned for Hill's reforms. In 1839, he was given responsibility for introducing his reforms and within a year the postal system was revolutionized. Hill still had his enemies among the politicians and was sacked by Robert Peel (see p.63) in July 1842. He was immediately appointed director of the London and Brighton Railway and made considerable improvements to their service before being re-appointed to the Post Office in 1846. By the time of his death, Sir Rowland Hill was recognised as one of the great practical reformers of his generation. He was awarded a knighthood in 1860 and is buried in Westminster Abbey.

25. Henry VIII (1491-1547)

St Bartholomew's Hospital, EC2
Sculptor Francis Bird, Stone, 1702

This is the only monument to Henry VIII in London. Two of his offspring, Edward VI and Elizabeth I, are commemorated in London (see pages 155 and 172) which is some indication of the big man's importance in British history. Henry was the second son of Henry VII and only became his heir on the death of his elder brother in 1502. His father died in April 1509 when Henry was not yet 18 and he spent the first years of his reign under the tutelage of a group of senior clerics among them William Warham, the Archbishop of Canterbury. He fulfilled his promise to his father by marrying Catherine of Aragon in June 1509, but the son born to them in January 1511 died in infancy.

Henry was a forceful and intelligent man and he soon took charge of his realm, replacing his old advisers with ambitious men such as Thomas Wolsey, and declaring war against France. Henry took a well-prepared army to France in 1513 and enjoyed victory in battle but was unable to derive any long-term advantage against a larger and wealthier adversary. Money soon ran out and Henry sued for peace in 1518, making much of his role as peacemaker in a war he had started.

The peace treaties and summits were to go down in history for their splendour but peace was short-lived and Henry's forces continued their campaign across northern France without any clear objective. At this time Henry gained favour with the Vatican for his refutation of Martin Luther, but when he sought an annulment of his marriage, having failed to produce a male heir, Pope Clement VIII was at the mercy of Catherine's nephew, Charles V, and could not grant his wish. Wolsey attempted an alliance with France in 1527, but the defeat of the French at Landriano in June 1529 brought an end to the plan, and to Wolsey, who died on his way to London to face charges of treason in 1530.

Henry had already separated from Catherine and was in love with Anne Boleyn. After the death of the Archbishop of Canterbury, William Warham, in August 1532, Henry replaced him with the more amenable Thomas Cranmer. In April 1533, Cranmer granted the divorce without recourse to Rome and Henry immediately married the pregnant Anne. Henry's 'break with Rome' was the most controversial aspect of his reign and he swiftly moved to strengthen his position by passing The Act of Succession and Act of Supremacy in 1534. The acts recognised his new daughter as heir and Henry as 'Supreme Head of the Church of England' making it an act of treason to deny this new state of affairs. Prominent clergymen, such as John Fisher and Thomas More (see p.319), were victims of this new orthodoxy.

Henry increasingly exploited the advance of the Reformation and tolerated the spread of evangelical preaching, that was to become recognised as Protestantism, as a means to strengthen his independence from Rome. Anne Boleyn, Thomas Cranmer and Thomas Cromwell all favoured the evangelical movement and this tide of change was to lead to the dissolution of the monasteries between 1536 and 1540, the banning of many traditional forms of worship and, most significantly, the authorization of an English Bible. The north of England rose up against these changes and the heavy taxes that Henry had imposed. Henry was never one to have scruples when dealing with his enemies and he lured the rebels into negotiation and then arrested and executed the ring leaders in a public display of brutality that was to end any further attempts at rebellion.

Anne Boleyn's failure to produce a son was to see her suffer a similar fate, having been accused of false charges of adultery in the spring of 1536. Within a fortnight of her execution Henry married the young Jane Seymour who was to bear him his long-awaited son, Edward, in 1537, but she died soon after. Henry now had less use for the Protestant movement and began reining in its more radical preachers, passing laws which recognised the Mass, confession and the celibacy of priests. For the rest of his reign Henry was content to halt any further religious reform and to play one religious faction against another in his court. The evangelical Cromwell was soon in the dock for treason having attempted to marry Henry to Anne of Cleves who Henry found unattractive. Cromwell, who had executed so many on Henry's behalf, was himself executed in July 1540. Henry found solace in the arms of the young and attractive Catherine Howard, who was the niece of Cromwell's rival, the Duke of Norfolk, but the evangelicals again won favour when they provided evidence of the young Queen's infidelity, leading to her execution in February 1542.

Henry married his sixth and final wife, the widow Catherine Parr, in June 1543. He spent the final years of his reign again seeking military glory against France. The ebb and flow of battle achieved very little and cost the country dear, but when the French fleet were repelled from the coast of England, Henry was able to declare himself before parliament in December 1545 as the country's saviour. As the King's health declined it was the evangelicals that assumed the upper hand and as he lay dying in January 1547 it was a Protestant group of advisers that he chose to provide counsel to his young son. This monument of Henry VIII stands outside St Bartholomew's Hospital, which he founded in 1539 having shut down St Thomas's during his dissolution of the monasteries

.

26. Sir William Wallace (1270-1305)

St Bartholomew's Hospital, EC2
Stone tablet, 1956

William Wallace was a young man when John Balliol was declared King of Scotland in 1292. Wallace remained loyal to Balliol when King Edward I of England won victory at Dunbar in 1296 and forced Balliol's abdication to become *de facto* king of Scotland.

There are a great many versions of how Wallace became involved in the struggle. Ayrshire legend claims it was an argument about the selling of fish which led to a fight and the killing of two English soldiers, while in Dundee it is claimed that Wallace killed the son of the town's English governor. Whatever the exact events, Wallace soon found himself at the head of a Scottish army which defeated the English at Loudon Hill and Scone and freed the land north of the Forth from English rule. The greatest victory for Wallace's rebel army was at Stirling Bridge in September 1297, but by this time many of the Scottish nobility had made peace with the English. After losing the Battle of Falkirk in 1298, Wallace left for France to attempt an alliance with Phillip IV. He returned to Scotland in 1303, by which time Robert Bruce had been forced to make peace with Edward. Wallace narrowly escaped capture at Elcho Wood but was later betrayed and handed over to the English. This tablet was placed in the wall of St Batholomew's Hospital in 1956, close to where William Wallace was hung, drawn and quartered after a summary trial in 1305. Wallace's head was placed on a pike at London Bridge and his body parts displayed in Scotland as a warning. The plaque reads, 'His example of heroism and devotion inspired those who came after him...'.

27. Protestant Martyrs
St Bartholomew's Hospital, EC2
Stone tablet, 1870

This simple stone tablet was placed on the wall of St Bartholomew's Hospital to commemorate the Protestant Martyrs who died here during the reign of Queen Mary. The memorial makes particular mention of three prominent clergymen – John Rogers, John Bradford and John Philpot – who were burned to death for their refusal to accept the Catholic faith. Mary I was the daughter of Henry VIII but was closer to her mother, Catherine of Aragon, who brought her up to be a devout Catholic. While her brother, Edward VI, passed laws favouring the Protestant faith, his half-sister privately observed Mass.

When Mary unexpectedly came to the throne she immediately sent key Protestants, such as the Duke of Northumberland, to the Tower and released Catholics such as the Bishop of Winchester. Protestant legislation was revoked in her first parliament and in November 1554 Cardinal Pole accepted her realm back into the Catholic faith. Mary's use of the 15th century Acts for the Burning of Heretics claimed the lives of nearly 300 Protestants and forced many more to flee to the continent to avoid persecution. Her brutal policy was remarkably successful, but after her death Elizabeth returned the country to the Protestant faith and 'Bloody Mary' became a symbol of Catholic repression summoned up whenever a monarch's Protestant commitment appeared to waver. John Foxe's book *Acts and Monuments* used the Protestant Martyrs to demonstrate the fundamental brutality of the Catholic Church and is one of the key texts for the Protestant Alliance which paid for this memorial.

28. Smithfield War Memorial
Grand Avenue,
Smithfield Market, EC1
Bronze and stone, 1921

This memorial is dedicated to all
those of Smithfield that lost their lives
in the First World War and has the
names of over 200 victims engraved
upon it. An additional plaque is
dedicated to those of the area that
lost their lives in later conflicts.

29. Golden Boy
Corner of Cock Lane and Giltspur Street, EC1
Bronze, Date not known

Pye Corner, at the junction of Cock Lane
and Giltspur Street, was an area known
for prostitution in medieval times and
has since then always been associated
with sin. It is claimed that the Great
Fire of London was extinguished
here in September 1666 and Puritan
preachers concluded that having
started in Pudding Lane and ended at
Pye Corner, the fire was a punishment
for the capital's gluttony. This fat gilt
boy was placed on the corner, after the
fire, to remind Londoners of the perils
of excess. The building on which the
boy stands has changed several times,
but until 1910 it was a famous public house, *The Fortunes of War*,
which served as a meeting place for the Victorian body snatchers who
provided cadavers for St Bartholomew's Hospital nearby.

30. Charles Lamb (1775-1834)

Giltspur Street, EC1

Sculptor William Reynolds-Stephens, Bronze, 1962, originally at Christchurch Greyfriars

The name of Charles Lamb is largely forgotten, but in his time he was a very widely read essayist, poet and novelist and friend to many other writers including Coleridge and Wordsworth. This bust once stood within Christ's Hospital where Lamb was a school boy. Lamb was obliged to leave school at 14 and seek employment in various clerical posts while also pursuing his literary interests.

Charles Lamb's life and work was inextricably linked with that of his older sister, Mary. The two siblings were bound by affection but also by the mental illness that afflicted both of them, and by the tragic circumstances of their mother's death. In September 1796, Mary suffered a severe attack of mania and murdered her mother with a carving knife. It was only due to the efforts of her brother that she avoided prison and he remained her guardian for the rest of his life.

Despite this tragedy, Mary and Charles enjoyed their life together and attracted a circle of literary and radical friends including Coleridge, Wordsworth, Hazlitt and Shelley. Charles was already recognised as a poet when he collaborated with his sister to write *Tales from Shakespeare,* which proved a great success when published in 1807. Using the pen name 'Elia', Charles found further fame as an essayist for *The London Magazine* in 1821. Lamb loved London and once wrote, 'The man must have a rare recipe for melancholy, who can be dull in Fleet-street. I am naturally inclined to hypochondria, but in London it vanishes like other ills.'

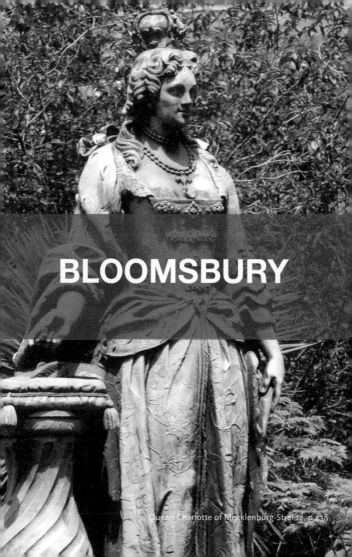

BLOOMSBURY

Queen Charlotte of Mecklenburg-Strelitz, p. 238

1. George I
2. Charles James Fox
3. Francis Russell,
   5th Duke of Bedford
4. Joseph Priestley
5. Queen Charlotte
6. Thomas Coram
7. Major John Cartwright

8. Dame Louisa Aldrich-Blake
9. Virginia Woolf
10. Mahatma Gandhi
11. Hiroshima Tree
12. Peace Stone
13. Rabindranath Tagore
14. Noor Inayat Khan
15. Richard Trevithick

Bloomsbury

From the Bloomsbury Gang of Whig politicians formed in 1765 by the 4th Duke of Bedford to the Bloomsbury Group of the 1920s, Bloomsbury has always been associated with England's liberal elite. Among the grand squares are some of the country's leading academic institutions including University College London, Birkbeck College and the British Museum, all of which attract students and academics to the area who provide custom for Bloomsbury's many antiquarian and second-hand bookshops. With the exception of the monuments to George I and Queen Charlotte, the monuments here reflect the area's liberal history with pride of place given to Whig politician Charles James Fox (see p.235) who was able to keep the flame of liberty alive during the repressive administration of Pitt the Younger (see p.256). Fox looks north along Bedford Place to where his aristocratic patron the 5th Duke of Bedford stands. Just off Russell Square sits a modest statue to the chemist and radical thinker Joseph Priestley who was forced into exile for his sympathy for the French Revolution.

Major John Cartwright (see p.240) is the only military man in the area, but he was a kindred spirit of Priestley, who refused to fight against American independence and is recognised here for his reform campaigning rather than for his military adventures. Near to Cartwright is the figure of Thomas Coram who dedicated his later years to helping London's destitute children. The values of 19th-century radicalism are continued in several 20th-century memorials in Tavistock Square, with Mahatma Gandhi taking centre stage – the surgeon Louisa Aldrich-Blake and the writer Virginia Woolf keeping the old man company. The Peace Stone and Hiroshima Tree confirm that this is a place dedicated to non-violence. Gordon Square now has its own monuments with the recent arrival of the poet Rubindranath Tagore and the Second World War spy, Noor Khan. The chapter ends with a plaque to the pioneering engineer, Richard Trevithick.

1. George I (1660-1727)
St George's Church, WC1
Sculptor Anonymous, Stone, 1730

George I came to the throne in 1714 having spent the first 56 years of his life as elector of the German state of Hanover. He was not ideal material for the crown as he could speak very little English, was a public cuckold who had imprisoned his wife and kept a number of mistresses. He found himself monarch because neither William nor Mary produced an heir. This tenuous claim to the crown meant that George was constantly under threat from the Jacobite descendants of James II, who arguably had a greater claim to the succession.

Despite these disadvantages, George proved a rather successful monarch who allowed parliament to claim greater powers than it had previously enjoyed. He was pragmatic in his dealing with politicians and even allowed Walpole to take office despite his initial objections. His wise and undramatic reign established the house of Hanover as the dynastic line and his son acceded to the throne with more certainty.

George I was considered a comic figure by the public, but his death in 1727 – while travelling in a coach to Hanover – was widely mourned. This is the only monument to the King in the capital and stands upon the spire of a Hawksmoor church. Horace Walpole described the monument's location as a 'master-stroke of absurdity'. There was an equestrian monument to him placed at the centre of Leicester Square in 1748, but as the area declined so the statue fell into disrepair and was removed in 1872.

2. Charles James Fox (1749-1806)

Bloomsbury Square, WC1
Sculptor Sir Richard Westmacott, Bronze, 1816

Charles James Fox was one of the most important politicians of his generation and yet he held office only fleetingly and was responsible for only one law, and that relating to libel. His early career was distinguished by his ability to remain a key figure in the reforming Whig party through his oratory, flamboyance and ability to win powerful friends. It was only in his later career, when the French Revolution so polarised British public opinion, that Fox showed his mettle by continuing his commitment to reform. William Pitt used the war against revolutionary France as a justification for stifling reform, and adopting draconian measures against radicals and was helped by the support of influential Whig figures such as Edmund Burke. Between 1793 and 1797 Fox and his allies continued to press for reform of the rotten boroughs, but were always outvoted by the Tories and their parliamentary allies. Other radicals such as Joseph Priestley (see p.237) faced considerable danger at this time, but Fox, with his aristocratic wealth and parliamentary immunity, was able to continue the fight. Although he failed to achieve any significant reform, his staunch support for William Wilberforce's anti-slave-trade movement was to help in the trade's abolition in 1807. Fox's continued advocacy of reform during the repressive years of William Pitt's government was to provide an important legacy to the Whig reformers of the late 18th and early 19th century, who eventually achieved some measure of parliamentary reform in 1832. This monument shows Fox in the garb of a Roman senator, one hand holding a copy of the Magna Carta.

3. Francis Russell, 5th Duke of Bedford (1765-1805)

Russell Square, WC1
Sculptor Sir Richard Westmacott, Bronze, 1809

This monument commemorates the aristocrat and politician Francis Russell who was a member of Charles James Fox's Whig government and an ally of the Prince of Wales (later George IV). The Duke's greatest legacy remains the planned streets and Georgian squares of Bloomsbury which were built on farm land belonging to the Bedford estate. Russell Square was laid out in 1800 under the Duke's patronage and the development of the east side of Tavistock Square was begun in 1803 shortly before his death. This monument eschews any association with the city the 5th Duke helped to create and instead concentrates on his interest in agriculture. A ploughshare and a sheaf of corn form part of the main design and agricultural scenes are depicted on the plinth. The figure of the Duke looks down Bedford Place towards Fox, his friend and political ally. The current Duke of Bedford has inherited the family fortune and is still one of this countries richest people according to the Sunday Times Rich List.

4. Joseph Priestley (1733-1804)
30 Russell Square, WC1
Sculptor Gilbert Bayes, Stone, 1914

Joseph Priestley was one of the first scientific chemists, the discoverer of oxygen, but also a non-conformist minister and radical thinker who was eventually forced into exile. Priestley was brought up in his aunt's non-conformist, liberal home and despite illness proved himself a brilliant scholar, eventually attending a Dissenting Academy where he studied to become a minister, but also acquired an interest in the natural sciences. This academy is now Manchester Harris College Oxford, where a picture of Priestly still hangs.

Throughout his career as a minister and teacher Priestley conducted experiments and advocated the use of scientific method to determine truth. He was interested in all manner of subjects and wrote books on science, religion and politics, and formed friendships with radicals such as Richard Price and future US president Benjamin Franklin, on his regular visits to London.

Priestley's Unitarian views and support for the American colonies created controversy, but his support of the French Revolution so enraged the population of his Birmingham parish that a mob ransacked his home and he was forced to flee to London. The capital provided only temporary refuge and in April 1794 Priestley embarked for the newly independent United States where he spent the final years of his life. Passing this modest statue above a doorway of the Royal Institute of Chemistry, few people would know that it commemorates an exiled revolutionary as well as an accomplished scientist.

5. Queen Charlotte of Mecklenburg-Strelitz (1744-1818)

Queen Square, WC1; Sculptor Anonymous, Lead, 1780

In the 19th century this was thought to be a statue of Queen Anne, but has since been recognised as Queen Charlotte, consort to George III. Born Charlotte Sophia of Mecklenburg-Strelitz, she married George III of England in 1761. She was not George's first choice, but the first to meet the exacting requirements of his mother. Despite George's reluctance the marriage was long and happy, producing 15 children, 13 of whom lived to adulthood and was only blighted by George's bouts of mental illness. The Queen was said to have African features inherited from the Moorish branch of the Portuguese royal family, to whom she was related. Allan Ramsay's painting is the only one to show Charlotte's African heritage and can be seen at the National Portrait Gallery.

6. Thomas Coram (1668-1751)

Brunswick Square, WC1
Sculptor William MacMillan, Bronze, 1963

Thomas Coram spent his early career as a sea captain in the American colonies and later made his fortune as a ship-builder and London merchant. He became a famous philanthropist having settled in London and been troubled by the number of abandoned children he encountered on his regular walks through the City.

Coram campaigned for some time to establish a foundling hospital and school but initially found little enthusiasm for the idea. Eventually he gained the support of Queen Caroline and obtained a Royal Charter from George II, establishing the Foundling Hospital in 1739. The hospital became one of the most popular charitable institutions with artists such as Hogarth and Handel donating works and performances. The Foundling Hospital's public displays of art provided the inspiration for the Royal Academy exhibitions. This monument stands outside The Foundling Museum on the site of one of the early foundling hospitals and is based on Hogarth's portrait. An earlier bust of Coram is located above the doorway. The museum is well worth visiting and has a moving collection of tokens left with abandoned children by desperate mothers.

7. Major John Cartwright (1740-1824)
Cartwright Gardens, WC1
Sculptor George Clarke, Bronze, 1831

John Cartwright came from a wealthy family and his brother Edmund was the inventor of the power loom. John joined the Royal Navy at the age of 18 and served with distinction in the colonies, although his career was hindered by his refusal to serve under the Duke of Cumberland (see p.258) against American Independence. Cartwright had great sympathy for the claims of the American people and when he returned to Britain he determined to argue for parliamentary reform in Britain. From the publication of his first book in 1776, he campaigned tirelessly for universal suffrage, annual parliaments and the general principles of liberty and representation. He founded several organisations with the purpose of spreading these ideas and used some of his fortune to fund radical publications including the satirical magazine *Black Dwarf*.

Cartwright was fighting for reform during the same repressive period in British politics as Joseph Priestley (see p.237) and Charles James Fox (see p.235) and was imprisoned for his troubles several times. He became known as the 'Father of Reform' and his efforts contributed greatly to the passing of the first Reform Act of 1832, just eight years after his death.

8. Dame Louisa Aldrich-Blake (1865-1925)

Tavistock Square, WC1

Sculptor A. G. Walker, Column & base by Edwin Lutyens, Stone, 1927

Louisa Aldrich-Blake was the daughter of the rector of Chingford. As a young girl Louisa had always shown an interest in medicine, but it required determination to become the country's first female surgeon in a male-dominated profession. She proved an outstanding student, graduating from the Royal Free Hospital and was the first woman to pass the surgery degree. She went on to become master surgeon at the Elizabeth Garrett Anderson Hospital and performed the first operation to remove cancer of the cervix. Aldrich-Blake was appointed dean of the school in 1914 and was made a dame in 1924. She died a year later at the age of 60.

9. Virginia Woolf (1882-1941)
Tavistock Square, WC1
Sculptor Stephen Tomlin (copy), Bronze, 2004

Virginia Woolf was born into a literary family, her father being the eminent writer and editor, Sir Leslie Stephen. She was educated at home amid her father's vast library and was both nurtured and harmed by her cloistered upbringing. Creativity, depression and mental breakdown were to be features of Virginia's life, and she was first admitted to a mental institution on the death of her father in 1904.

Virginia moved to Bloomsbury and it is here that she became the nucleus of the eponymous intellectual circle whose members included Lytton Strachey, Clive Bell, Leonard Woolf and John Maynard Keynes. Virginia married Leonard Woolf in 1912 and began the literary career that was to make her newly acquired name. Her first novel, *The Voyage Out*, was published in 1915 by her brother's publishing company, but in 1917 she and Leonard founded the Hogarth Press which published all her subsequent books. Her novels included *Mrs Dalloway* (1925), *To the Lighthouse* (1927) and *The Waves* (1931), establishing her reputation as one of the first great modernist writers, escaping the Victorian conventions of her father's library through disjointed narratives and psychological insight.

Virginia and Leonard both had affairs, most famously Virginia's with Vita Sackville-West who was the inspiration for *Orlando* (1928). Despite success, Virginia continued to suffer from depression. In 1941, having left London to escape the bombing which had destroyed her Bloomsbury home, she committed suicide. This bust was erected by the Virginia Woolf Society, close to her former home on the south side of Tavistock Square.

10. Mahatma Gandhi (1869-1949)
Tavistock Square, WC1
Sculptor Fredda Brilliant, Bronze, 1968

One of the key political figures of the 20th century and the father of Indian independence, Gandhi was born into a wealthy family and studied law at London University close to this monument. As a young man he showed little interest in politics but in South Africa he fought for the rights of the minority Indian population and developed a political strategy based upon civil disobedience (satyagraha) and non-violence (ahimsa). This strategy was not just politically expedient, but evolved from Gandhi's growing Hindu faith, which regarded violence as profoundly immoral. He returned to India in 1914 and began campaigning against specific injustices before going all out for full independence from British rule. Gandhi was beaten and imprisoned many times by the authorities but he never called for retaliation and withdrew from campaigning when violence occurred. He controversially refused to take sides during the Second World War and in 1942 launched the 'Quit India' campaign which led to Independence in August 1947. The blood shed in that year and the creation of Pakistan greatly troubled Gandhi and he sought to lessen the violence and encourage trust and co-operation between the two new states.

Gandhi was assassinated by a Hindu radical on 30th January 1948 after only six months of independence. His ideas have influenced many people and were adopted by both the civil rights movement in America and the ANC in South Africa. This large and rather ugly monument sits upon a hollow plinth where people still leave flowers and candles.

11. Hiroshima Tree
Tavistock Square, WC1
Memorial Tree, 1967

This tree was planted in 1967 in memory of those who died when America dropped the first atomic bomb on the Japanese city of Hiroshima on 6th August 1945. It is estimated that approximately 150,000 people were killed by the bomb – nicknamed 'Little Boy' by the Americans – and 75 per cent of the city's buildings destroyed. Many thousands were to suffer from the later consequences of radiation and even today Hiroshima's population suffers from a high level of birth defects. It is argued that the use of atomic weapons at Hiroshima, and three days later at Nagasaki, helped bring an end to the Second World War and as a result saved lives, but it is now known that Truman already knew of Emperor Hirohito's intention to surrender when the bombs were dropped.

Peace Stone

12. Peace Stone

Tavistock Square, WC1

Stone with bronze plaque, 1994

This stone (see below left) was dedicated in 1994 'To all those who have established and are maintaining the right to refuse to kill'. It is the only pacifist memorial in the capital and is a welcome change from places like Trafalgar Square (see p.3) which are almost entirely dedicated to military men and their achievements.

13. Rabindranath Tagore (1861-1941)

Gordon Square, WC1

Sculptor Shenda Amery, Bronze, 2011

Rabindranath Tagore was unknown outside Bengal until the age of 50. He had briefly studied law at nearby University College, but soon returned to his native India and dedicate himself to writing poetry, novels and music.

On a long boat trip from India to London Tagore began translating a selection of his poetry into English. WB Yates encountered the poems through a mutual friend and recognised their beauty and brilliance. With his charismatic personality, flowing locks and exotic dress, Tagore became an overnight literary success and within two years the first non-European to win the Nobel Prize for Literature in 1913. Tagore went on to found a school based upon his internationalist, pacifist philosophy. Despite his anti-nationalist beliefs, two of his songs are now the national anthems of India and Bangladesh.

14. Noor Inayat Khan (1914-1944)

Gordon Square, WC1

Sculptor Karen Newman, Bronze, 2012

Noor Khan was born to an Indian Muslim father and American mother and enjoyed a nomadic childhood. She studied at the Sorbonne and had just published her first children's book when war engulfed Europe. Khan worked as a wireless operator before joining the Special Operations Executive. In June 1943 she was dropped into France and communicated vital information from Paris before her betrayal and arrest in October of that year. She fought her captors, and even attempted escape, but was executed at Dachau Concentration Camp in September 1944.

15. Richard Trevithick (1771-1833)

Gower Street opposite University Street, WC1

Sculptor L. S Merrifield, Bronze plaque, 1933

This plaque is close to the site of the world's first passenger carrying steam locomotive which was the work of pioneering 19th century steam engineer, Richard Trevithick. Like many pioneers, Trevithick never made money from his engineering inventions. Two years after the failure of his railway project, he contracted typhoid and returned to his native Cornwall. He died penniless of pneumonia while working as an engineer in Dartford and was buried in a paupers grave. This fine plaque was unveiled on the centenary of his death.

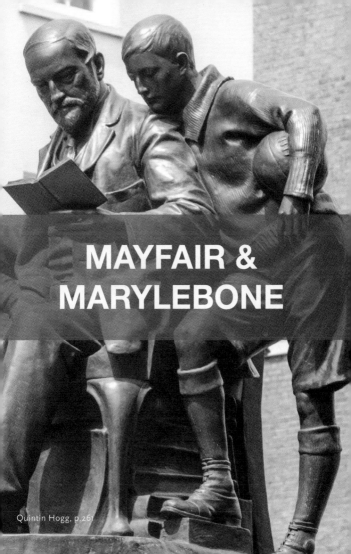

MAYFAIR &
MARYLEBONE

Quintin Hogg, p.261

1. Raoul Wallenberg
2. Dwight D. Eisenhower
3. American Eagle
   Squadron's Memorial
4. Franklin Delano Roosevelt
5. Roosevelt & Churchill – The Allies
6. Ronald Wilson Reagan
7. William Pitt the Younger
8. William George Frederick
   Cavendish-Scott-Bentinck

9. Prince William
   Duke of Cumberland
10. John Nash
11. Quintin Hogg
12. Field Marshal Sir George White
13. General Wladyslaw Sikorski
14. Joseph Lister
15. Edward Augustus,
    Duke of Kent
16. John Fitzgerald Kennedy

Mayfair & Marylebone

The fine squares of Mayfair and Marylebone were all created during the building boom of the early 18th century. The stability provided by the Hanoverian accession combined with the rapidly increasing population of London was to be the impetus for wealthy landowners, such as the Earl of Oxford and Duke of Portland, to build on their farm estates. In 1700 there was nothing but fields and cattle in this area but by 1778 one would recognise the same squares and streets that exist today. The area was originally developed for London's rich but the grand houses are now largely offices, shops and embassies.

The monument to Raoul Wallenberg is a little isolated, but is one of the best monuments in London and worth visiting. Further south, the heavily fortified American Embassy looks out over Grosvenor Square which has monuments to presidents Eisenhower, Roosevelt and Reagan and one to the American Eagle Squadron who fought as v in the Battle of Britain. The 'special relationship' between Britain and America is recognised in the bronze figures of Roosevelt and Churchill sitting on a bench on New Bond Street.

An enclave of Tory politicians and military men lies to the north with William Pitt the Younger on Hanover Square, while on Cavendish Square stands the lesser figure of William Bentinck, and a plinth which is all that remains of an equestrian monument to the Duke of Cumberland. Portland Place owes much of its beauty and grandeur to the work of John Nash and his bust can be found in the portico of All Souls Church. Quintin Hogg is commemorated close to the University of Westminster which he helped to found as the Regent Street Polytechnic. Given the fact that the Polish leader General Wladyslaw Sikorski was betrayed by the Allies it is perhaps fitting that his monument faces the rear end of the British soldier Field Marshal Sir George White's horse. At the junction with Park Crescent can be found monuments to the medical scientist Joseph Lister, the Duke of Kent and a bust of President John F. Kennedy.

1. Raoul Wallenberg (1912-1947)
Great Cumberland Place, W1
Sculptor Philip Jackson, Bronze, 1998

There are several monuments to those whose date of birth is not known, but Raoul Wallenberg is the only person whose date of death is still a mystery. Wallenberg was Swedish and studied architecture in the United States. After graduation he worked briefly in Palestine where he met many Jewish refugees and heard of the Nazi atrocities.

Wallenberg was not Jewish, but worked for a company owned by a Jewish Hungarian and used his Swedish passport to avoid the restrictions imposed on Jewish businesses. The persecution of Jews in Hungary had begun in 1938 and escalated to mass deportation to concentration camps by May 1944. Wallenberg was given diplomatic status by the American and Swedish governments to help save Hungarian Jews by the issuing of protective passports (Schutzpass). These passports were not legal but deterred the Hungarian authorities from sending many Jews to their deaths. There are accounts of Wallenberg climbing onto a death camp train to issue Schutzpässe while being threatened by Nazi guards. He saved thousands more lives by creating areas of diplomatic refuge in Budapest and used the threat of war crimes prosecution to stop further killings. It was not the Nazis but the Soviets who arrested Wallenberg in 1945, suspecting him of being an American spy. The Soviets claim Wallenberg died of natural causes while in custody in July 1947, but recent evidence suggests he was executed. It is estimated that Wallenberg saved the lives of up to 200,000 Jews.

2. Dwight D. Eisenhower (1890-1969)

Grosvenor Square, W1
Sculptor Robert Dean, Bronze, 1989

Eisenhower was born to an established farming family of Mennonites and attended West Point Military Academy despite his family's pacifist beliefs. By the First World War he was appointed lieutenant colonel, but never saw action. In the interwar years Eisenhower attained the rank of general and served under famous military names including Fox Connor, John Pershing, Douglas MacArthur and George Patton. His intelligence and administrative skill were recognised by the army, but it was during the Second World War that he rose to prominence. General Marshall appointed him as senior military strategist after Pearl Harbour and he went on to head military operations in Europe, then commanded 'Operation Torch' in north Africa, and oversaw the invasion of Italy which was successfully accomplished in February 1944. Eisenhower had won the trust of both Roosevelt and Churchill and was appointed to overall control of the successful invasion of Europe in June 1944. He retired from the army in 1948 and briefly held the position of Supreme Commander of NATO until he was persuaded to run as Republican candidate for president in 1952.

Dwight D. Eisenhower became the 34th President of the United States in January 1953 with the election slogan 'I like Ike'. During his two terms as President he ended the Korean War, developed America's nuclear arsenal, initiated the space race, increased the social security programmes begun by Roosevelt and built the interstate highway system. His 'Dynamic Conservatism' was liberal by today's standards as he began the process of desegregation in schools and the military and avoided involvement in Suez and Vietnam. Eisenhower's farewell speech in January 1961 is significant for its warning of the growing power of America's military. He coined the phrase 'military-industrial complex' to describe the dependency of America's economy upon military spending. Eisenhower enjoyed his retirement and spent a good deal of it on the golf course. He died in 1969 at the age of 78. This fine monument stands on a marble pavement which lists his military achievements. It was unveiled by Prime Minister Margaret Thatcher in 1989.

3. American Eagle Squadron's Memorial
Grosvenor Square, W1
Sculptor Dame Elizabeth Frink, Bronze, 1986

This monument stands in grateful memory to Eagle Squadron which was formed in September 1940. The squadron comprised of 244 American pilots who volunteered to join the Royal Air Force before their country entered the war, as well as 16 British pilots. The Squadron played a major part in the Battle of Britain and continued to serve until September 1942 when it was incorporated into the USAAF. During its existence the squadron suffered very high casualties, loosing 77 American and 5 British pilots.

4. Franklin Delano Roosevelt (1882-1945)

Grosvenor Square, W1
Sculptor Sir William Reid Dick, Bronze, 1948

Franklin Delano Roosevelt (FDR) was the only child of a wealthy New York family and after studying law at Harvard and Columbia embarked on a political career that was to take him to the White House. FDR served his political apprenticeship after winning a seat on the New York State Senate for the Democrats and working as assistant secretary for the navy before unsuccessfully running for Vice-President in 1920. Roosevelt was struck down by polio in 1921 which left him paralysed from the waist down, but he was able to hide his disability with the aid of walking sticks and leg braces. He continued to build his support within the Democratic Party, winning the governorship of New York in 1929 and becoming the 32nd President of the United States when he defeated the incumbent Herbert Hoover in 1932.

Roosevelt entered the White House on a wave of goodwill and a commitment to combat the Great Depression, declaring 'the only thing we have to fear is fear itself'. Roosevelt's administration greatly increased the role of government with a raft of policies, known as the New Deal, which regulated business practices, embarked on large public works to tackle unemployment, regulated agricultural prices and encouraged the establishment of trade unions, while at the same time reducing military spending. The policies were a success and Roosevelt's ebullient and confident personality created a New Deal Coalition of ethnic minorities, trade unionists, urban workers and southern Democrats that was to see him elected president an unprecedented four times.

This grand statue to FDR was raised by public subscription in this country in recognition of his support during the Second World War. Roosevelt was careful not to arouse America's strong isolationist sentiments, but introduced a series of measures – 'Arsenal for Democracy' and 'Lend Lease' – designed to assist Britain, France and China in their battle against the Axis Powers. Japan's attacked on Pearl Harbour in December 1941 gave Roosevelt the opportunity to join the Allies as he had always intended. FDR won a fourth term in office in 1944 but was already very frail and died just a few months before the declaration of victory in Europe which he did so much to secure. One of Roosevelt's greatest achievements was the founding of the United Nations which was designed as a forum for international relations and to limit conflict.

5. Roosevelt and Churchill – The Allies
Bond Street, W1
Sculptor Lawrence Holofcener, Bronze, 1995

This monument was erected by the Bond Street Association to commemorate 50 years of peace in Europe. The relationship between Roosevelt and Churchill was a complex one and fraught with difficulties, particularly concerning the third ally – Stalin. This monument is entitled 'The Allies', but has avoided featuring 'Uncle Joe'. Unpleasant historical realities, such as making alliance with one murderous dictator in order to defeat another, have been conveniently forgotten. These two giants of 20th-century history both have much finer monuments in London (see p.253 & 72).

6. Ronald Wilson Reagan (1911-2004)

Grosvenor Square, W1
Sculptor Chas Fagan, 2011

This most recent addition to Grosvenor Square commemorates the 40th US President, Ronald Reagan, whose two term presidency ran from 1981 to 1989. Reagan was born above a general store in Illinois. He was not academic but won a sports scholarship before becoming a successful sports radio commentator. Moving to California in 1937 he became an actor, most famously staring in 'Bedtime for Bonzo' (1951). Reagan started life as an enthusiastic Democrat but moved to the right after the war and co-operated with Hoover's anti-communist campaign as president of the actor's union during the McCarthy era. He went on to successfully serve as Govenor of California in the 1970's before running for President.

Reagan became president in 1981 with a simplistic message of patriotism, tax cuts, a strong military and a return to traditional values. His team helped delay the release of the Iranian hostages which greatly helped his victory. The hostages were eventually released on the day of Reagan's inauguration.

What became known as Reaganomics involved tax cuts for the rich, reducing welfare spending, cutting regulation and controlling money supply. This coincided with a 35% increase in military spending and a three fold increase in the National Debt during his presidency. Reagan's support of right wing regimes included arming Saddam Hussain's Iraq and eventually led to the Irangate Scandal which marred his second term of office. This bombastic monument perpetuates the myth that Reagan was responsible for Gorbachev's reforms and the disintegration of the Soviet Union and contains a piece of the Berlin Wall.

7. William Pitt the Younger (1759-1806)

Hanover Square, W1

Sculptor Francis Legatt Chantrey, Bronze, 1831

William Pitt the Younger became this country's youngest Prime Minister at the age of 24 in 1783 and proceeded to dominate British politics for 20 years. Pitt began his career as a Whig ally of Charles James Fox (see p.235). They two soon became rivals and Pitt was appointed Prime Minister with the support of the Tories and George III and in opposition to the Whig party. Pitt's position was initially tenuous but he won a decisive electoral victory in 1784 and kept his hold on power for nearly 19 years.

In his first administration Pitt stabilised the country's finances, reduced the national debt and improved Britain's administration of India through the India Act of 1784. He even attempted limited reform of the corrupt electoral system, but this was abandoned. The second phase of Pitt's government was concerned with the French Revolution which eventually led to war with Napoleon in February 1793. He was a strong wartime leader, but increasingly regarded any demand for worker's rights in Britain as a form of Jacobinism. As war raged on the continent, he suspended *habeas corpus* and passed a series of harsh laws which outlawed trade unions and all forms of radical political organisation. These measures remained in place for many years and put the cause of domestic reform back a generation.

Pitt was forced to resign in February 1801 when he attempted to pass a Catholic Emancipation Act to accompany the 1800 Act of Union which brought Ireland within the United Kingdom. He was returned to office in 1804 and despite the victory at Trafalgar was soon cast into despondency by Napoleon's victories at Alma and

Austerlitz. The disappointments of war and heavy drinking took a great toll on his health and he died in office in January 1806 aged 46. Pitt was a hero to many for his leadership during war and an enemy to others for his reactionary policies. When this monument was erected – 25 years after his death – radical Whigs attempted to pull it down. Pitt died unmarried and insolvent but Parliament paid his debts and buried him in his father's grave in Westminster Abbey.

8. William George Frederick Cavendish-Scott-Bentinck (1802-1848)

Cavendish Square, W1
Sculptor Thomas Campbell, Bronze, 1851

William (usually known as George) Bentinck was the second surviving son of the Fourth Duke of Portland. He retired from the Hussars in 1822 and began working as a private secretary to his uncle, the Foreign Secretary George Canning. In 1828 Bentinck inherited his father's Commons seat as a moderate Whig supporting parliamentary reform and Catholic emancipation. He later joined Robert Peel's Conservative party but took little part in politics, concentrating instead on his racing stables. It was the repeal of the Corn Laws that finally stirred Bentinck to action. He joined forced with Disraeli and fought fiercely to prevent the end of corn tariffs. They failed to stop the law's repeal in 1846, but ended Peel's political career. Bentinck was too liberal in his thinking for the Conservative party, of which he was now leader, and he resigned in 1847 – dying of a heart attack soon after in September 1848.

9. Prince William Duke of Cumberland (1721-1765)

Cavendish Square, W1
Sculptor not known, Stone plinth, lead statue (missing),
1770 (removed 1868)

The plinth that stands in the centre of Cavendish Square is all that remains of the equestrian statue of William Duke of Cumberland that stood here for nearly 100 years. The third son of George II (see p.330), William Augustus was created Duke of Cumberland in 1726. He joined the army in 1742 and was soon fighting on the continent, taking part in the War of Austrian Succession (1740-1748) against the French. After his defeat at the Battle of Fontenoy (1745) he was sent home to deal with the French-inspired Jacobite uprising, driving Charles Stuart and his army back into Scotland before fighting the decisive battle of Culloden in April 1746. The Duke became known as the 'Butcher Cumberland' in Scotland, but he was widely praised and awarded a substantial income for his victory.

He never enjoyed similar success against the French, losing the Battle of Lauffeld (1747) and ten years later the battle of Hastenbeck, and he returned home in ignominy having been forced to sign the Convention of Kloster-Zeven which his furious father rejected. Cumberland retired from public life to pursue his interest in botany, and introduced many new species to Windsor Great Park. He continued to take some part in politics behind the scenes and was instrumental in attempts to return William Pitt to the premiership, before his premature death in October 1765. Cumberland was popular with his men and the monument that once stood here was erected by Lieutenant General William Strode who served under him.

10. John Nash (1752-1835)

All Souls, Langham Place, W1
Sculptor Cecil Thomas, Stone wall-bust, 1956

The most important architect of his generation – the son of a humble London millwright – John Nash did more than any man since Wren (see p.212) to influence the landscape of London. Nash was apprenticed to the architect Sir Robert Taylor as a young man, but abandoned his work and settled in Wales when he inherited a fortune from a wealthy uncle. The fortune was lost through unwise investments and he was forced to return to his architectural work,

establishing a successful country practice with the landscape gardener Humphrey Repton. Nash returned to London in 1792 and became rich designing stucco-clad, Palladian houses made from brick for London's rich and famous. He was nearly 60 when he came to the attention of the Prince of Wales and was appointed architect to develop the farmland called Marylebone Park. Over the next 18 years, assisted by James Pennethorne and Decimus Burton, extensive tracts of central London were developed under Nash's guidance. Parks were landscaped, while streets, terraces, crescents, town houses and villas sprang up in a golden age of architecture. Much of his legacy can still be seen, including Regent's Park and the grand terraces that enclose it, Portland Place, Regent Street, Carlton House Terrace, The Mall and finally St James's Park. Nash provided the initial designs for Trafalgar Square, nearby Haymarket Theatre and the Royal Mews. He was also director of the company responsible for Regent's Canal which extends across London from West to East.

Outside London, Nash built Brighton Pavilion, the onion-domed oriental fantasy about which the Reverend Sydney Smith said 'The dome of St. Paul's must have come down... and pupped'. It continues to remain the most significant feature of the city today. Nash's greatest failure was his work on Buckingham Palace which began in 1825 and was altered many times due to the changing whims of the King. Nash received considerable public ridicule as the costs mounted and he was replaced by Edward Blore after the King's death in 1830. Today only the west wing remains from his original design. One of Nash's most prominent achievements is Marble Arch, originally designed as a triumphant arch for Pall Mall but moved to its current location at the end of Oxford Street during the reign of Queen Victoria. Nash retired to his grand estate on the Isle of Wight and died there in 1835. This fine bust stands in a niche of Nash's All Soul's Church and just ten minutes walk north are some of his finest buildings. As in his own time, these grand crescents are almost exclusively owned by the very rich.

11. Quintin Hogg (1845-1903)

Langham Place, W1
Sculptor Sir George Frampton, Bronze, 1906

Quintin Hogg was the Eton-educated son of James Hogg, the last director of the East India Company. Just like Thomas Coram a century before (see p.239), Hogg was troubled by the poverty and suffering he saw in London and started his philanthropic work by teaching children in the street. With the help of his friend Arthur Kinnaird and his sister Annie, Hogg opened his first school in a rented room near Charing Cross in 1864, which proved a great success. Hogg was a fine sportsman and had a sense of fun, often giving street children rides in his father's carriage. His work was not always easy and on several occasions he was nearly killed by street robbers.

Hogg not only continued to extend the scope of his philanthropic work but prospered in his business dealings as a successful tea and sugar merchant. The passing of the 1870 Education Act by William Forster (see p.118) made the Ragged Schools less important and in 1882 he opened the Regent Street Polytechnic to provide educational, sporting and social facilities for working adults. The polytechnic was very popular and Hogg soon introduced morning classes and then a day school. As one of the first aldermen of London County Council, Quintin Hogg promoted the idea of polytechnics and helped establish 12 by the time of his early death in 1903. This monument is close to the University of Westminster which was the original site of his polytechnic. Hogg was the grandfather of the Conservative politician Quintin Hogg who became Lord Hailsham.

12. Field Marshal Sir George White (1835-1912)
Portland Place, W1
Sculptor John Tweed, Bronze, 1922

Educated at Sandhurst, this son of Irish gentry joined the Inniskillings in 1853 and soon saw action during the Indian Mutiny of 1857. White was promoted to second-in-command of the Gordon Highlanders and during the Second Afghan War (1878-80) overran several positions when outnumbered by the enemy. For his heroics at Charasiah and Kandahar, White was awarded the Victoria Cross. He participated in the Nile Expedition (1884-5) with the Gordon Highlanders and was promoted to major-general for his service during the Burmese War (1885-7). Having succeeded Lord Roberts (see p.53) in Burma, White took over from him in India as Commander-in-Chief. He was knighted in 1897 and returned to England a year later but was soon dispatched to Natal at the start of the Second Boer War (see p.90) in 1899. After several victories against the Boers his forces were surrounded at Ladysmith and forced to endure a siege of 119 days. White returned to England after the war in ill health but was appointed governor of Gibraltar (1900-04) and promoted to field marshal in 1903. He became governor of Chelsea Hospital in 1905 and died there in 1912. Sir George White's only son, Jack White, followed his father into the army and was decorated, but became disillusioned with the military and became a radical figure – fighting for the Republican cause in Ireland and for the International Brigade in the Spanish Civil War (see p.152).

13. General Wladyslaw Sikorski (1881-1943)

Portland Place, W1
Sculptor Faith Winter, Bronze, 2000

General Wladyslaw Sikorski was one of Poland's great military and political figures whose life and death were to have a dramatic effect upon the fate of the Polish nation. Sikorski was born in a country that had been partitioned between Russia, Prussia and Austro-Hungary since the time of Napoleon. During the First World War he abandoned his engineering studies to fight for the Austro-Hungarian army against Russia, believing that the defeat of Russia would afford the best opportunity of establishing Polish independence. Sikorski proved an able soldier and soon adapted his skill to fight directly for independence which was achieved with the collapse of the partitioning powers in 1918. The Second Polish Republic was immediately embroiled in the Polish Soviet War (1919-21) and, under the leadership of Jozef Pilsudski, Sikorski played a major role in the battle of Warsaw which secured peace in 1921. Within a year Sikorski became prime minister on a wave of popular support and served in several governments before Pilsudski, his former ally, staged a coup in May 1926 and he was forced from public office.

Sikorski was exiled in Paris when Germany invaded Poland in 1939 and he became the head of the exiled Polish government. The army of over 80,000 exiled Poles was vital to Britain's survival during the first years of the war and Polish pilots played a key part in the Battle of Britain. Sikorski became the symbol of a future independent Polish nation in the same way as De Gaulle (see p.105) represented French liberation. When the Soviet Union joined the Allies, Sikorski was persuaded to make a pact with Stalin and thousands of Polish prisoners of war were released from Soviet camps to join the allied campaign in North Africa. In January 1942 Sikorski was told of Stalin's plans to occupy large areas of Poland and serious divisions arose in the Allied camp. In April 1943 details emerged of the Soviet massacre of Poles in Katyn at the start of the war and the ensuing row gave Stalin the pretext to cut diplomatic contact with Sikorski's government and threaten Britain and America with Soviet withdrawal from the Allied struggle. The brave Poles, with Sikorski as their leader, who had been vital in 1940, were now a major hindrance to Allied unity.

In July 1943 General Sikorski's plane mysteriously crashed just after taking off from Gibralter and with his death the problem of Poland was resolved. One Polish airman who witnessed the crash exclaimed 'this is the end of Poland', and so it was to be. Sikorski's successor, Stanislaw Mikolajczyk, lacked authority and was excluded from the conferences of Tehran, Yalta and Potsdam, when Poland was effectively given to the Soviet Union. The exact cause of the plane crash that killed Sikorski has never been established. The unveiling of this statue to him, just after the collapse of the Soviet Union, does nothing to erase the betrayal of the Polish people which his name evokes.

14. Joseph Lister (1827-1912)
Upper Portland Place, W1
Sculptor Thomas Brock, Bronze, 1924

Joseph Lister was the son of a physicist but originally studied the arts before taking up medicine and graduating with honours in 1852. In 1856 Lister was appointed assistant surgeon to James Syme at Edinburgh Royal Infirmary and married Syme's daughter. After becoming a surgeon at the infirmary in 1861 Lister started work trying to reduce the level of infection in the operating theatre. At that time post-operative infection, called ward fever, killed nearly half of all patients. Lister was influenced by the work of the Hungarian surgeon, Ignaz Semmelweiss, who made the link between hygiene and infection, and Louis Pasteur's scientific paper suggesting that living organisms in the air caused infection.

By 1867 Lister had developed a carbolic acid spray which almost eradicated infection. In England Lister's results were treated with scepticism but they were well received in Prussia and his methods used to great affect during the Franco-Prussian War of 1870. Lister demonstrated his methods in Germany and the United States, but it was not until he accepted the chair of Clinical Surgery at King's College London in 1877 that his methods gained acceptance in Britain. He was recognised for his achievements with a baronetcy in 1883 and received of the Order of Merit in 1902. The last years of Lister's life were marred by the death of his wife in 1893 which effectively marked the end of his active career. This monument to the medical pioneer stands close to his London home at 12 Park Crescent.

15. Edward Augustus, Duke of Kent (1767-1820)

Park Crescent, W1
Sculptor S. S. Gahagan, Bronze, 1827

Like his siblings, Edward Augustus, fourth son of George III, had a difficult relationship with his father. He joined the army in 1785 and trained in Germany under a hated governor. His flight back to England only exacerbated his father's disapproval. He was promptly despatched to Gibraltar with the 7th Royal Fusiliers, with whom he travelled to Canada and North America. By 1799 Edward had been made Commander-in-Chief of British forces in North America and enjoyed a comfortable life with his long-term French mistress.

After a short spell back in Gibraltar as governor, he was ordered home in 1803 having nearly caused a mutiny. His life changed irrevocably on the death of Princess Charlotte, George IV's daughter, in 1817, which placed the Hanoverian succession in jeopardy. All Charlotte's uncles now attempted to sire an heir. The Duke gave up his French mistress – for the greater good – and married Princess Victoire of Leiningen in 1818, a daughter arriving the following year. He died in 1820 and so failed to see his infant daughter Victoria become the Queen who would rule Britain and her empire for over sixty years (see p.109).

While fathering the heir to the throne is perhaps the Duke's greatest achievement, there is considerable doubt about Victoria's parentage. It is known that Princess Victoire had a long affair with her secretary, Sir John Conroy, and her daughter introduced the haemophilia gene to the Royal family where it had not previously existed on either side.

16. John Fitzgerald Kennedy (1917-1963)

Marylebone Road, W1
Sculptor Jacques Lipchitz, Bronze bust, 1965

John Fitzgerald Kennedy was the charismatic 35th president of the United States whose rapid ascent to the White House and brief period in office are forever marred by his assassination on the streets of Dallas in 1963. JFK had all the attributes of a presidential candidate including a Harvard education, distinguished war record, good looks and a way with words, but this would have amounted to nothing without the money and political influence of his father Joseph. Joseph Kennedy was one of America's richest men, having made his fortune on the money markets, the selling of liquor and his control of several movie studios. Kennedy Snr was a close friend and financial supporter of Roosevelt (see p.253) and was determined to see one of his sons become president. The death of Joseph's eldest son during the Second World War placed all expectations on JFK and he duly became a Democratic congressman for Boston and was elected to the Senate in 1953, the same year he married Jacqueline Bouvier.

JFK was occasionally required to compromise his principles for the sake of family and political alliances – he did not vote for civil rights legislation, in order to keep southern senators' support, and avoided all criticism of Republican senator Joseph McCarthy because he was a family friend. In July 1960 JFK won the Democratic nomination for president and with his father financing and organising the campaign he became the youngest-ever and first Catholic president. The Kennedy administration lasted for just over a thousand days but in that time acquired a glamorous reputation; the media referred to Kennedy's White House as 'Camelot'. His domestic policy was called the 'New Frontier' and was marked by support for civil rights legislation, reflation of the economy and increased federal funding for medical care and education. In reality, JFK was restricted on the domestic front by a Republican Congress, but many of his reforms were passed after his death under President Johnson.

Kennedy's foreign policy revolved around the politics of the Cold War. It began with his unsuccessful support for the overthrow of Castro which resulted in the Bay of Pigs incident and escalated to the Cuban Missile Crisis, when Kennedy blockaded Cuba to prevent the installation of Soviet missiles. In Europe, America was forced to resort to airlifts to prevent the blockade of Berlin and Kennedy subsequently made his famous speech in that city. The new President was becoming more adept at handling the Soviets by the autumn of 1963, but his support of the South Vietnamese government and introduction of 18,000 troops to the region was to lead to a disastrous war in years to come.

Many facts have emerged since November 1963 about Kennedy's presidency and character. It is now known that he suffered from chronic back pain and several other illnesses that were hidden from the public, and that he conducted numerous affairs behind the walls of the White House. Kennedy also had some troubling connections with organised crime through his friendship with Frank Sinatra. This bust stands as a monument to the more noble public face of John F. Kennedy and was unveiled by his brothers Robert and Edward a few years after his tragic death.

HYDE PARK CORNER,
BELGRAVIA & VICTORIA

Animals In War Memorial, p.272

Hyde Park Corner, Belgravia & Victoria

1. Animals In War Memorial
2. 7th July Memorial
3. Achilles
4. George Gordon Byron,
   6th Baron Byron
5. Cavalry of Empire
6. Bomber Command Memorial
7. Royal Artillery War Memorial
8. Arthur Wellesley,
   1st Duke of Wellington
9. Machine Gun Corps
10. Constitution Arch
11. Australian War Memorial
12. New Zealand Memorial
13. Sir Robert Grosvenor
14. Elias George Basevi
15. General Don Jose De San Martin
16. Prince Henry The Navigator
17. Christopher Columbus
18. Simon Bolivar
19. Marshal Ferdinand Foch
20. Suffragette Fellowship
21. Henry Purcell
22. Queen Victoria

Hyde Park Corner, Belgravia & Victoria

When Kensington and Knightsbridge were villages on the outskirts of London, Hyde Park Corner was the site of a modest toll gate into the city. The area was transformed by the ambitions of George IV to create a grand entrance into Hyde Park and by the arrival of the Duke of Wellington who bought nearby Apsley House in 1817. The Duke's grand house was to become surrounded by monuments to the great man, with Achilles arriving in 1822, closely followed by Wellington Arch (now Constitution Arch) and finally a vast statue of the Duke was placed on top of the arch in 1846.

It was not until 1887 – over 30 years after the Duke's death – that politicians found the courage to remove Wellington's statue to Aldershot, replacing it with one of more modest proportions and renaming the arch. More recent monuments have all been of a military nature, the Australian and New Zealand Memorials have now been joined by one to Bomber Command which is as bombastic as it is controversial. Lord Byron's monument stands apart from the rest to the north, which is perhaps fitting given his dislike of Wellington. A recent addition is the Animal War Memorial – the inspiration of popular writer Jilly Cooper.

Just a few minutes walk from Hyde Park Corner is Belgrave Square, which contains a monument to the Second Earl of Grosvenor who commissioned Thomas Cubitt (see page 354) to build houses for London's wealthy here in the 1820s. The Latin American embassies in the area help to explain the other monuments on the square which all have an association with that part of the world, from explorers such as Henry the Navigator to Simon Bolivar. The only exception being the bust to the architect Basevi which is located in the private garden at the centre of the square. The monument to Marshal Foch stands alone on Buckingham Palace Road, but as one of the great military men of the First World War is worth visiting along with Purcell and the Suffragette Fellowship and the recently erected monument to the young Queen Victoria.

1. Animals In War Memorial

Brook Gate, Park Lane, W1
Sculptor David Backhouse, Bronze and Portland stone, 2004

This memorial to the animals that died in wars and conflict in the 20th century was inspired by Jilly Cooper's book, *Animals in War*. The author and other like-minded animal lovers started a fund in 1998 which raised over £1 million for the project. The monument consists of a semicircular wall of Portland stone depicting all kinds of animals serving man in wartime, from glow worms (used for light in the trenches) to carrier pigeons. The central area is occupied by statues of two heavily laden mules struggling to reach a breach in the wall where a bronze dog and horse are waiting. The monument seems to divide people between those that think such a monument is long overdue and is a reflection of a wiser less man-centred view of the world, and those that think it is a testament to the mawkish sentimentality of the British when it comes to animals. The reader can decide on which side of the fence they stand.

2. 7th July Memorial
Park Lane, W1
Architects: Carmody Groake, Cast stainless steel, July 2009

This permanent memorial to the victims of the 7 July 2005 London Bombings, in which 52 people were killed, was unveiled in Hyde Park on the fourth anniversary of the attack.

The monument comprises of 52 solid columns, representing a victim with details inscribed on each and clustered into four groups, to signify the four locations around London where the attacks took place. A plaque at the far eastern end of the memorial lists the names of the innocent victims.

3. Achilles

Park Lane, W1
Sculptor Sir Richard Westmacott RA, Bronze, 1822

This huge monument was erected through public subscription by 'the women of England to Arthur Duke of Wellington and his brave companions'. The 20-foot high bronze sculpture represents Achilles in martial pose with sword and shield in hand, but is actually a copy of one of the horse tamers on the Monte Catallo in Rome. The monument cost the vast sum of £10,000 and was cast from French cannon won at Salamanca, Vittoria, Toulouse and Waterloo. Achilles was the first public monument to depict a nude man and caused such controversy that a fig leaf was later added to save the warrior's modesty which over the years has been removed by vandals on several occasions. Achilles was also the first of many public monuments to Wellington and as such was criticised and lampooned by radicals who disliked the Duke and the reactionary politics he represented. Lord Byron's friend, the radical journalist Leigh Hunt, described Achilles as 'manifesting the most furious intentions of self defence against the hero whose abode it is looking at'.

4. George Gordon Byron, 6th Baron Byron (1788-1824)

Hyde Park Corner, SW1

Sculptor Richard C. Belt, Bronze, 1880

Lord George Gordon Byron was born on the eve of the French Revolution and like many of his English contemporaries his imagination was inspired by the idea of revolution and by the rejection of the political and social order in his own country. Byron was to become one the most recognised romantic poets of his generation, but he was a figure of scandal with a colourful personal life. Byron's family was both aristocratic and chaotic – his father, John 'Mad Jack' Byron, spent the family fortune and young Gordon was brought up in modest circumstances in Aberdeen, with the further disadvantage of a club foot which was to trouble him throughout his life. At the age of ten he inherited his great-uncle's fortune and was able to complete his education at Harrow and Trinity College, Cambridge. Despite his disfigurement, Byron was a seductive character who embarked on a series of affairs including a passionate love affair with a junior choir boy.

In 1809 Byron published his first book of poetry which was indifferently received, but his comic poem ridiculing his critics was a success and he embarked on a tour of southern Europe with a burgeoning reputation. Between 1809 and 1811 Byron travelled across the Mediterranean enjoying numerous affairs and writing of his adventures in *Childe Harold's Pilgrimage* (1812) which was followed by *The Giaour*, *The Bride of Abydos*, *The Corsair* and *Lara*, all published soon after his return to England.

Byron assumed his seat in the Lords on his return and used his position to argue for radical causes such as the Luddites and against reactionary politicians such as Lord Castlereagh and the Duke of Wellington; both of whom he lambasted in his poetry. Byron's complicated private life led him into a brief marriage and the scandal surrounding his separation was to drive him into permanent exile in 1816. Byron fled to Venice and began writing *Don Juan* (1819-24), loosely based on his own romantic adventures – he claimed to have slept with 250 woman in his first year in the City. He was joined in Italy by his radical friend Leigh Hunt and Shelley and together they published a radical journal called *The Liberal* to avoid England's repressive laws. Byron was always attracted to radical causes and he joined the fight for Italian independence.

By 1823 Byron was bored of his life in Italy and welcomed the chance to fight for Greek independence against Ottoman rule. He landed in Missolonghi and spent his own money refitting the Greek fleet and establishing a brigade of fighters under his command. Byron was never to see battle as he fell ill and died of fever in April 1824. Lady Caroline Lamb described Byron as 'mad, bad and dangerous to know' and despite his recognised genius as a poet he was not commemorated in Westminster Abbey until the 1960s. The marble for this monument was provided by the Greek government in recognition of his efforts, and shows the poet with his favourite dog 'Boatswain'. Byron's friend Trelawny claimed the statue bore no resemblance to the poet.

5. Cavalry of Empire
Hyde Park, SW7
Sculptor Captain Adrian Jones, Bronze, 1924

This brutal depiction of St George slaying the dragon is dedicated to the cavalry regiments of the First World War. The cavalry were for many centuries the most prestigious regiments of the army and cavalry regiments were important in the Crimean and South African Wars. The First World War was the first to employ mechanised tanks, aircraft and static trench positions. This new form of warfare left the cavalry obsolete, and with the exception of one or two engagements they played little part in the conflict.

6. Bomber Command Memorial

Green Park, W1
Sculptor Philip Jackson, Stone and Bronze, 2012

The history of Bomber Command is one marred with controversy for the policy of 'area bombing' adopted by Churchill, outlined by Lord Charles Portal as head of Bomber Command and carried out with enthusiasm by Arthur 'Bomber' Harris. In February 1942 directive 22 authorised Bomber Command to 'use your forces without restriction'. Following the initial bombing of Lubeck, Rostock and Cologne, Bomber Command laid waste to many German cities, culminated in the firebombing of Dresden on the 13th February 1945 – killing as many as 100,000 civilians and leading to considerable criticism, even within Bomber Command. Churchill quickly distanced himself from the campaign and pointedly failed to mention Bomber Command in his final war speeches.

This vast building with brass figures of eight airmen avoids any of the controversy surrounding Bomber Command, but rightly pays tribute to the brave young men that flew the planes and the sacrifices they made in the heat of conflict. It is a pity that one of the most controversial aspects of the war has been commemorated with one of the largest and most triumphant monuments.

7. Royal Artillery War Memorial

Hyde Park Corner, SW1
Sculptor Charles Sargeant Jagger and Lionel Pearson, 1925

This marble memorial with a bronze figure on each side and a vast howitzer gun at its centre is dedicated to those of the Royal Regiment of Artillery killed or injured in World War One. The monument is notable for its harsh depiction of war with one figure that of a dead soldier, draped in his greatcoat, with the words 'Here was a Royal fellowship of Death' from Shakespeare's Henry V. During the Second World War, 30,000 members of the Royal Artillery were killed and in 1949 a further three panels were added to commemorate their loss. It is claimed that the stone gun on this memorial is aimed towards the Somme in northern France.

8. Arthur Wellesley, 1st Duke of Wellington (1769-1852)

Hyde Park Corner, SW1
Sculptor Sir Joseph Edgar Boehm, Bronze, 1887

This monument stands where Constitution Arch was originally located and replaces the vast equestrian statue by Matthew Cotes Wyatt that was on top of the arch until 1883 (see Constitution Arch page 280). This monument shows the Duke upon his horse, Copenhagen, and surrounded below by soldiers from the 1st Guards, 42nd Royal Highlanders, 23rd Royal Welsh Fusiliers and the 6th Inniskilling Dragoons. For further details see Wellington's monument in the City (page 198).

9. Machine Gun Corps (Boy David Memorial)

Hyde Park Corner, SW1

Sculptor Francis Derwent Wood RA, Bronze, 1922

By the start of the First World War machine guns were used in all infantry battalions. The army introduced special training centres in November 1914 to develop tactics for the use of these new weapons and in October 1915 the Machine Gun Corps (MGC) was established and attached to every army brigade.

The MGC were equipped with the new and powerful Vickers guns and throughout the war cut a deadly swathe through the battlefields of northern France. The effectiveness of the new weapons made the machine gunners particular targets for enemy fire and they were called 'The Suicide Club' for the heavy casualties they suffered during the conflict, with over 60,000 killed or injured.

After the war, machine guns became lighter and more widely deployed within the army and the MGC was no longer necessary as a unique fighting force. The corps was disbanded in 1922 and this memorial erected in the same year. It shows the naked figure of David resting upon a sword with two Vickers guns on either side. The biblical inscription reads, 'Saul has slain his thousands; But David his tens of thousands'. Questions were asked in the House about the monument, amid complaints that it glorified war.

The first machine gun was designed and produced by Sir Hiram Maxim in Clerkenwell, just a few miles from where this monument stands. The Maxim Gun Factory was financed by Edward Vickers and it is his name that was used on the later models of the gun used by the MGC. A plaque to Maxim can be seen on the site of his factory in Hatton Gardens to this day.

10. Constitution Arch (Formerly Wellington Arch)
Hyde Park Corner, SW1
Sculptor Decimus Burton, Bronze, 1828 (moved here 1883)

This grand arch was commissioned by George IV in 1825, along with Marble Arch, to commemorate victory over Napoleon. Decimus Burton began work in 1826 but as the King's funds depleted, the elaborate exterior was abandoned for a simpler and cheaper design. It was erected opposite Wellington's residence, Apsley House, in 1828 and became known as Wellington Arch. In 1846 Matthew Cotes Wyatt's massive 8.5-metre high equestrian monument to the Duke was transported from his workshops on Harrow Road to Hyde Park Corner with a military escort of 500 guardsmen and placed on top of the arch.

Decimus Burton, who had planned a quadriga for the top of the arch, objected to the lack of proportion of the statue and others complained that the horse did not resemble the Duke's famous Copenhagen. The arch and the monument parted ways when the arch was moved to the top of Constitution Hill, and Wyatt's monument was eventually dispatched to Aldershot where it stands to this day. Constitution Arch underwent a further transformation in 1912 when Burton's initial plan for a quadriga was completed by the soldier-turned-sculptor, Captain Adrian Jones. The work was funded by the Jewish businessman, Lord Michelham, in memory of Edward VII. The king had promoted the interests of the Jewish community during his reign. There are several other monuments to Edward VII in London (see p.93).

11. Australian War Memorial

Hyde Park Corner, SW1
Sculptor Janet Laurence &
architectural firm Tonkin Zulaikha Greer, Granite, 2003

This beautiful monument was funded by the Australian government, who commissioned the design of Australian artist Janet Laurence in partnership with the architectural practice Tonkin Zulaikha Greer in 2002. The monument consists of a 40-metre long sweeping curve of granite which is 3.4 metres at its highest point and weighs 200 tons. The monument commemorates the sacrifice of over 100,000 Australian lives in the two World Wars. The 24,000 Australian towns from which these people came are inscribed in small type, while the 47 battlegrounds upon which they shed their blood is inscribed in a much larger script, making them visible from some distance. The main inscription reads 'Whatever burden you are to carry we also will shoulder that burden'. The monument has a constant flow of water over the stone and lights illuminate it from below at night. Large crowds gathered to see the unveiling of the monument by Queen Elizabeth and Australian Prime Minister John Howard.

12. New Zealand Memorial
Hyde Park Corner, SW1
Sculptor Paul Dibble, John Hardwick-Smith (Architect)
Bronze, 2006

Consisting of 16 cross shaped columns rising at an angle from a grass verge, this monument is one of the most original to be found in the capital. From a distance the crucifix shape is evident at the top of each column, but closer up can be seen detailed markings which include text and symbols representing the links between Britain and New Zealand. The memorial was unveiled on Armistice Day, which gives some indication that while this is not only a war memorial, the sacrifice made by New Zealand soldiers in two world wars and other conflicts, is an important part of the annual commemoration. History has undergone some editing to emphasise the friendly links between Britain and New Zealand. The 1840 Treaty of Waitangi, which granted Maori land rights, is engraved upon one of the columns, but there is no mention that the treaty was largely ignored, resulting in 25 years of intermittent conflict. For more details of this conflict see the New Zealand memorial in Greenwich (see p.324).

13. Sir Robert Grosvenor, 1st Marquess of Westminster (1767-1845)

Belgrave Square, SW1
Sculptor Jonathan Wylder, Bronze, 1999

Sir Robert Grosvenor was the 2nd Earl of Grosvenor and acquired the title 1st Marquess of Westminster in 1831 from William IV for his change of allegiance to the Whig cause. He spent much of his time on his lands near Chester and the family's country home of Eaton Hall. Employing master builder Thomas Cubitt, Grosvenor transformed farmland to the west of London into the grand Regency squares of Mayfair, Belgravia and Pimlico. This statue was commissioned by the current 6th Duke of Westminster.

14. Elias George Basevi (1794-1845)

Private Garden, Belgrave Square, SW1
Sculptor Jonathan Wylder, Bronze, 2002

Elias George trained as an architect with Sir John Soane and was one of his favourites. Like his mentor, Basevi's work was of a classical style, inspired by his travels to Greece and Italy. Many of his major works are outside London, most notably the Fitzwilliam Museum in Cambridge. He did design several grand squares in West London including Belgrave Square. Basevi met a premature and violent end, falling from the ceiling of Ely Cathedral while inspecting its restoration.

15. General Don Jose De San Martin (1778-1850)
Belgrave Square, SW1
Sculptor Juan Carlos Ferraro, Bronze, 1994

Don Jose De San Martin was born in a province of what is now Argentina, but at the time of his birth was a colony of Spain. San Martin was educated in Spain and joined the Spanish army, seeing battle against the French in Africa and Spain. He rose to the rank of lieutenant colonel before fleeing Spain in 1811 to join the revolutionary army of Argentina fighting Spanish rule. When San Martin arrived in Buenos Aires in 1812, the fledgling government was under threat from the Spanish forces and he was employed to build an army to defend the city. He soon devised an audacious plan to drive out the Spanish by crossing the Andes into Chile and attacking the Spanish stronghold in Peru.

San Martin formed an alliance with Bernardo O'Higgins (see page 379) – the deposed leader of Chile – and between 1817 and 1821 began the arduous series of battles that were to liberate Chile, Peru and his beloved Argentina from Spanish rule. San Martin had no political ambition and he retired in 1824 to briefly live on his farm in Chile, before leaving for France after the death of his wife. He was to spend his remaining years in Europe and only returned once to South America before his death in 1850. This rather ugly monument was a gift of the British community in Argentina.

16. Prince Henry The Navigator (1394-1460)
Belgrave Square, SW1
Sculptor Simpões de Almeida, Bronze, 2002

Prince Henry the Navigator was the third son of King John I of Portugal. Henry persuaded his father to mount an attack upon the Muslim port of Ceuta, on the North African coast. The Portuguese successfully took the city in August 1415 and Henry was able to oversee the vast riches that flowed through the Saharan trade routes. In 1420, Henry was appointed as governor of the order of Christ which was based at Tomar at the southern tip of Portugal. As well as practicing a devout Catholic faith, Henry established a centre for navigation and map-making at Sagres and financed numerous voyages of exploration. These voyages succeeded in discovering and occupying the Madeira Islands, the Azores and helped establish trade routes in Africa which circumnavigated Muslim lands. Within 30 years of Henry's death Portuguese ships had sailed beyond the southern tip of Africa and soon established trade routes with the Indies. Henry was far less successful as a soldier and his expedition to Tangier in 1437 was a military failure, but his achievements at Sagres were to change the world. The monument lies within the gardens of Belgrave Square and can only be seen through the gates.

17. Christopher Columbus (1446-1506)
Belgrave Square, SW1
Sculptor Tomas Banuelos, Bronze, 1992

Christopher Columbus is thought to be Italian in origin, but his early life is not well documented and there is still some disagreement as to his year of birth – this monument states it to be 1446. It is fairly certain that he spent his early years as a merchant seaman and acquired skills in navigation and map-making. In the late 15th century the disintegration of the Mogul Empire and the rise of Islam threatened the long-established trade routes with India and attempts were made to find new routes eastward through Africa. Columbus devised a plan to voyage west across the Atlantic Ocean to India based upon a false calculation of the earth's size and very poor knowledge of its landmass.

Columbus spent years petitioning the Spanish crown and in 1492 they granted the ships and provisions he required. After five weeks sailing, Columbus and his crew discovered land on 12th October and went on to explore the islands that are now known as San Salvador and Cuba. Columbus believed these lands to be part of the Indian subcontinent – a misconception he held till his death. He returned to Spain as a hero and embarked on a further three voyages, but was to prove a less successful administrator than explorer and was removed from his position as governor in 1500. Columbus is a hero to many who regard him as the discoverer of the Americas, but others have criticised the conquest of these lands. This bronze statue of a seated Columbus was a gift of the Spanish government to commemorate the 500th anniversary of the discovery of the New World.

18. Simon Bolivar (1783-1830)

Belgrave Square, SW1
Sculptor Daini, Bronze, 1973

Simon Bolivar came from a wealthy and privileged background, and inherited a fortune when he was left an orphan as a child. He was educated by tutors and inculcated with the ideas of the European Enlightenment. As a young man Bolivar travelled in Europe and for a while became a figure in the court of Napoleon. On his return to Venezuela he allied himself to the revolutionary cause and through military action drove the Spanish forces out and declared independence in 1813.

The liberation was short-lived and civil war allowed the royalist army to again claim Venezuela for the Spanish crown in 1815. Bolivar fled to Jamaica, where he formed a new revolutionary army and again returned to do battle with the Spanish, culminating in victory and the establishment of Greater Columbia (which included present-day Columbia, Panama, Ecuador and Venezuela) in 1819, with Bolivar as its first president. Bolivar continued his war against the Spanish and managed to drive them from neighbouring Peru. He was less successful as a politician than a revolutionary soldier and failed to unite the continent as one nation, encountering rebellion and an attempt on his life. He died of tuberculosis just months after relinquishing power in 1830 having established himself in South America as El Libertator. The monument, which stands on the corner of Belgrave Square, does very little justice to the great man and looks more like a toy soldier adopting a ludicrously wooden posture.

19. Marshal Ferdinand Foch (1851-1929)

Grosvenor Gardens, SW1
Sculptor G. Malissard, Bronze, 1930

Ferdinand Foch's childhood was filled with stories of his forefathers' Napoleonic battles. Foch enlisted during the Franco-Prussian War (1870) and experienced the bitterness of defeat and occupation. Foch became a career soldier, attained the rank of captain and entered staff college in 1885. By the start of World War One, he was a lieutenant general and assumed command of the XX Corps. Despite initial retreat he managed to hold the German advance and prevent them crossing the Meurthe. Following this success Foch was appointed head of the Ninth Army and again stemmed the German advance and counter-attacked during the Battle of the Marne which greatly strengthened Allied resolve. In October 1914 he became commander of the northern section of the front and held his line before suffering heavy casualties at the Battle of the Somme (1916) leading to his brief removal from the front. The failure of Foch's successor, General Nivelle, and the support of Prime Minister Clemenceau saw Foch's return and by March 1918 he was Allied Supreme Commander, accepting German surrender on 11th November 1918. A tough negotiator, the harsh terms of the Treaty of Versailles, owe much to his influence.

Foch became a national hero in France and was the first foreign soldier to be made a field marshal in the British army. Since his death in 1929, he has received some criticism for his offensive strategy, but there is little doubt that he was a great soldier. This fine monument is a copy of one that stands in Cassel, France.

20. Suffragette Fellowship
Christchurch Gardens, SW1
Sculptor Edwin Russell, Bronzed fibreglass, 1970

The Suffragette Fellowship was established in 1926 to preserve the history and spirit of the struggle for women's emancipation and the right to vote, that was fought in the early 20th century. The Suffragette's stopped their campaign at the start of World War One but the threat of renewing the struggle directly lead to women securing the vote when peace returned. The Fellowship funded this monument and maintains an archive related to the struggle. The memorial was unveiled by Fellowship treasurer and former suffragette, Lilian Lenton.

21. Henry Purcell (1659-95)

Christchurch Gardens, SW1
Sculptor Glynn Williams, Bronze, 1995
Son of a musician in the court of Charles II, Henry Purcell's musical talent was soon evident. In 1679 he was appointed organist at Westminster Abbey, Dr John Blow resigning the post in deference to his brilliance. Purcell benefitted from Royal patronage but was also much involved in Restoration London's vibrant concert scene, composing smaller pieces, operas, stage and chamber music. He worked with dramatists including John Dryden and wrote several pieces for the newly established 'Musical Society'. Purcell caught a chill and died at the age of 36. He is buried close by the organ in Westminster Abbey.

22. Queen Victoria (1819-1901)

Victoria Square, SW1
Sculptor Catherine Laugel, Bronze, 2007
This most recent monument to Queen Victoria is situated in a square which bares her name and was completed in 1839, at the beginning of her long reign. The monument depicts the young queen as she would have looked at the time and contrasts with the more familiar image of the Queen as an elderly widow.

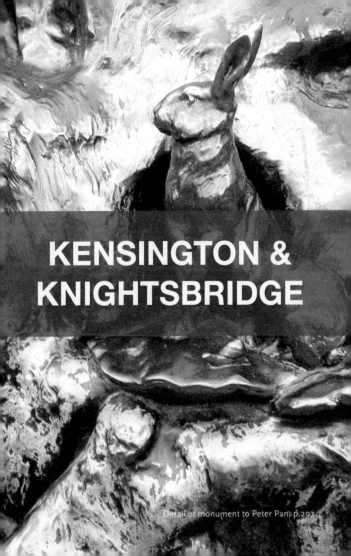

KENSINGTON & KNIGHTSBRIDGE

Detail of monument to Peter Pan, p.297

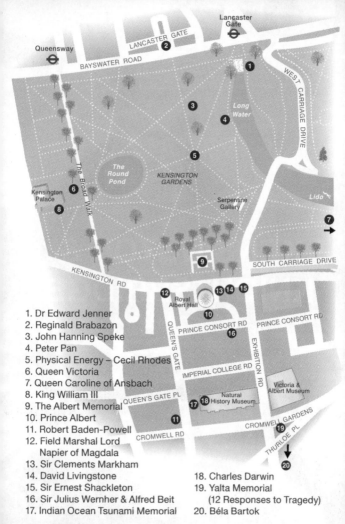

1. Dr Edward Jenner
2. Reginald Brabazon
3. John Hanning Speke
4. Peter Pan
5. Physical Energy – Cecil Rhodes
6. Queen Victoria
7. Queen Caroline of Ansbach
8. King William III
9. The Albert Memorial
10. Prince Albert
11. Robert Baden-Powell
12. Field Marshal Lord
    Napier of Magdala
13. Sir Clements Markham
14. David Livingstone
15. Sir Ernest Shackleton
16. Sir Julius Wernher & Alfred Beit
17. Indian Ocean Tsunami Memorial
18. Charles Darwin
19. Yalta Memorial
    (12 Responses to Tragedy)
20. Béla Bartok

Kensington & Knightsbridge

Most of the monuments in and around Hyde Park and Kensington Gardens have a royal or imperial theme. The Albert Memorial is the largest in London and as much an expression of a widow's grief as it is a statement of the Prince Consort's achievements. A further grand monument to the prince stands behind the Albert Hall. Queen Victoria's monument by Kensington Palace shows her as the young Queen Albert married in 1840. A more recent monument to a much earlier monarch, William III, stands in Kensington Palace.

Victoria's reign was much concerned with the British Empire and there are a great many monuments which touch on this theme. Reginald Brabazon established the Empire Movement and was helped in his patriotic mission by Lord Baden-Powell who has a monument on Queen's Gate. Field Marshal Napier of Magdala fought in many of the most important wars of empire, including the defeat of the Abyssinian king in 1868.

The Royal Geographical Society commemorates a more benign aspect of Victoria's reign with monuments to a number of famous explorers. Wernher and Beit made their fortune in the South African diamond mines and gave part of their fortune to Imperial College's Department of Mining, outside which their busts stand. Both men knew and worked with the founder of Rhodesia, Cecil Rhodes, who is commemorated in the large equestrian figure, 'Physical Energy'. The monuments to Peter Pan and the pioneer of vaccination, Dr Edward Jenner, are all the more charming for having no connection with royalty or empire although they are joined by a modest urn to Queen Caroline.

Further afield, the monuments to the eminent scientist Charles Darwin and the Hungarian composer Béla Bartok are worth the walk to visit,- as are the monuments to the Indian Tsunami and the equally tragic Yalta Memorial, which commemorates the treaty that repatriated many people to the Soviet Union after the war.

1. Dr Edward Jenner (1749-1823)

Italian Garden, Kensington Gardens, W8
Sculptor W. Calder Marshall, Bronze, erected in Trafalgar Square
in 1858, moved here in 1862

Edward Jenner was a country doctor who pioneered and promoted the inoculation of cowpox virus against the widespread and deadly scourge of smallpox. The word he used for this treatment was 'vaccination' (from the Latin for cow), which was later adopted by Pasteur for all forms of immunisation. Despite his critics, Jenner proved the efficacy of his treatment from his country practice in Gloucestershire and eventually won the support of Parliament for widespread vaccination. Jenner saved many millions of lives with his research, but his interests were far wider than medicine. He was an enthusiastic geologist and fossil hunter and in 1819 found the first remains of a dinosaur now known as a Plesiosaur. He became a member of the Royal Society not for his medical work but for his paper on the nesting habits of cuckoos. Jenner was taught by the famous John Hunter (see p.27) as a medical student and they remained life-long friends, working together on subjects such as hibernation and migration. Jenner was also fascinated by balloon flight and launched one of the first hydrogen balloons in 1784, the sight of which is said to have terrified local labourers. Jenner was an incredible man and one untouched by vanity or pomp. He would no doubt have been indifferent to the movement of his statue from Trafalgar Square to its present site in the Italian Garden of Kensington Gardens in 1862. His place on the square was taken by a monument to the soldier Sir Henry Havelock (see p.16).

2. Reginald Brabazon, 12th Earl of Meath (1841-1929)

Lancaster Gate, W2
Sculptor Herman Cowthra, Stone, 1934

Brabazon started his career as a soldier and after a brief period in the diplomatic service, with postings in Germany, Holland and France, he retired while still in his 30s to devote himself to good causes. Brabazon founded the Metropolitan Public Gardens Society in 1880 which promoted parks and green spaces and introduced the now familiar idea of a green belt around London to limit the capital's expansion – Meath Garden in Bethnal Green still bears his name.

Those readers who hated compulsory games during their time at school have Brabazon to blame – his Physical Education Bill of 1890 was rejected by Parliament, but persuaded school governors to introduce physical education into the weekly curriculum. Brabazon became a supporter of the Scout movement and a friend and ally of its founder, Baden-Powell (see p.303). He founded his own movement, the *Legion of Frontiersmen*, in 1904 and later established *The Duty and Discipline Movement*, which had the rather vague purpose of combating 'indiscipline' and giving 'support to all legitimate authority'.

The Earl of Meath will be best remembered for his *Empire Movement*, which sought to promote 'Responsibility, Sympathy, Duty and Self-Sacrifice' and introduced 'Empire day', a patriotic celebration on 25th May. Brabazon's emphasis upon physical and mental discipline and respect for authority seems anachronistic in the 21st century, but there is no doubt that he was a generous and kind man.

3. John Hanning Speke (1827-1864)

Italian Garden, Kensington Gardens, W8,
Granite obelisk, 1864

John Hanning Speke was a commissioned officer who served in the Punjab and the Crimea and travelled in the Himalayas and Tibet before being injured while exploring Somaliland. In December 1856 he joined Richard Burton's expedition to search for the great lakes of Africa and the source of the Nile. In February 1858 they were the first Europeans to reach Lake Tanganyika. Speke later set out on his own and in July 1858 became the first explorer to reach the source of the Nile, which he named Lake Victoria.

Speke's claims were rejected by Burton and he set out again with Captain James Grant to prove his discovery. On his return to England in 1862, Speke was fêted by the British public, but because of his poor notes he failed to convince several key figures, including his rival Burton. On the day they were scheduled to meet to debate the matter publicly, Speke was killed by his own gun while grouse shooting. Although Speke achieved where David Livingstone had failed (see p.306), his journal reveals him to be a lesser character: 'Now I had made up my mind never to sit upon the ground as the natives and Arabs are obliged to do, nor to make my obeisance in any other manner than is customary in England.' Speke left a bloody legacy in the form of his Hamitic hypothesis which claimed that Tutsi people (Hamites) were a superior race to the Hutus (Bantus). This theory was a divisive element in the genocide that took place in Rwanda in the 1990s.

4. Peter Pan

Kensington Gardens, SW7
Sculptor Sir George Frampton, Bronze, 1912

Situated on the west bank of the Long Water, this statue of 'the boy who never grew up' is one of the few in London to be dedicated to a fictional character. It was commissioned by the author of Peter Pan, J.M. Barrie, who had recently enjoyed great success with the stage play. The statue appeared on the 1st May 1912, as if by magic, having been installed in the dead of night. It was the author's intention to make the appearance of the statue as magical as the tale. The location of the statue is also of significance, for it is here that Peter Pan first appears to Wendy. Barrie lived on Bayswater Road and used his local park and the children that played there as inspiration for his play.

The art nouveau style of the sculpture and its sudden appearance led to some disquiet. It was thought by some to be a piece of self-publicity by Barrie to promote his book and questions about the statue were asked in the House of Commons. It was only the popularity of the statue, particularly with children, that ensured its survival. There are seven other replica statues distributed throughout the world, although the one in Liverpool has recently been taken down due to vandalism. The London statue has been damaged many times – perhaps the vandals are inspired by the mischievous Greek god of the woodland from whom Peter Pan gets his name?

5. Physical Energy – Cecil Rhodes (1853-1902)
Lancaster Walk, Kensington Gardens, SW7
Sculptor George Frederic Watts, Bronze, 1908

This sculpture is the work of G.F. Watts who created the 'Heroes Wall' in Postman's Park (see p.222). Watts regarded his work as representing the energy of the 'age of empire' and it was used as the centrepiece for the memorial to Cecil Rhodes in Cape Town. The monument's association with the man has faded with time, but still offers an opportunity to mention the most successful empire-builder of the late 19th century.

Sent away to Africa because of his frail health, Cecil Rhodes established a successful fruit farming business before concentrating on the Kimberley diamond mines in 1871 and founding the De Beers Mining Company in April 1880, which was the basis of his fortune. It was at this time that Rhodes entered politics, becoming prime minister of the Cape in 1890 and passing measures to serve the interests of the mining industry, such as the Glen Grey Act, which deprived the black population of their land. In 1895, and with the financial support of Beit (see p.308), Rhodes attempted a disastrous coup in the Transvaal to overthrow the Boer government and helped bring about the Second Boer War a few years later. Undaunted, Rhodes established the British South Africa Company, which went on to occupy the Mashonaland, defeating the indigenous tribes and so creating Rhodesia in 1897. Ironically, it was a disturbed Polish aristocrat, Catherine Radziwill, who gave Rhodes his greatest problems. Her stalking and false accusations were to lead to a court case which contributed to Rhodes's final illness and premature death.

6. Queen Victoria (1819-1901)

Broad Walk, Kensington Gardens, SW7
Sculptor Princess Louise, Marble, 1893

This is one of the seven statues dedicated to Queen Victoria in London. It is remarkable because it is the work of her daughter, Princess Louise, who was a skilled sculptor and a pupil of Joseph Boehm. The statue is close to that of her beloved Prince Albert and shows the Queen as a young monarch. The largest and most extravagant monument to Victoria can be found in front of Buckingham Palace (see p.109).

7. Queen Caroline of Ansbach (1683-1737)

South-east corner
of Serpentine, W2
Sculptor Reginald Blomfield
Stone Urn, 1990

Caroline of Ansbach was the German princess who became the Queen consort of George II. She was a patron of Robert Walpole and important in securing the position of the Hanoverian dynasty in Britain. She commissioned the damming of the Westbourne river to create the Long Water and Serpentine, by which this urn now stands.

8. King William III (1650-1702)

Kensington Palace, W8
Sculptor Heinrich Baucke, Bronze, 1907

This statue commemorates William III, who deposed James II in 1688 – an event that has become known as the 'Glorious Revolution'. The monument is, however, less about the events of 1688 and far more about the politics of the early 20th century. It was presented by Kaiser Wilhelm II to his uncle Edward VII, no doubt to remind him of the historic links between the two nations that were by then on opposite sides of international alliances.

The attempt proved a failure and only seven years after this gift was presented the two countries were confronting each other on the battle fields of northern Europe. Edward VII was the last monarch of the House of Saxe-Coburg-Gotha; his successor, King George V, replaced the German-sounding title with the more British 'Windsor' during the First World War. For a more detailed account of the Glorious Revolution of 1688 and William III's part in it, refer to his monument on St James's Square (see p.102) and the monument to James II on Trafalgar Square (see p.8).

9. Prince Albert – The Albert Memorial (1819-1861)

Kensington Gardens, opposite Royal Albert Hall, SW7
Architect: Sir G. Gilbert Scott (monument)

Sculptors: John Foley (statue), P. Macdowell (Europe), John Bell (America), J. H. Foley (Asia), W. Theed (Africa), W. Calder Marshall (Agriculture), Thomas Thornycroft (Commerce), J. Lawlor (Engineering), J. Weekes (Manufacturing), H. H. Armstead, J. Birnie Philip, J. F. Redfern (Friezes & other sculpture) Material: Red, Pink & Grey Granite; Marble; Bronze Gilt; 1875

There is no larger or more extravagant monument to be found in the capital than that to the memory of Prince Albert, consort to Queen Victoria.

Prince Albert was a great influence upon the Queen and can take credit for many of the achievements of her reign. Britain had embarked on the world's first industrial revolution when George III was king, but it was not until the coronation of Victoria, with the considerable encouragement of Prince Albert, that the royal family embraced the middle-class virtues of industry and progress. It was Prince Albert who organised the Great Exhibition to celebrate Britain's industry, which took place in Hyde Park in 1851. When it was suggested that a memorial be erected to the Prince at the time of the exhibition he dismissed the idea, writing: '... I would much rather not be made the prominent feature of such a monument, as it would both disturb my quiet rides in Rotten Row to see my own face staring at me, and if (as is very likely) it became an artistic monstrosity, like most of our monuments, it would upset my equanimity to be permanently ridiculed and laughed at in effigy.'

This monument, constructed after Albert's sudden death from typhoid at the age of only 42, is as much an expression of a widow's grief as it is a celebration of Albert's achievements. Standing 180 feet in height and involving the work of a vast number of the county's leading sculptors and craftsmen, the monument took over 20 years to complete and cost £120,000, an enormous sum. The Prince is depicted by John Foley, sitting with a catalogue of the Great Exhibition in hand and is the centre of a vast Gothic shrine with friezes depicting artists, musicians and writers (both English and German) while above him are depictions of the celestial. At each corner of the shrine, separate sculptures represent Agriculture, Commerce, Engineering and Manufacture and a further group of four statues stand further out, representing Europe, America, Asia and Africa. It is arguable whether the monument is a grand Victorian statement or the 'artistic monstrosity' which Albert dreaded. By the 1990s the monument had fallen into disrepair and was covered in scaffolding for several years – there were even plans for its demolition. In 1994 English Heritage took charge of its restoration at a cost of over £10 million and the monument can again be seen in all its bombastic glory. There is a second statue commemorating Prince Albert in Holborn (see p.184).

10. Prince Albert

Steps of Albert Hall, SW7
Sculptor Joseph Durham
Bronze, 1858

This monument is easily forgotten, being located behind the Royal Albert Hall and so close to the grand Albert Memorial. It was first placed in the gardens of The Royal Horticultural Society, but was moved to its present site in 1899.

11. Robert Baden-Powell (1857-1941)

Queen's Gate (near Hyde Park Gate), SW7
Sculptor Donald Potter, Granite, 1961

This monument stands outside the head quarters of the British Scout movement which Baden-Powell founded in 1908. Baden-Powell was always interested in the outdoor life and as a boy would escape from his boarding school to camp in the nearby woods. He put his survival skills to good use as a soldier during the Second Boer War and became a hero of the Siege of Mafeking (1899-1900).

Baden-Powell used his new-found celebrity to write books about military scouting and trained new recruits, who lacked the skills of self-sufficiency, common-sense and initiative, to be useful soldiers. Like many Victorian military men, Baden-Powell found the new century a bewildering place. He became concerned that society was becoming weak and degenerate and that people were losing their individuality and enjoyment of life. It was from his concern for the young and a desire to share some of his scouting experiences as a soldier, that Baden-Powell wrote *Scouting for Boys* in 1908. Widespread interest in this book led to the formation of the Boy Scouts and Girl Guides movements, with the first World Scout Jamboree taking place in Olympia in 1920. Today it is easy to mock Baden-Powell and his movement, but there are still millions of scouts around the world as demonstrated by the many who visit the Queen's Gate offices. Some of Baden-Powell's attitudes continue in modern essentialist thinking such as the recent 'Iron John' movement in the US. Baden-Powell was a skilled artist and also an enthusiastic thespian.

12. Field Marshal Lord Napier of Magdala (1810-90)
Queen's Gate, SW7
Sculptor Sir Joseph Boehm, Bronze, erected in Carlton House
Gardens in 1891, moved here in 1920

Robert Cornelis Napier was born in Ceylon at the height of the British Empire. Despite not being a member of the famous Napier military family, he rose rapidly within the British army and gained a reputation as a skilled administrator and brave soldier. The Indian population was beginning to rebel against the yoke of British rule and Napier was involved in the Sikh Wars (1845-49) and took part in the relief of Lucknow (1858) during the Indian Mutiny under General Outram (see p.137). He later served in the North West Frontier District and saw action in Peshawar and Afghanistan. His most famous military campaign was the expedition to Ethiopia in April 1868 to release hostages held by the Abyssinian king Tewodros II and capture Magdala. The conflict's swift resolution made Napier a national hero and he was raised to the peerage. The situation was a little more complicated than the British public's adulation might suggest. Napier had defeated a poorly equipped army with the use of modern guns and the Abyssinians were seeking the protection of Britain from other Muslim neighbours and did not want war. To make matters worse, after victory Napier had supervised the removal of a valuable treasure from Magdala. The prime minister, William Gladstone, expressed dismay at Napier's actions but did nothing for fear of a scandal. Today there is still a campaign to return the Abyssinian treasures, nearly 150 years after they were looted. This equestrian statue of Napier is a replica of one that formerly stood in Calcutta.

13. Sir Clements Markham (1830-1916)

Royal Geographical Society, Exhibition Road, SW7
Sculptor F. W. Pomeroy
Bronze, 1921

Sir Clements Robert Markham was born into a highly regarded clerical family, his great grandfather having served as Archbishop of Canterbury. Markham had a brief spell in the Navy before he travelled to Peru to explore the eastern slopes of the Andes and developed an abiding interest in the country and its history. After his travels, Markham joined the Indian civil service and while acting as an administrator also explored the sub-continent. In 1875 he went on his only Arctic expedition which made him an enthusiast for polar exploration and an important supporter of later Arctic expeditions as president of the Royal Geographic Society.

Markham was the key proponent of the Discovery expedition and supervised the building of the ship in Scotland and chose the crew, which included Captain Scott and Shackleton (see pages 97 and 307). It was Lady Markham who launched the Discovery on the Tay in March 1901. Markham was not only an explorer but also an influential historian who wrote on all manner of subjects, from the Greek traveller Pytheas to the reign of Richard III, as well as several important books about the culture and history of Peru. His knowledge of Peruvian medicine enabled him to save many lives by introducing the use of quinine as a cure for malaria in colonial India. This bust of Markham was a gift from the Peruvian government in recognition of his work and stands outside the Royal Geographic Society which he served for many years.

14. David Livingstone (1813-1873)

Royal Geographical Society, Exhibition Road, SW7
Sculptor T. B. Huxley-Jones, Bronze, 1953

LIVINGSTONE

Livingstone was a Scottish missionary who became the greatest African explorer of his generation. He spent over 30 years of his life exploring the continent, acting as missionary, doctor, explorer, scientist and anti-slavery activist. As a child, Livingstone worked in a cotton mill while continuing his education through evening classes, eventually qualifying as a medical doctor. It was his Methodist faith that persuaded him to become a missionary doctor in southern Africa in 1840.

After settling in Africa and marrying the daughter of a fellow missionary, Livingstone began exploring the continent. Unlike John Speke (see p.296), Livingstone considered the Africans as his equals and in the course of his travels learnt several native languages. He covered almost a third of the continent and received a gold medal from the Royal Geographical Society for crossing the entire African continent from west to east. He was the first European to see Victoria Falls and contributed to the discovery of the source of the Nile. It was in November 1871 that Henry Stanley uttered the famous words 'Dr Livingstone, I presume?', having been sent by the New York Herald Tribune to provide assistance to Livingstone in his last, troubled expedition. Stanley provided Livingstone with vital supplies, but the years of struggle had begun to take their toll. Livingstone died in April 1872. In accordance with his wishes, his heart was buried in Africa while his body was laid to rest in Westminster Abbey. This bronze statue was erected 80 years after his death.

15. Sir Ernest Shackleton (1874-1922)

Royal Geographical Society, Exhibition Road, SW7
Sculptor C. Sargeant Jagger, Bronze, 1932

Ernest Shackleton determined to lead a life of exploration from an early age and went to sea at 16 against the wishes of his father, who wanted him to train as a doctor. On leave in London in 1900, Shackleton was chosen to go with Captain Robert Scott (see p.97) to the South Pole on the famous *Discovery* expedition. On 30th December 1902 Scott, Shackleton and Wilson came within 400 miles of the South Pole, the furthest South then achieved. The reaching of the South Pole had captured the public's imagination and Shackleton now became determined to make it to the Pole with his own expedition, setting out in command of the *Nimrod* in 1907. He set out to cross the ice with a small team and reached within 97 miles of the South Pole in January 1909, before turning back after running out of food. Shackleton was awarded the Royal Geographic Society gold medal for his heroic failure but his achievement was soon eclipsed by Roald Amundsen's successful arrival at the South Pole in December 1911. Shackleton commanded another voyage to circumnavigate the South Pole between 1914-16 on the appropriately named *Endurance*. The ship became trapped in the ice in 1915 and Shackleton was forced to make an incredible journey across 800 frozen miles to South Georgia to get aid. It was this dramatic rescue which assured Shackleton's place in history as a great British hero. He died of a heart attack after embarking on a third expedition in January 1922.

16. Sir Julius Wernher (1850-1912) & Alfred Beit (1853-1906)

Royal School of Mines, Prince Consort Road, SW7

Sculptor Paul Montford, Stone, 1910

The busts of Julius Wernher and Alfred Beit commemorate two men who came from Germany in the 1870s and made their fortune in the diamond and gold mines of South Africa – founding Wernher, Beit and Co. which became De Beers in 1888.

Wernher and Beit gave substantial sums to various educational and colonial causes including the Royal School of Mines where their busts stand today. A good deal of Julius Wernher's art collection can be seen at Ranger's House in Greenwich.

17. Indian Ocean Tsunami Memorial

Darwin Centre Garden, The Natural History Museum, SW1

Sculptor Carmody Groarke, 2011

Over 225,000 people are estimated to have lost their lives when a vast body of water engulfed the coastal regions of South East Asia on 26th December 2004. This simple 115 tonne stone commemorates the 155 Britons who died that day. The Tsunami was the most devastating natural disaster in living memory and it is fitting that this monument should stand in the grounds of the Natural History Museum.

18. Darwin (1809-1882)

Main Staircase of The Natural History Museum, SW1
Sculptor Sir Joseph Boehm, 1885

Charles Darwin was born into an eminent Shrewsbury family – the grandson of both Josiah Wedgewood and biologist Erasmus Darwin. The young Charles was uncertain of his path and did not excel at Edinburgh University or with his later theological studies at Cambridge.

Darwin's life changed when he embarked on *The Beagle* at the age of 22 to explore the wildlife of the southern hemisphere. During the long voyage he read Lyall's *Principles of Geology* which was already beginning to question the traditional creationist explanation of life's origins.

As Darwin collected specimens he became fascinated by the diversity within similar species and particularly among those of the Galapagos Islands. He returned to England in 1836 and began working on a theory that would explain the change of species through adaptation to the environment. He proposed that the survival of the fittest led to the adaptation or 'evolution' of each species over time. Darwin was aware of the controversial nature of his theory and did not publish *On the Origin of Species* until 1859. Despite criticism and ridicule, Darwin's theory was soon widely accepted and later verified by the discoveries of DNA and gene technology in the 20th century.

This monument was erected on the steps of The Natural History Museum soon after Darwin's death. It was moved in 1927 and remained in an obscure part of the museum until its reinstatement to its original location on the 200th anniversary of Darwin's birth in 2009.

19. Yalta Memorial
(12 Responses to Tragedy)
Cromwell Gardens, SW7
Sculptor Angela Connor, Bronze, 1982

In February 1945 the Allied powers
met in Yalta to negotiate the future
shape of Europe. Soviet troops
were within 40 miles of Berlin and
Stalin was able to secure all his
major demands. This monument
commemorates those displaced
citizens returned to their country of
origin under the terms of the treaty,
often to face Soviet prosecution,
imprisonment and death. Just over a year after Yalta, Winston
Churchill gave his famous 'Iron Curtain' speech which was to
presage the beginning of the Cold War.

20. Béla Bartok (1881-1945)
Outside South Kensington Tube, SW7
Sculptor Imre Varga, Bronze, 2004, moved 2011

This monument is a copy of one
that stands in Budapest and
commemorates the influential
Hungarian composer and pianist, Bela
Bartok, who stayed in nearby Sydney
Place on his visits to London. He had
a great passions for the folk music
of Hungry and helped establish the
discipline of ethnomusicology. Bartok
was implacably hostile to fascism
and he and his family left for the US
in 1940, never to return. He died in
September 1945.

CHELSEA

King Charles II, p.315

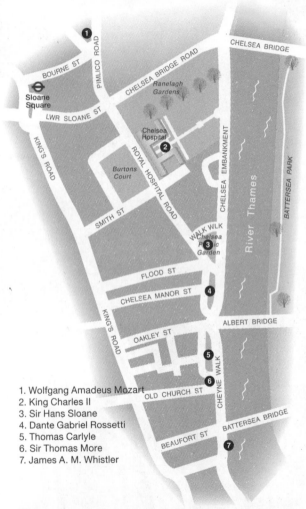

1. Wolfgang Amadeus Mozart
2. King Charles II
3. Sir Hans Sloane
4. Dante Gabriel Rossetti
5. Thomas Carlyle
6. Sir Thomas More
7. James A. M. Whistler

Chelsea

Chelsea was probably founded as a settlement by the Saxons and there are records of the manor of Chelsea which precede the Domesday Book. The manor was acquired by Henry VIII in 1536 and has enjoyed royal associations since that time. The monuments to Sir Thomas More and Sir Hans Sloane reflect the status of Chelsea as a residential area. Both men were buried in Chelsea Old Church – where More's monument stands – alongside many prominent figures of the 17th and 18th centuries.

Chelsea Royal Hospital was completed by Wren in 1694 and is a further reminder of the area's history of royal patronage and contains a monument to Charles II – after whom the King's Road is named. Amadeus Mozart stayed here as a child prodigy, when Chelsea was still a modest village and a monument to him stands in Orange Square. It was not until the 19th century that Chelsea ceased to be a separate village and was subsumed into the capital during a period of rapid urban expansion.

It was during the late-19th century that Chelsea became known as an artist's colony with painters Rossetti, Turner, Whistler and Singer Sargent, and writers George Meredith, Algernon Swinburne, Leigh Hunt and Thomas Carlyle among the artists to call Chelsea their home. The monuments to Rossetti and Carlyle stand on Cheyne Walk – where both men lived and where the Pre-Raphaelite movement was born. Further along and tucked away beside Battersea Bridge is the monument to James Whistler who was one of the founders of the Chelsea Arts Club. The monuments are a reminder of Chelsea's bohemian past but during the 20th century property prices increased and those with a talent for making money, rather than art, colonised the smart terraced houses.

1. Wolfgang Amadeus Mozart (1756-1791)

Orange Square, SW3
Sculptor Philip Jackson, Bronze, 1994

Wolfgang Amadeus Mozart was a rare example of a genius born into circumstances which developed his talents to their full potential. Mozart's father, Leopold, was a recognised musician and teacher and both young Wolfgang and his sister were given a rigorous musical education. The Mozart family toured Europe and Amadeus and his sister performed for many royal courts and spent time in both Paris and London.

In April 1764 the Mozart family briefly settled in London and Amadeus performed for George III (see p.6) on the fourth anniversary of his ascension to the throne. Mozart learned a great deal in London, being influenced by the Italian music that was so popular in the capital, and making a life-long friend of the composer Johann Christian Bach who was 30 at the time of their first meeting.

London's interest in 'the little German boy' began to wane and the family left England for the continent in August 1765. Wolfgang was never to return to these shores, making his reputation and establishing his genius in Vienna and Prague. Having spent his youth under the strict but loving control of his father, Mozart was to lead a troubled, chaotic but remarkably creative adult life. He died from a mysterious fever at the age of 35 in December 1791, leaving behind him over 600 musical compositions, from symphonies and operas to piano sonatas and quartets. This diminutive 20th-century monument depicts Mozart as the child prodigy during his time in London and stands not far from where the family lived in Chelsea.

2. King Charles II (1630-1685)

South Court, Chelsea Hospital, Royal Hospital Road, SW3
Sculptor Grinling Gibbons (1648-1721), Bronze, 1676 (erected 1692)

This monument to King Charles II in Roman costume was presented to the King by his loyal servant Tobias Rustat, who also presented a second equestrian statue which stands in Windsor Castle, and a third statue to commemorate his brother James II (see p.8). This marks Rustat as one of history's greatest royal sycophants, but his loyalty was to be rewarded when Charles II returned to the throne in May 1660. Rustat was given a well paid place at court and became a wealthy business man who funded many worthy causes, including Jesus College, Cambridge. The preference for Roman costume to depict British monarchs may stem from the idea in Roman Law of Divine Right, rather than British Common Law which defines the monarch's power as stemming from the will of his subjects. It was this difference in law which was at dispute during Charles I's trial. This interpretation is given further weight by the fact that the statue of Charles II shows him holding a baton, which is a symbol of imperial authority.

Every year on May 29th the statue is wreathed in oak leaves to commemorate the king's escape from the battle of Worcester in 1651, when it is said he hid in Boscobel Oak to avoid Cromwell's troops. Originally gilded, it was bronzed in 1782 and re-gilded in 2002. Charles II sired at least 14 illegitimate children, many of whom were given an aristocratic title. Both Camilla Parker-Bowles and Princess Diana descend from Charles II's illegitimate offspring. Prince William will be the first monarch since Queen Anne in 1714 to have a direct hereditary line to the Stuarts.

3. Sir Hans Sloane (1660-1753)

Chelsea Physic Garden, Royal Hospital Road, SW3
Sculptor John Michael Rysbrack (1693-1770), White marble, 1732

Hans Sloane was a scientist, naturalist and physician who gave this site to the Apothecaries' Society in 1722 on condition that they supply the Royal Society with specimens. If the establishment of this fine botanical garden had been Sloane's only achievement it would have been noteworthy, but this was only a small part of this incredible man's exploits.

During his long life Sloane travelled widely and amassed one of the greatest collections of plants, animals, antiquities, coins and many other objects of his time which became so large that it filled much of his house and required a full-time curator. Sloane opened his collection to many leading naturalists and so helped the development of many fields of natural science. On his death at the age of 93, his collection formed the founding core of the British Museum and later the Natural History Museum.

The original of this sculpture stands in the foyer of The British Museum in recognition of his importance in the founding of this great institution. Those with a love of chocolate should also be thankful to Hans Sloane. As a young man he journeyed to Jamaica and was introduced to the cocoa bean which he found unpalatable. It was Sloane who formulated a recipe for milk chocolate which was later to be used by the Cadbury brothers.

4. Dante Gabriel Rossetti (1828-1882)

Chelsea Embankment Gardens, SW3
Architect J. P. Seddon, Sculptor Ford Madox Brown
Bronze and Stone, 1887

Fountains are not really the subject of this book, but this ornate piece does include a fine bronze medallion representing Rossetti holding a quill pen, by his fellow Pre-Raphaelite and teacher Ford Madox Brown. Dante Gabriel Rossetti was born in 1828 to an illustrious family. His father was the exiled Italian patriot and scholar, Gabriele Rossetti and his sister, Christina, was a renowned poet.

Rossetti was both a painter and poet, whose work sought to recapture the richness and purity of medieval art. In both his paintings and his poetry his main theme was love, but he also tackled Christian subjects. As a student at the Royal Academy he met William Holman Hunt and John Millais, with whom he founded the Pre-Raphaelite Brotherhood in 1848.

As befits a romantic artist, Rossetti had many lovers. His most famous muse was Elizabeth Siddal, who became his wife in 1860. When she died of laudanum poisoning after only two years of marriage, Rossetti was consumed with grief and buried her at Highgate cemetery with the only draft of a book of his poems. Seven years later, and facing penury, Rossetti was granted permission to disinter her body and remove the book for publication.

After Elizabeth's death, Rossetti moved to 16 Cheyne Walk (close to this fountain) and established what he described as a 'temple to aestheticism'. This involved living with a great many exotic animals including a zebra, raccoon and kangaroo. He died in poverty in 1882. His paintings can still be seen in Tate Britain.

5. Thomas Carlyle (1795-1881)

Chelsea Embankment, SW3
Sculptor Sir Joseph Boehm, Bronze, 1882

This monument commemorates the Scottish-born historian and essayist Thomas Carlyle, who was one of the leading intellectual figures of the Victorian Era. In an age of reason and progress Carlyle struck a sceptical note, influenced by his Scottish Calvinist upbringing and his interest in German philosophy. His idiosyncratic style of writing captured the public imagination, contrasting as it did with the detached style of historians such as Macaulay.

Carlyle moved to London with his formidable wife in order to write his three volume history of the French Revolution which appeared in 1837. The first draft of the work was mistakenly burned by the maid servant of his friend John Stuart Mill – a mistake for which Mill paid his friend £100. A stone medallion on 24 Cheyne Row marks his long residence at the address where he established his reputation with philosophical works such as *Sartor Restartus* (1834), and *On Heroes and Hero Worship* (1841). Like his near neighbour, Rossetti, Carlyle was deeply affected by the death of his wife in 1866 and virtually disappeared from public life.

Ironically for a historian, history has not been kind to Carlyle. His praise of heroes as the driving force of history was to be discredited in the 20th century by the rise of Fascism and Soviet Communism, particularly when it was discovered that Hitler was a keen reader of Carlyle and kept a copy of his biography of Fredrick II by his bedside. The writer Henry James rather cruelly described the elderly Carlyle as 'the same old sausage, fizzing and sputtering in its own grease.'

6. Sir Thomas More (1478-1535)

Chelsea Embankment, SW3
Sculptor L. Cubitt Bevis, Bronze, 1969

This unusual painted statue is a contemporary work situated outside Chelsea Old Church where More worshiped and close to the farm house where he lived when Chelsea was still a rural hamlet. More was a scholar who as a young man wrote *Utopia* (1516) and became a close friend of Desiderius Erasmus and Hans Holbein. He considered joining the priesthood, but his talents and temperament led him to a political career within the court of Henry VIII. In 1518 he became a Privy Councillor and by 1529 he had risen to the position of Lord Chancellor.

Moore's fall came when Henry demanded changes that would sanction his divorce. He was an ardent Catholic and could not accommodate his master and so resigned in 1532. In April 1534 More was imprisoned for failing to swear to the Act of Succession and the Oath of Supremacy and in 1535 he was executed for treason. His final words were: 'The King's good servant, but God's First.' More has become a Catholic martyr and was canonised in 1935 – 400 years after his death. This statue was unveiled by one of his successors as Speaker of the House, Dr Henry King, in July 1969. History has been kind to More but several biographers have painted a more complex picture of the man. His religious faith not only inspired his defiance to the king, but led him to zealously persecute Lutherans when Lord Chancellor. He sent six dissenters to the stake and even interrogated a number in his own home. There is another monument to More in Holborn (see p.192).

7. James A. M. Whistler (1834-1903)
Battersea Bridge Gardens, SW3
Sculptor Nicholas Dimbleby, Bronze, 2005

James Whistler was born in Lowell Massachusetts, but at one time claimed to have been born in Russia, stating 'I shall be born when and where I want'. This was typical of Whistler's combative nature. In 1879 he sued Ruskin for libel and later published his collected writings under the title *The Gentle Art of Making Enemies* (1890).

It is true that Whistler spent part of his childhood in Russia, but he was largely brought up in America. After his father's death and a failed attempt to follow a military career, he left America to pursue his dream of becoming an artist. In Paris he perfected his technique and style, strongly influenced by Ingres, with a simple pallete and the use of line and form taking precedence over colour.

In 1859 Whistler left Paris in bad health and with mounting debts. Chelsea was a bohemian enclave at the time and he settled here, painting many pictures of the old Battersea Bridge and helping found the Chelsea Arts Club. In 1862 his portrait *The White Girl* helped secure his reputation and he enjoy great success for the last 20 years of his life, only marred by his legal action against Ruskin and the death of his wife, Beatrix Godwin, in 1888. By the time of Whistler's death his paintings were already being collected by major galleries. Examples of his work can be seen in Tate Britain, just a few miles from this recently erected monument.

GREENWICH

View from the Royal Observatory

321

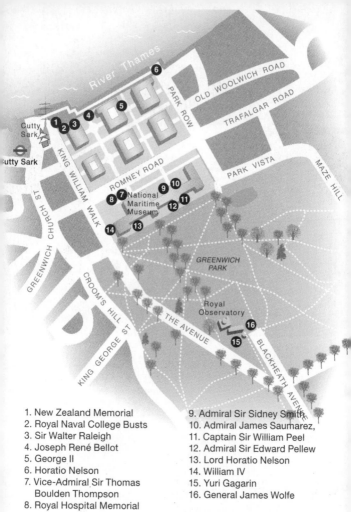

1. New Zealand Memorial
2. Royal Naval College Busts
3. Sir Walter Raleigh
4. Joseph René Bellot
5. George II
6. Horatio Nelson
7. Vice-Admiral Sir Thomas Boulden Thompson
8. Royal Hospital Memorial
9. Admiral Sir Sidney Smith
10. Admiral James Saumarez,
11. Captain Sir William Peel
12. Admiral Sir Edward Pellew
13. Lord Horatio Nelson
14. William IV
15. Yuri Gagarin
16. General James Wolfe

Greenwich

General James Wolfe sailed from Greenwich in 1759 for the Battle of Quebec that was to prove his last. His monument was unveiled at the highest point in Greenwich Park in 1930 and looks out upon a landscape that would astound the 18th-century warrior with the distant towers of Canary Wharf dominating the skyline. He would recognise the distant monument of George II who was a great admirer of the young Wolfe's exploits, but the monument to his other contemporary, Captain Cook, that formerly stood in the grounds of the National Maritime Museum has recently moved out of London.

It is the Hanoverian dynasty and the naval men who fought their battles that predominate in Greenwich. Admiral Nelson was the greatest of these and has three monuments, the finest being the bust inside Queen's House. William IV, the 'sailor king', was the best man at Nelson's wedding, but was prevented from taking command of a ship because of fears about his competence. His monument stands close to Nelson's in its own garden. Within the National Maritime Museum are three monuments to naval men who worked with Nelson – the Admirals Smith, Saumarez and Pellew – and one to the Victorian Captain Sir William Peel. At the front of the museum is a column in memory of Sir Thomas Thompson who was a protégé of Nelson's, and an obelisk to the 20,000 seamen patients of Greenwich Naval Hospital.

At the entrance to what used to be the Royal Naval College are reliefs commemorating many great sailors and closer to the Thames are Victorian obelisks, one in memory of those who lost their lives in the last significant war against the Maori and the other commemorating Joseph Bellot for his courage during the 1851 expedition to find Franklin. Sir Walter Raleigh is the only Tudor among the many Hanoverians but he is recent arrival, having been moved from Whitehall in 2002. The most recent monument commemorates the first man to see the Earth from outer space – the Soviet cosmonaut Yuri Gagarin.

1. New Zealand Memorial (1863-4)

River front near Greenwich Pier, SE10
Sculptor n/a, Granite

There were 13 wars during the 19th century which are collectively known as the New Zealand or Maori Wars. This obelisk commemorates those who lost their lives in one of the last battles of the conflict. The wars resulted from the gradual displacement of the native Maori tribes of New Zealand by white settlers. The 1840 Treaty of Waitangi protected the Maori lands but the settler occupation continued and in 1843 the first of the New Zealand Wars was fought. The Maori tribes were skilled warriors and during the Northern (1845-6), the Wellington-Hutt (1846) and Whanganui (1847-48) Wars, they fought the settlers to a standstill. Having achieved very little by military means, an uneasy peace was kept for 12 years until the growing settler population led to the First Taranaki War (1860-1), another unsuccessful attempt to drive the Maori from the land which led to stalemate after 12 months of fighting.

Until this time the settlers had largely fought unaided, but from 1860 they were assisted by Royal Naval ships based in the Australian colonies. This monument commemorates those who lost their lives during the Battle of Gate Pa, in April 1864, which was part of the last major war fought in New Zealand, finally driving the Maori from their land. The crews from HMS *Curacoa*, *Miranda*, *Esk* and *Harrier* were heavily involved in the bloody campaign which involved hand-to-hand fighting. The victory enforced the New Zealand Settlements Act of 1863 which confiscated about 4 million acres from the Maori.

324

2. Royal Naval College Busts
Greenwich Visitor Centre, Cutty Sark Gardens, SE10
(entrance to the Old Royal Naval College)
Date: 1874-75
Above the entrance to the Royal Naval College at the Greenwich
Visitor Centre are busts of great naval heroes:

A) George Anson (1697-1762) – He defeated the French off Cape
Finisterre in 1747 and was made a full admiral a year later. He
attained the position of admiral of the fleet in 1761.

B) Sir Francis Drake (1540-1596) – Drake voyaged to Africa where
he sold slaves and spent much of his career fighting the Spanish
fleet under the patronage of Elizabeth I. In 1579 he was the first to
sail the Pacific Ocean and was knighted in 1581. He is best known
for his successful battle against the Spanish Armada in 1588.

C) Captain James Cook (1728-79) – see p.88.

D) Admiral Charles Howard (1536-1624) – Lord Howard of
Effingham was an admiral and courtier who, along with Drake,
played a key role in the defeat of the Spanish Armada.

E) Robert Blake (1598-1657) – He fought for the Parliamentarians
during the Civil War and later did battle with the Dutch and
Spanish. Blake was the first English Admiral to keep a fleet at sea
during the winter and developed several naval techniques.

F) Vice-Admiral John Benbow (1653-1702) – Benbow had a
reputation for his reckless command against pirates, the French
and the Spanish. While serving in the West Indies in 1702 he
suffered a mutiny while chasing four French vessels and was fatally
injured. He became known as Brave Benbow for his heroic death.

G) John Montagu, Fourth Earl of Sandwich (1718-1792) – Montagu was first lord of the Admiralty during the American Revolution and promoted Britain's naval exploration. An inveterate gambler, he would eat meat between bread while at the gaming tables and so gave his name to the sandwich.

H) Admiral Lord George Rodney (1719-1792) – Perhaps the greatest of Britain's 18th-century admirals, he distinguished himself against the French and Spanish during the Seven Years War and the American War of Independence. In 1781 he became Vice-Admiral of Great Britain.

I) Admiral Adam Duncan (1731-1804) – Duncan's defeat of the Dutch at Camperdown in 1797 was one of Britain's great naval victories for which he was given a baronet. Duncan was a mentor to Nelson who kept a portrait of him in his cabin.

J) Admiral Cuthbert Collingwood (1748-1810) – He fought under Howe and Jervis during the first naval engagements of the French Revolutionary wars and was made vice-admiral in 1799. Collingwood was second-in-command at Trafalgar.

K) Admiral Richard Howe (1726-1799) – Howe played a major part in the Seven Years War and the American War of Independence against the French. Howe's relief of Gibraltar in 1782 gained him the post of Lord of the Admiralty. He successfully commanded the first naval battle against revolutionary France in 1794.

L) Horatio Nelson (1758-1805) – see p.17.

M) Admiral John Jervis (1735-1823) – Jervis commanded the Mediterranean fleet in 1795, won a crushing victory against the Spanish off Cape St Vincent in 1797 and blockaded the French fleet at Brest in 1799. As first Lord of the Admiralty he did much to fight corruption in the navy.

3. Sir Walter Raleigh (1552-1618)

Outside Greenwich Visitor Centre, Cutty Sark Gardens, SE10
Sculptor William Macmillan, Bronze, 2002, unveiled in Whitehall 1959

As a young man, Walter Raleigh embarked upon a naval expedition which was little more than piracy. Later, as a soldier, he crushed a Catholic rebellion in Ireland which earned him a knighthood and brought him into the court of Queen Elizabeth. He became one of her favourites and used his royal influence to shamelessly enrich himself. Raleigh, using royal patronage, embarked on an expedition to the New World between 1584-89. The adventure failed to colonise America but brought the potato and tobacco to Europe. It is said that when Raleigh first smoked, his servant doused him with ale, thinking he was on fire.

Raleigh's fall began when Elizabeth discovered his affair with one of her ladies-in-waiting. He was sent to the Tower and when released banished on another expedition. The Queen died in 1603 and Raleigh was even more out of favour with King James I. He was sent to the Tower, where he began his book *History of the World*. After 12 years, Raleigh was sent on a further expedition to South America, but failed to return with the promised treasure and was executed in 1618. As was the custom in Tudor times his preserved head was given to his wife – a grisly token which she kept until her death nearly 30 years later.

This monument was erected over 350 years after Raleigh's execution. The delay may be explained by the complexity of Raleigh's character; he was both courageous and brutal, an embodiment of renaissance culture and a flagrant opportunist.

4. Joseph René Bellot (1826-1853)

River front near Greenwich Pier, SE10
Sculptor Philip Hardwick, Red Aberdeen granite, 1855

Joseph René Bellot is a name that has largely been erased from the history books. The obelisk that stands outside the Maritime Museum commemorates his role in one of the expeditions in search of John Franklin (see p.95). Franklin set forth in May 1845 to navigate the Northwest Passage, with over 180 men and two well stocked ships. He and his men disappeared and the search to find them captured the Victorian imagination, with 30 rescue expeditions undertaken between 1847 and 1880.

Joseph René Bellot was second-in-command of *The Prince Albert*, which set sail from Aberdeen in May 1851 under the captaincy of William Kennedy. At one stage in their adventures, when attempting to enter Port Leopold, Kennedy was left stranded. Bellot established winter quarters at Batty Bay and then returned to find Kennedy who had fended for himself on the ice for five weeks. William Kennedy's account of their unsuccessful expedition to find Franklin gave a good account of Bellot's actions and he was promoted to lieutenant. He immediately embarked on a further expedition to find Franklin, but died when crossing ice in August 1853 at Wellington Channel. The stone used for the obelisk originates from Aberdeen, from where Kennedy and Bellot sailed in 1851.

It was later discovered that Franklin and his men met a terrible fate when their ships became trapped in the ice and they were forced to abandon them, eventually starving to death. Joseph Bellot also has a crater on the moon in his name.

5. George II (1683-1760)
Old Royal Naval College Gardens, SE10
Sculptor J. M. Rysbrack, Marble, 1735
It is fitting that this much eroded statue is made from marble captured from a French ship in the Mediterranean as its subject was a military man, whose greatest personal achievements were his military exploits against the French.

George was the last British monarch to lead his men into battle and spent much of his time talking of military matters and explaining in details his military achievements. His last battle was at Dettingen in 1743 which was the first battle for the young James Wolfe (see p.340), whose statue now looks down upon his king from Greenwich Park. George's wife, Caroline of Ansbach (see page 299), is said to have been by far her husband's intellectual superior and to have had a very great influence upon his decision-making. The situation was recognised by politicians at the time who sought to win favour with the Queen in order to influence the King. After her death in 1737, George II proved an ineffectual political strategist – failing to manipulate parliament (as his son was later able to). It was on the battlefield that his reign had its greatest successes, with the defeat of the Jacobites at Culloden in 1746 and the triumphs of Clive in India and Wolfe in North America. The latter part of his reign marked the ascendancy of Pitt the Elder in parliament and it was to Pitt's leadership that these victories were credited. George II died in October 1760. There is also a statue to him in Golden Square (see p.32).

6. Horatio Nelson (1758-1805)

Outside The Trafalgar Tavern, Park Row, SE10

Sculptor Lesley Pover, Bronze, 2005

This monument to Nelson (see p.17) looks out across the Thames and is remarkable for the ample dimensions attributed to the naval man's breeches, prompting one wit to remark 'so that's what they mean by Nelson's column'. The monument was commissioned by the Trafalgar Tavern and was unveiled by that other great Englishman, the interior designer Lawrence Llewellyn-Bowen.

7. Vice-Admiral Sir Thomas Boulden Thompson (1766-1828)

Old Royal Naval College, SE10, Stone

This stone column commemorates one of the great naval men of the Napoleonic Wars, who went to sea at the age of 12, was a lieutenant at 16 and took command of his first ship at 20. It was at the Battle of the Nile on 1st August 1798 that the 50-gun *Leander*, with Thompson at the helm, played a major part in the defeat of the French. The success of the campaign was marred by the later capture of the *Leander* and Thompson was court-martialed for the loss of his ship, but quickly acquitted and awarded a knighthood. In the spring of 1799 he was given command of the much larger ship, *Bellona*, and took part in the blockade of the French at Brest in 1801, later joining Nelson for his attack on the Danish fleet. Thompson did some harm to his reputation when he ran the Bellona aground within reach of the Danish guns, resulting in considerable casualties. It was the courage Thompson showed under fire and the loss of his own leg in battle that saved his reputation.

Thompson's career at sea was over, but he did serve as a naval administrator and was made a rear-admiral in 1809. He worked as a treasurer for Greenwich Hospital for many years and also represented Rochester in parliament from 1807 to 1818. Thompson was married to the eldest daughter of the pioneer of Sunday Schools, Robert Raikes (see p.126). This stone column, in the former grounds of the hospital where Thompson worked for many years, gives an account of his deeds. The names of the two ships he commanded, the *Leander* and *Bellona*, are engraved on either side of the column.

8. Royal Hospital Memorial (1749-1869)

Old Royal Naval College, SE10
Sculptor n/a, Portland stone, 1892

The Greenwich Royal Hospital stood on this site from 1694 until 1869 to provide residential care for seamen wounded in battle. The gardens of the hospital also served as a burial ground for former inmates and over 20,000 Marines and Royal Navy men are thought to have been interred here. Several of the more prominent stones are still to be seen just a little further back from the road and close to the National Maritime Museum. Many of the remains were moved from the grounds when the hospital became the Royal Naval College, and reinterred at East Greenwich Pleasaunce where a tablet was placed in their memory. Among the famous naval men to have seen out their days here was Vice-Admiral Hardy who was Nelson's second-in-command on board the Victory.

9. Admiral Sir Sidney Smith (1764-1840)

Upper foyer, National Maritime Museum, SE10
Sculptor Thomas Kirk
Marble, 1845

Sidney Smith joined the Navy at the age of 12 and saw action in the American War of Independence. In 1780, at Cape St Vincent, Smith demonstrated his bravery and continued to distinguish himself against the French at the Battles of Chesapeake and Saintes. Following the Versailles treaty of 1783, Smith served as a commander with the Swedish Navy in 1790 and was given a knighthood by the Swedish king for helping to defeat the Russians. Six British officers had died on the Russian side which made Smith an unpopular figure among his fellow officers.

When war recommenced with France, Smith was given his own ship and special orders and successfully lifted the Siege of Acre (Syria) in 1799 – helping to drive the French from Egypt. He returned to England in 1801 but his achievements were overshadowed by those of Nelson at Copenhagen. After Trafalgar, Smith served in a number of roles in the Mediterranean; beating the French at the Battle of Maida, accompanying Admiral Duckworth in negotiations with the Turks in February 1807 and organising the passage of the Portuguese fleet to Brazil to avoid capture by the French in 1808. He even lent his services to Wellington at Waterloo – making provision for the treatment of the wounded and negotiating the return of King Louis XVIII to Paris.

Smith spent the final years of his life in Paris to avoid his English creditors. Although under-valued by the Royal Navy, Napoleon accurately said of him, 'That man made me miss my destiny'.

10. Admiral James Saumarez, 1st Baron de Saumarez (1757-1836)

Upper foyer, National Maritime Museum, SE10
Sculptor Sir John Steell, Marble, 1854

James Saumarez was born in 1757, in Guernsey, to an established naval family. He began his career at the tender age of 13 and rapidly gained promotion. He commanded his first ship in 1778 when his senior officers were injured and was promoted to commander in 1781 for his bravery during the Battle of Dogger Bank. His actions contributed significantly to Admiral Rodney's victory over the French at the Battle of Saintes in April 1782. He played a major part in the naval battles against revolutionary France and was knighted for his capture of the French frigate *La Reunion* in 1793. In 1795 Saumarez took command of the 74-gun *Orion* and fought under Admiral Jervis at the Battle of Cape St Vincent and the Blockade of Cadiz and helped secure Nelson's victory at the Battle of the Nile in 1798, where he was wounded.

Having taken command of the 80-gun *Caesar*, Saumarez was given responsibility for restraining the French fleet at Brest and was made Rear Admiral for his services in 1801. One of his greatest naval triumphs was the defeat of a much larger French and Spanish fleet in July 1801 at the Battle of Algeciras. As the threat from Napoleonic France began to lessen Saumarez provided valuable service in the naval conflict with Russia in the Baltic between 1809 and 1814. The Treaty of Vienna marked the end of Saumarez's active career but he went on to serve in the Admiralty and was made a Vice-Admiral of Britain in 1821. Unlike many of his naval contemporaries, Saumarez died peacefully in his bed in 1836, having been awarded a peerage a few years earlier.

11. Captain Sir William Peel (1824-1858)

Upper foyer,
National Maritime Museum, SE10
Sculptor William Theed, Marble, 1860

Sir William Peel, was the third son of Prime Minister, Sir Robert Peel (see p.63). Peel joined the navy in 1838 and attained the rank of captain by the age of 24. In 1849 he took leave of absence to travel in the Middle East and Africa and published an account of his travels *A Ride Through the Nubian Desert.* Peel resumed his naval career in 1852 and was soon posted to the Crimea, where he established a reputation as a fearless and daring officer. His advice to his soldiers to 'disregard fire in the battery, by always walking with head up and shoulders back', was not sensible, but earned him the respect of his troops. He was awarded a Victoria Cross for his disposal of a live shell at Sebastopol in October 1854 (the medal is still on display at the National Maritime Museum). Peel went on to play a major part in the Battle of Inkerman in November 1854, but it is not surprising that his courage and disinclination to duck resulted in severe injury in June 1855. He soon recovered and went on to serve in India, playing a part in the Relief of Lucknow where he was again badly wounded. He did not return home but was struck down with smallpox at the age of only 33 while recovering from his injuries.

Throughout his time in the Crimea, Peel was ably assisted by his ADC, midshipman Edward St John Daniel, who rescued his captain on several occasions and who was also awarded the VC. Daniel was stripped of the medal in 1861 for what was described as 'taking indecent liberties' and later served in the New Zealand Wars (see p.324). He died of natural causes on Hokitika Island in 1868, just ten years after the captain he served so well.

12. Admiral Sir Edward Pellew, Lord Exmouth (1757-1833)
Upper foyer, National Maritime Museum, SE10
Sculptor Patrick MacDowell, Marble, 1846

Edward Pellew joined the Royal Navy at only 13 and rose to prominence at a time when Britain was first fighting revolution in America and then confronting Napoleonic naval power. He first distinguished himself in the Battle of Valcour Island in 1776 and later fought with General John Burgoyne (see p.91) at Saratoga, where he was captured and repatriated. In 1793 Pellew was given command of the 36-gun *Nymphe* and quickly made his reputation by capturing a French frigate and the secret naval code on board.

The dying French captain had attempted to swallow the code, but ate the wrong paper. Pellew was knighted for his capture of the ship and its secrets and given command of the much larger 76-gun *Indefatigable* in 1795. It was at the command of this giant ship that Pellew inflicted great damage upon the French fleet.

One of Pellew's greatest acts of heroism was not in battle, but rescuing passengers from a grounded ship near Plymouth. Pellew was a very strong swimmer and swam to the stranded ship with a line which was used to rescue the passengers. His courage earned him a baronetcy. In 1802 he became an MP, but continued his career, commanding vessels in the East Indies between 1804-09. In 1816 Pellew led an Anglo-Dutch fleet against the Barbary state that was trading in slaves. Their bombardment of Algiers was to secure the release of over a thousand Christian slaves. A gold-plated trophy was given to Pellew by his officers to commemorate this action – it can be seen in one of the glass cases close to where this statue stands today. The Pellew Group of barren Australian islands are named after him.

13. Lord Horatio Nelson (1758-1805)

Queen's House, Greenwich, SE10
Sculptor Sir Francis Leggatt Chantrey
Marble, 1835

This is one of the four busts Chantrey made for Greenwich Hospital. The other busts were of the admirals Duncan, Howe and Vincent. There are several monuments to Nelson in Greenwich but his most important monument is, of course, in Trafalgar Square (see p.17).

14. William IV (1765-1837)

King William Walk, Greenwich Park, SE10
Sculptor Samuel Nixon
Foggit Tor granite, 1844 (in the City), moved here 1938

William IV was known as the 'sailor King', because he spent much of his life in the navy. William saw limited active service during the American War of Independence and in the West Indies but spent much of his career on land, as Lord High Admiral, in whose uniform he is commemorated. When William insisted on commanding the Channel Fleet in 1828, there was such protest that he resigned his position.

William IV's main achievement as king was not being like his brother, George IV (see p.13). His reign witnessed the passing of the Reform Bill (1832), the abolition of slavery in the colonies (1833) and reform of the Poor Laws (1835), but the changes were driven by politicians and popular political movements – the monarchy becoming a symbolic, rather than actively political institution. William's only intervention into politics was his dismissal of Melbourne's Whig ministry in 1834. In the following elections, Melbourne was returned to power and this proved the last time a British monarch dismissed a government. William sired ten children by his long-term mistress before coming to the throne. As a King he proved less fertile, his two daughters by Queen Adelaide died in infancy. On his death in 1837 the crown passed to his niece, Victoria. The House of Hanover would not permit a female monarch and so William's reign marked the end of the royal family's direct link with the German Principality.

15. Yuri Gagarin (1934-1968)

The Royal Observatory,
Greenwich Park, SE10
Sculptor Anatoly Novikov
Zinc-alloy, 2013

Yuri Gagarin was the first man to look down upon our planet from outer space when his Soviet space craft orbited the earth on 12th April 1961.

Gagarin was not just a hero of the Soviet Union and when he visited London, just months after his successful flight, vast crowds came out the greet him. He was too valuable to be allowed into space again, but tragically died in 1968 while testing a MiG-15 fighter plane. This monument was a gift from the Russian space agency to mark the 50th anniversary of his flight and was unveiled by his daughter who, unlike her father, lived to see the US moon landings in 1969 and the fall of the Soviet Union. It was temporarily placed on Pall Mall, but has now found permanent residence in the grounds of the Royal Observatory.

16. General James Wolfe (1727-1759)
Greenwich Park, SE10 (next to The Royal Observatory)
Sculptor Dr Tait Mackenzie (1867-1938), Bronze, 1930

The statue of James Wolfe stands at the highest point in Greenwich Park. Wolfe joined the army at only 16, and took part in his first battle at Dettingen, against the French, in 1743. The courageous young soldier soon made a name for himself and gained the favour of George II (see p.330) who was greatly impressed with accounts of Wolfe's exploits. Wolfe saw action against the Spanish and Bourbon armies and put an end to the Jacobite claim to the throne at Culloden in 1746.

James Wolfe embarked from Greenwich in 1759 to strengthen Britain's claims upon Canada against those of the French monarchy. On arrival, in order to surprise the French force, Wolfe led his army over the cliffs and a fierce battle commenced on the Plains of Abraham, where Wolfe took a bullet and died. The French were defeated and General Montcalm met his end the following day.

Wolfe's body was embalmed and returned to Greenwich. He is buried at nearby St Alfege's Church in the family vault. There is an impressive monument within Westminster Abbey which was erected 13 years after his death. This imposing monument was presented by the Canadian people in 1930 and was unveiled by the Marquis de Montcalm, a descendant of the vanquished French general. Wolfe's victory secured Canada for a great many hardy Scottish migrants from whom the sculptor Dr Robert Tait Mackenzie could count himself a descendent.

DISTANT
AND ALONE

*There are many interesting
monuments that stand alone
and usually have some particular
connection with their location.
The isolation of these commemorative
statues is not indicative of the
obscurity of their subjects, for
among notables reviewed here can be
found William Gladstone, Sigmund
Freud and Karl Marx.*

Richard Green, see p.374

DISTANT & ALONE

Central

1. Sir John Cass
2. Children of the Kindertransport
3. Peter Pan
4. Samuel Pepys
5. Site of Scaffold – Trinity Square
6. Emperor Trajan

North

7. Charles Dibdin
8. Sigmund Freud
9. Karl Heinrich Marx
10. Sir Hugh Myddleton
11. Edgar Allan Poe
12. Oliver Tambo *(off map)*
13. Sir Sydney Waterlow
14. Isaac Watt
15. John Wesley

North-west

16. Sir John Betjeman
17. Richard Cobden
18. Edward Onslow Ford
19. Anne Frank
20. Sir Isaac Newton
21. Robert Stephenson

West

22. Isambard Kingdom Brunel
23. Thomas Cubitt
24. Charles II
25. Charles Dickens
26. Henry Vassall-Fox,
    3rd Baron Holland
27. William Hogarth *(off map)*
28. Andrea Palladio &
    Inigo Jones *(off map)*
29. Ladbroke Grove Rail
    Disaster Memorial
30. General Francisco
    de Miranda
31. Cardinal John Henry Newman
32. Mrs Sarah Siddons
33. St Volodymyr the Great

South-west

34. Marc Bolan
35. John Colet
36. Edward VII *(off map)*
37. Johnny Haynes
38. William Huskisson
39. Sir John Everett Millais
40. Peter Osgood
41. Fred Perry *(off map)*
42. Peter Scott
43. Haile Selassie *(off map)*
44. Sir Henry Tate *(off map)*
45. Tradescant Family Memorial

South-east

46. Edward Alleyn (off map)
47. Robert Aske (off map)
48. Dr Robert Bentley Todd
     (off map)
49. Ernest Bevin
50. Colonel Samuel
     Bourne Bevington
51. William & Catherine Booth
     (off map)
52. Circle Dray Horse
53. Crimean Memorial (off map)
54. Brass Crosby
55. Thomas Guy
56. Guy the Gorilla (off map)
57. Alfred the Great
58. Peter the Great
59. James Hulbert
60. Sir Leonard Hutton
61. Captain Christopher Jones
62. Alexander McLeod (off map)
63. John Keats
64. William R. Morris,
     Viscount Nuffield
65. Joseph Paxton (off map)
66. Dr Salter –
     Dr Salter's Daydream
67. James Walker
68. Duke of Wellington (off map)

East

69. Queen Alexandra
70. Clement Attlee
71. Bethnal Green Memorial
72. General William Booth
73. The Champions (off map)
74. Michael von Clemm
75. Edward VII
76. Sir Robert Geffrye
77. William Gladstone
78. Richard Green
79. George Lansbury
80. Robert Milligan
81. John Rennie
82. Bradley Stone (off map)
83. Virginia Settlers Memorial
84. Sir Corbet Woodall (off map)

Outskirts

85. Sir John Alcock &
     Sir Arthur Whitten Brown
     (off map)
86. Queen Anne (off map)
87. Job Henry Drain (off map)
88. Bobby Moore (off map)
89. Bernardo O'Higgins (off map)

CENTRAL

1. Sir John Cass (1661-1718)
31 Jewry Street, EC3
Sculptor Roubiliac, 1751

This statue to the wealthy merchant, Alderman and philanthropist, stands outside the Sir John Cass Foundation which he founded in 1748. The original monument is now in the Guildhall, this is a copy that was installed in 1998.

2. Children of the Kindertransport

Liverpool St Station, EC2
Sculptor Frank Meisler, 2003

This monument commemorates the nearly 10,000 Jewish children that were granted refuge in Britain after the terrible events of *Kristallnacht* in November 1938. The children arrived by train at Liverpool Station from Holland – one of their number was the sculptor, Frank Meisler.

3. Peter Pan

Great Ormond Street Hospital, WC1N
Sculptor Diarmud Byron O'Connor, 2000

Great Ormond Street Children's hospital is partly funded from the proceeds of J. M. Barrie's most famous work. This statue of the boy 'who never grew up' was erected in the millenium year and since 2005 has company with the addition of Tinkerbell.

4. Samuel Pepys (1633-1703)

Seething Lane Gardens, EC3
Sculptor Karin Jonzen, 1983

Samuel Pepys was a naval administrator who would have disappeared into the dustbin of history had he not kept a diary which chronicled his life in 17th century London. Pepys lived in Seething Lane and it is in this garden that he recounts burying state papers and his parmesan cheese when the Great Fire of London threatened.

5. Site of Scaffold – Trinity Square

Trinity Place, EC3

Trinity Square has a memorial area which marks where prisoners from the Tower of London were executed between 1388 and 1747. The square also contains a more recent memorial to merchant seamen who died in the two World Wars (see picture opposite) and close by is a statue of Emperor Trajan (see next page).

6. Emperor Trajan (53-117)

Trinity Place, EC3; Bronze, 1980

Close to Trinity Square is the only statue of a Roman Londoner in the form of Emperor Trajan. The monument was reclaimed from a scrap yard by the vicar of All Hallows' Church and erected here in 1980.

NORTH

7. Charles Dibdin (1745-1814)

St Martin's Gardens, NW1; Stone, 1889

The actor, theatre impresario and writer of sea songs, Charles Dibdin, was a resident of Camden. He was a popular public figure in his day and his patriotic songs did much to inspire jingoism during the Napoleonic Wars. He was granted a pension for his services but died in relative poverty.

8. Sigmund Freud (1856-1939)

Adelaide Rd, NW3

Sculptor Oscar Nemon, Bronze, 1970

Sigmund Freud was the father of psychoanalysis, which attempts to explain the complex forces that underlie human personality. He brought into the public realm ideas of the subconscious, sexuality, ego and repression that were to profoundly shape the 20th century and a method of treating psychological problems through analysis that was to spawn a wide array of treatments. Freud spent much of his life as professor of neurology at Vienna University, but as a Jew he was forced to flee Nazi Austria in 1938. He spent his last years at 20 Maresfield Gardens which is close to this monument and is now home to the Freud Museum.

9. Karl Heinrich Marx (1818-1883)

Highgate Cemetery, NW6

Sculptor Laurence Bradshaw, Bronze, 1956

Karl Marx was a German philosopher who spent much of his life in exile in London, supported by his wealthy, businessman friend

Friedrich Engels. Marx devised a way of understanding politics that identified antagonistic economic classes and regarded the conflict between these classes as being the primary engine for progress through revolution. This predetermined historical process would ultimately lead to a utopian communist state. Marx died in London long before his ideas were adopted during the Russian revolution and embodied in the Soviet state. This monument to Marx was unveiled at the height of the Cold War in 1956 and long before the fall of the Berlin Wall, which marked the end of Communism as a powerful force in world history.

10. Sir Hugh Myddleton (1560-1631)

Islington Green, N1

Sculptor John Thomas, Marble, 1862

In the early 17th century Myddleton built an underground water system which brought fresh water into London from Hertfordshire to supply the capital's growing population. The project took four years to complete and was one of the largest engineering achievements of its time. This now eroded monument was unveiled by William Gladstone in 1862.

11. Edgar Allan Poe (1809-49)

Fox Reformed, Stoke Newington High St, N16

Sculptor Ralph Perrott, Stone, 2011

The famous American novelist, poet and man of letters spent three years of his short and troubled life as a student in Stoke Newington before returning to America. Poe was born in Boston to actor parents, but his father abandoned the family and his mother soon died, leaving him in the care of John and Francis Allan from Richmond. He had a difficult relationship with his new guardians and John Allan withdrew financial support from Poe, forcing him to abandon his studies at the University of Virginia. He soon found success with his narrative poem *The Raven*. Poe's subsequent dark, gothic tales of horror, in some way mirrored his own difficult life which involved the death of two wives and his own mysterious death at the age of 40, having been found delirious on the streets of Baltimore. This bust sits on the front of the *Fox Reformed* wine bar in Stoke Newington and was unveiled by the actor Steven Berkoff.

12. Oliver Tambo (1917-1993)

Albert Road Recreation Ground, Muswell Hill, N22

Sculptor Ian Walters, Bronze, 2007

Tambo was a close friend of Nelson Mandela who succeeded him as President of the African National Congress. He spent 30 years in exile from South Africa in this area of London and died just as Apartheid ended.

13. Sir Sydney Waterlow (1822-1906)

Waterlow Park, N19

Sculptor Frank Taubman, Bronze, 1900

Sir Sydney Waterlow inherited the family printing company and later made a fortune in banking. He worked as a councillor, member of parliament and served as Lord Mayor of London. Waterlow gave his 30-acre estate to the London County Council in 1889 as a 'garden for the gardenless'. His statue stands in the park that bears his name.

14. Isaac Watt (1674-1748)

Abney Park Cemetery, N16

Sculptor Edward Hodges Baily, Stone, 1845

Watts was a famous theologian and hymn writer. As a non-conformist he was unable to study at Oxford or Cambridge and instead attended the Dissenting Academy in Stoke Newington and spent much of his life in this area after his studies.

15. John Wesley (1703-1791)

49 City Road Chapel, N1

Sculptor J. Adams Acton, Bronze, 1891

This monument to the founder of Methodism stands in the City Road Chapel which was built under Wesley's instruction. There is another monument to Wesley in the grounds of St Paul's Cathedral (see p.211).

NORTH WEST

16. Sir John Betjeman (1906-1984)

St Pancras Station, N1
Sculptor Martin Jennings, 2007

John Betjeman was very much an Englishman, writing poetry about Ovaltine and Sturmey-Archer bicycles. He became Poet Laureate in 1972. This fine monument stands in St Pancras Station which Betjamin helped to save from developers as the founder of the Victorian Society. Betjeman is depicted in characteristic attire, holding his hat, and looking towards the station's fine roof. Words of his poetry are inscribed around his feet.

16

17. Richard Cobden (1804-1865)

Camden High Street, NW1

Sculptors W & T. Wills

Sicilian Marble, 1868

Richard Cobden was a wealthy calico trader
who formed the Anti-Corn-Law League (see
Robert Peel p.63 and Lord Bentinck p.257).
Once the Corn Laws were repealed, Cobden
became a Liberal MP and a fierce opponent
of Palmerston's aggressive foreign policy.
Napoleon III was the largest contributor to this
monument, which is now very badly eroded.

18. Edward Onslow Ford (1852-1901)

Abbey Road, NW8

Sculptor A. C. Lacches, Bronze, 1903

Ford was one of the most successful sculptors of the Victorian era.
His memorial was erected by friends and admirers and stands by
the Abbey Road pedestrian crossing made famous by *The Beatles*.
Ford was responsible for many fine monuments including his
statue of Rowland Hill in the City of London (see p.223) and several
fine busts in Westminster Abbey (see p.80).

19. Anne Frank (1929-1945)

British Library, NW1

Sculptor Doreen Kern, Bronze, 1999

This bust was unveiled in the courtyard
of the British Library to mark the 70th
anniversary of Anne Frank's birth. Her vivid
account of the Frank family's life in hiding
during the Nazi occupation of Amsterdam
was first published in 1947. She was killed
in a German concentration camp just before
the war's end.

20. Sir Isaac Newton (1642-1727)

British Library, NW1

Sculptor Eduardo Paolozzi, 1995

This monument to Newton takes as its inspiration William Blake's depiction of the mathematician planning the universe. There is another monument to Newton in Leicester Square (see p.25).

21. Robert Stephenson (1803-59)

Euston Station, NW1

Sculptor Baron Marochetti, 1871

Robert Stephenson was one of the great 19th-century engineers. This monument stands in Euston Station, the terminus for the London to Birmingham railway for which Stephenson was the chief engineer. He also helped his father, George, complete the famous Rocket locomotive.

WEST

22. Isambard Kingdom Brunel (1806-1859)

Paddington Station, W2

Sculptor John Doubleday, Bronze, 1982

Paddington station was designed by Brunel as the grand terminus of the Great Western Railway and was completed in 1854. This recent monument to Brunel can be found on platform 1. A larger monument to the great engineer is on the Embankment (see p.119).

23. Thomas Cubitt (1788-1855)

Denbigh Street, SW1

Sculptor William Fawkes, Bronze, 1995

Cubitt was the most important and successful builder of the 19th century. He was responsible for the design and building of many areas of London, including parts of Bloomsbury, Belgravia and much of Pimlico – where this monument stands.

24. Charles II (1630-1685)

Soho Square, W1

Sculptor Caius Gabriel Cibber, 1681

Carved by Caius Gabriel Cibber (also responsible for the bas reliefs on The Monument), this statue of Charles II once stood in the centre of the square. A decline in the condition of the garden in the mid-19th century saw its removal. The monument came into the hands of W.S. Gilbert the lyricist, whose widow returned it to the square in 1938.

25. Charles Dickens (1812-1870)

Ferguson House, Marylebone High Street, W1

Sculptor Eastcourt J. Clark, 1960

Dickens (see p.46) lived in a house that stood at the junction of Marylebone High Street and Marylebone Road for many years. Several of his novels were written here including *David Copperfield* and *A Christmas Carol*. On the wall of Ferguson House can be found this relief featuring the author in the company of characters from his novels.

26. Henry Vassall-Fox, 3rd Baron Holland (1773-1840)

Holland Park, W11

Sculptor G. F. Watts & Edgar Boehm, 1926

On the north side of the park, Lord Holland's seated statue rises from the centre of a small pond. Educated at Eton and Oxford, Lord Holland was a major figure in Whig politics in the early 19th century. His uncle was the great Whig orator Charles James Fox (see p.235).

27. William Hogarth (1697-1764)

Chiswick High Rd, junction with Turnham Green Rd, W4

Sculptor Jim Mathieson, Bronze, 2001

This monument commemorates Hogarth's long residence in Chiswick and depicts the artist with his dog, Trump. See p.28 for more about Hogarth.

28. Andrea Palladio (1508-80) & Inigo Jones (1573-1652)

Chiswick House, W4

Sculptor Michael Rysbrack, Stone, 1730

Chiswick House is a palladian masterpiece designed by one of its finest English exponents, Lord Burlington. The external staircase to the house has a figure of the founder of this style of architecture, Andrea Palladio, to the left. One of his English devotees, Inigo Jones, is to be found to the right. The Inigo Jones Gateway stands within the grounds of Chiswick House, having been bought by Lord Burlington in 1738 from its original location of Beaufort House which was being demolished.

29. Ladbroke Grove Rail Disaster Memorial

Memorial Garden, Canal Way, W10

Sculptor Richard Healy, Stone, 2001

This stone tablet stands close to the site of the Ladbroke Grove Rail Disaster which killed 31 people on 5th October 1999. The ashes of two of the victims are buried beneath this simple monument.

30. General Francisco de Miranda (1750-1816)
Corner of Fitzroy St & Grafton Way, W1
Sculptor Rafael de la Cova, Bronze, 1990

Miranda was born in Spanish occupied Venezuela and after serving in the Spanish navy fought for Venezuelan independence. Miranda spent 14 years in exile in London and lived in this house for much of that time. After a failed coup attempt in his homeland he was captured by the Spanish and died while in prison in Cadiz.

31. Cardinal John Henry Newman (1801-1890)
Brompton Oratory, SW3
Sculptor Léon-Joseph Chavalliaud, 1896

The Cardinal's statue is a small feature of this High Renaissance, Early Baroque church (consecrated in 1884) which was the first Catholic church to be built in London since the Reformation. Newman began his career as an Anglican churchman, but was always trying to move towards Rome and played a key role in the Oxford Movement which attempted to reintroduce many aspects of Catholic worship to the Anglican Church. Newman suffered a spiritual crisis which forced him to abandon his position in Oxford in 1843 and eventually join the Catholic Church in 1845. He was to serve the Catholic faith with renewed conviction, becoming a cardinal in 1889.

32. Mrs Sarah Siddons (1755-1831)

Paddington Green, W2
Sculptor Léon-Joseph Chavalliaud
Marble, 1897

Sarah Kemble was born into an theatrical family and began her acting career in the provinces. By the mid-1780s Sarah Siddons was an established actor and socialite, her portrait painted by both Gainsborough and Reynolds. Reynold's painting was the inspiration for this white marble sculpture which was unveiled by another great actor, Sir Henry Irving (see p.24).

33. St Volodymyr the Great (960-1015)

Outside Holland Park Station, W11
Sculptor Leonard Moll, 1988

Standing on a circular plinth the statue of St Volodymyr the Great was erected by the Orthodox Church to commemorate 1,000 years of Christianity in Russia. Volodymyr was originally a pagan prince who brought Christianity from Constantinople (Istanbul) in 988 and baptised the people of Kievan Rus' on the banks of the Dnieper River. More recently, this statue was the focal point for Ukrainians demonstrating their support of Viktor Yushchenko, who lost the presidential election in the Ukraine amid much controversy.

SOUTH WEST

34. Marc Bolan (1947-77)

Queen's Ride, Barnes, SW13
Sculptor Jean Robillard, Bronze, 2002

This bust stands at the spot where glam rock star Marc Bolan died in a car crash just two weeks from his 30th birthday. The sycamore tree was widely believed to be the immovable object hit by Bolan's car, but in fact the car hit a metal railing which has since been removed. The spot became a shrine to fans long before this monument was unveiled by the singer's son on the 25th Anniversary of the tragic accident.

35. John Colet (1467-1519)

St Paul's School, SW13
Sculptor Sir Hamo Thornycroft, 1898

John Colet was ordained deacon in 1497 and soon after became a priest. He inherited a substantial fortune, the great part of which he used for the endowment of St Paul's School, originally located in the City of London, near the cathedral after which it is named. His monument is in the grounds of the school and is not open to the public.

36. Edward VII (1841-1910)

Tooting Broadway, SW17
Sculptor L. F. Roselieb, Bronze, 1911

The first decade of the 20th century was also that of Edward VII's reign, unknowingly marking the demise of an older way of life which would change irrevocably with the First World War. The largest monument to Edward VII can be found at Waterloo Place (see p.93).

37. Johnny Haynes (1934-2005)

Craven Cottage (Fulham FC), SW6
Sculptor Douglas Jennings, 2008

Johnny Haynes was a footballer of the old school. Fulham's legendary number 10 shirt scored 158 goals for the club and earned 56 caps for England before retiring in 1970.

38. William Huskisson (1770-1830)

Pimlico Gardens, SW1
Sculptor John Gibson, Stone, 1836

William Huskisson was a Tory politician and head of the Board of Trade. He has the dubious distinction of being the first person to be killed by a train – he was struck by Stephenson's Rocket during the opening of the Liverpool to Manchester Railway. The monument stood on several sites before finding a home in Pimlico Gardens.

39. Sir John Everett Millais (1829-1896)

John Islip Street, SW1
Sculptor Sir Thomas Brock, Bronze, 1904

A founder of the Pre-Raphaelite Brotherhood, Millais went on to establish himself as a conventional and sentimental portrait painter. His saccharine-sweet portrait of a Victorian boy, 'Bubbles', became famous as the image of Pear's soap. He was knighted in 1895 and became President of the Royal Academy a year later.

40. Peter Osgood (1947-2006)
Stamford Bridge, West Stand, SW6
Sculptor Philip Jackson, 2010

Peter Osgood signed for Chelsea as a teenager and spent most of his career at the club, scoring nearly 300 goals and acquiring the knickname 'Ossie'. His autobiography was called 'Ossie – King of Stanford Bridge'. Despite his legendary status he was band from the club when Ken Bates was the owner, but welcomed back under Abramovich. After Osgood's sudden death from a heart attack, his ashes were spread at the Shed End of Stamford Bridge.

41. Fred Perry (1909-95)
All England Lawn Tennis Club, Church Rd, SW19
Sculptor David Wynne, 1984

Until Andy Murray's victory in 2013, Fred Perry was the last British man to win a singles title at Wimbledon back in 1936. Despite his achievements Perry was never fully embraced by the stuffy British tennis establishment and he became a US citizen in 1938 and fought in the US airforce during the Second World War.

42. Peter Scott (1909-89)

Wetlands Centre, Barnes, SW13
Sculptor Nicola Godden, Bronze, 2000

This Monument commemorates the naturalist and artist who founded the Trust which established this important Wetlands Centre. Peter Scott is the son of the famous artic explorer who is also commemorated with a London monument (see p.97).

43. Haile Selassie (1896-1975)

Cannizaro Park, Wimbledon, SW19
Sculptor Hilda Seligman, (moved here 1980's), Stone, 1957

In June 1936 Emperor Heile Selassie of Abysinia appealed to the League of Nations for assistance following the invasion of his country by Italy's Fascist army. The Emperor had already been driven from his country and had taken refuge with a sympathetic Wimbledon family. Dr Seligman and his household provided refuge to Selassie and his retinue until 1941 when the Italians were driven from his country with the help of British forces. The bust is the work of Mrs Seligman and remained in the grounds of their house until its demolition – it was then moved to Cannizaro Park. Many Londoners claim to have met the great man and the Emperor's exile has become part of Wimbledon folk lore.

44. Sir Henry Tate (1819-1899)

Brixton Library, Effra Road, SW2
Sculptor Sir Thomas Brook, Bronze, 1905

Henry Tate made a considerable fortune from the refining of sugar and became one of the great Victorian philanthropists. He funded the establishment of the Tate Gallery on Millbank, Liverpool University Library and the public library outside which this bust stands.

45. The Tradescant Family Memorial

St Stephen's Terrace, Stockwell, SW8
Sculptor Hilary Cartmel, Stone, 1988

John Tredescant and his son of the same name, were famous gardeners who travelled the world collecting plant species, many of which are now popular garden plants. They lived and worked in this area and are both buried in St Mary's Lambeth, which is now the Garden Museum.

SOUTH EAST

46. Edward Alleyn (1566-1626)

Old College Dulwich, SE21
Sculptor Louise Simson, Bronze, 2005

Edward Alleyn was the most famous actor-manager of the Elizabethan age, particularly renowned for his performances of Christopher Marlow's work. Alleyn purchased the land that surrounds this monument in 1605, founding a school which later became Dulwich College.

47. Robert Aske (1619-1689)

Pepy's Road, SE14
Sculptor W. Croggan, Coade Stone, 1836

Robert Aske was a successful merchant and philanthropist who established several almshouses and helped found the Haberdashers' Aske's School, outside which his monument stands. His statue is one of the few to be made from Coade stone (see Coade Stone Lion on page 154).

48. Dr Robert Bentley Todd (1809-1860)
King's College, Denmark Hill, SE5
Sculptor Matthew Noble, Marble, 1862

This statue commemorates the Irish doctor who helped to found King's College Hospital. The monument was unveiled at the hospital's original location, just off the Strand, but it moved to Denmark Hill with the hospital in 1913. Todd wrote many medical papers and was an expert in the study of paralysis.

49. Ernest Bevin (1881-1951)
Tooley Street, SE1
Sculptor E. Whitney Smith, Bronze, 1955

Ernest Bevin had very little education but became a trade unionist and Labour politician who founded the Transport and General Workers Union. Bevin was Minister for Labour in the wartime coalition government. He was made Foreign Secretary in Clement Attlee's government but died before the defeat of Labour in the 1951 election.

50. Colonel Samuel Bourne Bevington (1832-1907)
Tooley Street, SE1
Sculptor Sydney Marsh, Bronze, 1910

Samuel Bevington was a local businessman and philanthropist who employed, and gave help to, many in Bermondsey and was the area's first mayor. This monument was erected soon after his death and shows Bevington in his mayoral finery.

51. William (1829-1912)
& Catherine Booth (1829-1890)
Denmark Hill, SE5
Sculptor G. E. Wade, Bronze, 1929

The monuments to William Booth and his wife, Catherine, stand outside the training offices of the Salvation Army which they founded in 1861. There are several monuments to William Booth in Whitechapel (see p.373).

52. Circle Dray Horse

Queen Elizabeth Street, SE1
Sculptor Shirley Pace, Bronze, 1987

This monument commemorates the Courage Dray Horse Stable
which stood on this site – the horses being used to transport the
heavy casks of beer from the brewery. The area is now occupied by
smart flats and visitors are more likely to see a Porsche than a dray
horse on the narrow streets.

54

56

53. Crimean Memorial

Royal Artillery Parade Ground, Woolwich, SE18
Sculptor John Bell, Iron, 1860

The Royal Artillery left Woolwich in 2008, but their grand barracks, and this monument to the fallen of the Crimea, remain. The sculptor was also responsible for the Guards Monument in Central London (see p.100).

54. Brass Crosby (1725-1793)

Harmsworth Park, SE1

Stone Obelisk, 1771

Brass Crosby was a magistrate sent to the Tower for refusing to convict a printer for publishing the proceedings of parliament. The law prohibiting the reporting of events in parliament was eventually repealed following a long campaign by John Wilkes (see p.173).

55. Thomas Guy (1644-1724)

Guy's Hospital, SE1

Sculptor Peter Scheemakers, Brass, 1733

Thomas Guy was a bookseller and businessman who made a good deal of his fortune printing and selling English Bibles and a further fortune from South Sea stock. He was well known as a philanthropist and built three wards at St Thomas's before founding the hospital which bears his name in 1721.

56. Guy the Gorilla (1946-1978)

Crystal Palace, SE20

Sculptor David Wynne, Bronze, 1962

This statue commemorates the most popular attraction at London Zoo for 30 years, until his death in 1978. A further statue, by the sculptor William Timym, now stands in the Zoo itself as a tribute to this gentle giant.

57. Alfred the Great (849-899)

Trinity Church Square, SE1

Sculptor Anonymous, Stone, c.1395

The origins of this statue are unclear but it is believed to be a likeness of the Anglo-Saxon king Alfred the Great. It was moved here from the old Palace of Westminster in 1822, but has some claim to being the oldest outdoor monument in London.

58. Peter the Great (1672-1725)
Glaisher Street, Deptford, SE8
Sculptor Mihail Chemiakin, Bronze, 2001

This unusual monument commemorates the brief stay of Tsar Peter the Great in Deptford in 1698. The young Tsar attempted to remain incognito but, standing over two meters tall and with a large retinue, this proved difficult. During his stay at the house of John Evelyn the young Tsar enjoyed a wild time and severely damaged the house and its gardens. Peter was an autocratic and domineering character who ordered the torture and killing of his oldest son but also transformed Russia into a major European power. This monument is as eccentric as its subject and has an unusual cartoon quality.

59. James Hulbert (d.1720)
Fishmonger's Hall, London Bridge, SE1
Sculptor Robert Easton, Marble, 1978

James Hulbert was a successful fishmonger who founded the Fishmonger's Almshouses at St Peter's Hospital, Southwark. His investment in the South Sea Company was sold just before the stock crashed which greatly increased the value of his estate and enabled a much larger almshouse to be built.

60. Sir Leonard Hutton (1916-90)
Harleyford Road, The Oval, SE11
Sculptor Walter Ritchie, Brick, 1993

This monument commemorates the great Yorkshire and England Cricketer. Hutton was the first professional to captain England in 1952, won the Ashes the following year and was knighted in 1956.

61. Captain Christopher Jones (1570-1622)
St Mary the Virgin Church, Rotherhithe, SE16
Sculptor Jamie Sargeant, Sandstone, 1995

This sculpture of St Christopher commemorates the Captain of *The Mayflower* which took the first pilgrims to America in 1620. Captain Jones is buried in the grounds of St Mary's.

62. Alexander McLeod (1832-1902)

Powis Street, Royal Arsenal Co-operative Soc, SE18
Sculptor Alfred Drury, Terracotta, 1903

This monument stands on the site of the former Royal Arsenal Co-operative Society building and commemorates one of its founders.

63. John Keats (1995-1821)

Guy's Hospital Garden, SE1
Sculptor Stuart Williamson, Bronze, 2007

An alcove from old London Bridge has stood in the grounds of Guy's Hospital since 1861. In 2007 it acquired a permanent resident in the form of the studious figure of poet John Keats who studied to be a surgeon at the hospital before dedicating himself to poetry. It was unveiled by the Poet Laureate Andrew Motion and also commemorates Dr Robert Knight who worked at Guy's and loved the poetry of Keats.

64. William R. Morris, Viscount Nuffield (1877-1963)
Guy's Hospital, SE1
Sculptor Maurice Prosper Lambert, Bronze, 1944
William Morris began his career repairing bicycles in Oxford before
adapting his skills to the manufacture of cars. Morris made a fortune
from the car company which carried his name and was a major
benefactor to Guy's Hospital, where his monument now stands.

65. Joseph Paxton (1803-1865)
Crystal Palace, SE20
Sculptor W. F. Woodington, Marble, 1869
Paxton was an architect and the Duke of Devonshire's head gardener
whose design of a colossal glass building was chosen to house the
Great Exhibition of 1851. Paxton supervised the construction of his
Crystal Palace in Hyde Park and its move to Sydenham after the
exhibition closed. He went on to serve as MP for Coventry.

66. Dr Salter – Dr Salter's Daydream (1873-1942)
Cherry Garden Pier, SE16
Sculptor Diane Gorvin, Bronze, 1991, stolen November 2011
Dr Salter, and his wife Ada, did much for the residents of
Bermondsey, providing medical care to the poor of the area. Dr
Salter also served as the local MP. When their daughter, Joyce, died
from Scarlet fever there was widespread grief. The Monument that
stood here showed the seated figure of Dr Salter with his daughter
and cat opposite. The seated figure was stolen in 2011 and the rest
of the monument has been placed in storage. A board remains
which tells the family's sad story and is hopefully safe from those
'who know the price of everything, but the value of nothing'.

67. James Walker (1781-1862)
Greenland Dock, Sculptor Brunswick Quay, SE16
Sculptor Michael Rizzello, Bronze, 1990
James Walker was the Victorian civil engineer responsible for
Greenlock Dock and Vauxhall Bridge.

68. Duke of Wellington (1769-1852)

Wellington Square, Woolwich, SE18

Sculptor Thomas Milnes, Marble, 1848 (Tower of London),
Moved here 1863

A further monument to the 'Iron Duke' (see p.198 for more
information).

EAST

69. Queen Alexandra (1809-1898)

Courtyard of London Hospital, E1

Sculptor George Edward Wade, Bronze, 1908

Queen Alexandra was the long suffering wife of Edward VII. She
was also a patron of London Hospital and introduced the *Finsen
Light* cure for lupus into this country from her native Denmark. She
has another monument on Marlborough Road (see p.107).

Distant and Alone

70. Clement Attlee (1883-1967)
Queen Mary University Library, E1
Sculptor Frank Forster, Bronze, 1988
Clement Attlee was a social worker who became a Labour
politician. He served in Churchill's coalition government and
was the country's first post-war prime minister. Between 1945-
51 Attlee's government established the National Health Service,
nationalised many industries, carried through education reforms
and granted independence to India and Pakistan.

71. Bethnal Green Tube Disaster Memorial
South East exit of Bethnal Green Station, E2
Sculptor Harry Paticas, Stone and Bronze, 2013
This memorial has resulted from a long campaign to
commemorate the 173 people who died on March 3rd 1943 in a
crush, as people tried to enter Bethnal Green tube station which
was being used as an air raid shelter. The tragedy was hushed up
at the time for fear of damaging moral and partly because the panic
was triggered by the noise of an anti-aircraft battery which was
launched close to Victoria Park. The perseverance of local people
who lost loved ones has resulted in this impressive monument
unveiled 70 years after that tragic night.

72. General William Booth (1829-1912)

Mile End Road, E1

Sculptor George Edward Wade, Bronze, 1927

William Booth was a methodist preacher who founded the Salvation Army in 1865. This bust stands on the site of Booth's first open air service, following the practice of John Wesley (see p.211). In 1979, a second monument to Booth was unveiled close by, based on a copy of the monument that stands on Denmark Hill in South London (see p.364).

73. The Champions

West Ham FC, E13

Sculptor Philip Jackson, Bronze, 2003

West Ham players figured strongly in England's 1966 World Cup winning team. This monument shows Bobby Moore upon the shoulders of fellow West Ham players Martin Peters and Geoff Hurst, with Everton's Ray Wilson making up the quartet.

74. Michael von Clemm (1935-1997)

Cabot Square, E14

Sculptor Gerald Laing, Bronze, 1998

Michael von Clemm was an American who came to England to study anthropology before becoming a successful investment banker. Clemm helped establish the Eurodollar Market and contributed to the transformation of Docklands in the 1980s. He also helped raise the money required to establish the famous Roux brothers' first restaurant.

75. Edward VII (1841-1910)
Whitechapel Road, E1
Sculptor W. S. Frith, Stone and Bronze, 1911
Edward VII encouraged the acceptance of Jewish refugees into the country at the turn of the century and the integration of those Jews already established here. This elaborate column was erected in gratitude to the King by the Jewish community of east London. There is a much larger equestrian monument to Edward on Waterloo Place (see p.93).

76. Sir Robert Geffrye (1613-1704)
Geffrye Museum, E2
Sculptor John van Nost, Lead, 1723
Robert Geffrye was a successful ironmonger who left provision for the establishment of an almshouse in his will. The almshouse moved away from London and the building has since become the Geffrye Museum. This monument is a 1913 copy of the John van Nost original.

77. William Gladstone
Bow Church Yard, E3
Sculptor Albert Bruce-Joy, Bronze, 1882
This is one of the few monuments to be unveiled while its subject was still alive. This tribute was the gift of the local match manufacturer Theodore Bryant. The hands on this monument have been painted red in protest at the terrible conditions of the local match factories which killed and disabled many, mostly female, factory workers.

78. Richard Green (1806-1863)
East India Dock Road, E14
Sculptor E. W. Wyon, Bronze, 1866
Richard Green was a ship owner and philanthropist who showed concern for the welfare of seamen. Green's efforts were exceptional given the widespread harsh practices of other ship owners (see Samuel Plimsoll on page 136). Unlike those of his rivals, Green's funeral attracted large crowds.

75

76 Rob. Geffryes Kn^t Alderman

77 GLADSTONE

78

80

79. George Lansbury (1859-1940)
Bow Rd, Junction Harley Grove, E3
Bronze, 1955

This simple plaque commemorates the
Labour politician who lived in a house on this
site for 23 years. He campaigned for women's
suffrage, relief for the poor and helped to
usher in the modern welfare state which he
never lived to see. His daughter is the famous
Hollywood actor, Angela Lansbury.

80. Robert Milligan (1746-1808)
West India Quay, E14
Sculptor Richard Westmacott, Bronze, 1875

Robert Milligan was deputy chairman of the West India Dock
Company and instrumental in the opening of the West India Dock
in 1802 which was the main arrival point for sugar from the West
Indies. Milligan's monument has moved several times but since the
mid-1980s has found its place on the dock which he did so much to
establish.

81. John Rennie (1761-1821)
Spirit Quay in Wapping, E1
Sculptor John Ravera, Bronze, 1992

Rennie was one of the great Georgian engineers, designing
Southwark, Waterloo and London bridges and helping to create
the system of East London Docks that were to transform Britain's
economy.

82. Bradley Stone (1970-94)
Caxton Street North, E16
Sculptor Ann Downey, Bronze, 1995

Bradley Stone was an East End boxer who died two days after
winning a fight at Bethnal Green's York Hall. This monument
stands outside the boxing club where Stone trained.

83. Virginia Settlers Memorial
East India Dock Road, E14
Sculptor Wendy Taylor, Stone, 1951

This tablet was a gift from the Virginian people and commemorates the three ships that left from Blackwall in 1606 to establish the colony of Jamestown. The monument to Captain John Smith has a more detailed account of the voyage and initial settlement (see p.207).

84. Sir Corbet Woodall
Twelvetrees Crescent, E3
Sculptor A. G. Walker, Bronze, 1926 moved 1969

Woodall was an engineer who became director of the *Gas, Light and Coke Company*. This monument originally stood outside Beckton Gas Works, but moved when the gasworks closed.

OUTSKIRTS

85. Sir John Alcock (1892-1919) & Sir Arthur Whitten Brown (1861-1948)
Bath Road, Heathrow Airport, TW6
Sculptor William McMillan, Limestone, 1954

This monument commemorates two pioneering airmen who were the first to cross the Atlantic in a single flight in 1919. Both men were knighted for their achievement. Sadly, Alcock had little time to enjoy his triumph, dying in a plane crash just a few months after the historic flight.

86. Queen Anne (1665-1714)
Market Place, Kingston, KT1
Sculptor Francis Bird, Lead, 1706

Francis Bird was also responsible for the monument of Queen Anne that stands outside St Paul's (see p.218).

87. Job Henry Drain (1895-1975)
Broadway, Barking IG11
Sculptor Steven Hunter, Bronze, 2009
John Drain was a local hero who won the Victoria Cross for the courage he displayed during World War One.

88. Bobby Moore (1941-93)
Wembley Stadium, HA9
Sculptor Philip Jackson, 2007
At the entrance to the new Wembley Stadium stands this monument to the captain of the 1966 World Cup winning England team. Moore played for West Ham for many years and earned 108 caps for his country.

89. Bernardo O'Higgins (1778-1842)
Bridge Street, Richmond, TW9
Stone, 1998
This bust commemorates Chile's first President who helped liberate the country from Spanish rule. O'Higgins was of Irish decent and spent several years studying in Richmond as a young man.

General Index

Index

Subject Index

Index

Index

About us:

Metro is a small independent publishing company with a reputation for producing well-researched and beautifully-designed guides on many aspects of London life. In fields of interest as diverse as shopping, bargain hunting, architecture, the arts, and food, our guide books contain special tips you won't find anywhere else.

How to order:

The following titles are available to buy from our website (P&P free). Alternatively, you can call our customer order line on 020 8533 7777 (Visa/Mastercard/Switch)

www.metropublications.com

LONDON'S PARKS AND GARDENS
COVER MORE THAN TWENTY-FIVE PERCENT OF THE CAPITAL – THAT'S A LOT MORE GRASS BETWEEN TOES THAN ANY OTHER CITY IN EUROPE

LONDON'S CEMETERIES
SPEND THE DAY WITH KARL MARX, ENID BLYTON, KEITH MOON AND MANY MORE

LONDON'S CITY CHURCHES
SEE THE SCORCH MARKS OF THE GREAT FIRE, OR VISIT AN ALTAR BY HENRY MOORE

LONDON'S HOUSES
FROM WORKHOUSE TO ROYAL PALACE, COME IN, CLOSE THE DOOR AND STEP BACK IN TIME...

LONDON'S HIDDEN WALKS
THE LONDON WE KNOW IS JUST THE SURFACE!

Volume 1

LONDON'S HIDDEN WALKS
EXPLORE LONDON AND DISCOVER HOW 2000 YEARS OF HISTORY HAVE SHAPED THIS CITY

Volume 2